A Dialectical Psychology

A Dialectical Psychology

Allan R. Buss
University of Calgary

IRVINGTON PUBLISHERS, INC., New York

HALSTED PRESS Division of
JOHN WILEY & SONS, Inc.

New York   London   Sydney   Toronto

Distributed by Halsted Press
A division of John Wiley & Sons, Inc., New York

Library of Congress Cataloging in Publication Data

Buss, Allan R
  A dialectical psychology.

  Includes index.
  1. Psychology—Philosophy. 2. Dialectic. 3. Humanistic psychology. 4. Social psychology. I. Title.
BF38.B87   150′.1   79-11813
ISBN 0-470-26737-2

Printed in the United States of America

for Stella

Contents

Preface   ix
1. The Structure of Psychological Revolutions   1
2. The Fact-Theory Relationship and Marx's Epistemology   13
3. The Historical Context of Differential Psychology and
   Eugenics   27
4. Psychology's Future Development as Predicted from
   Generation Theory   43
5. The Historical Roots of the Individual-Society Dialectic   53
6. Development of Dialectics and Development of Humanistic
   Psychology   75
7. Counter-Culture and Counter-Psychology   89
8. Humanistic Psychology and the Liberal Tradition: Maslow's
   Theory   101
9. Theories of Cognitive Development: Piaget, Marx and
   Buck-Morss   115
10. Conceptual Issues in Life-Span Developmental Methodology   127
11. Educational Theory and Values: Mastery Learning and
    Computer-Assisted Instruction   149
12. The Trait-Situation Controversy and the Concept of
    Interaction   161
13. A Conceptual Critique of Attribution Theory   169
14. A Metascience Critique of Attribution Theory   187
    Index   203

Preface

The individual-society dialectic has been obliterated and ignored for too long by psychologists. The social, historical, and developmental dimensions of psychological ideas should not, and indeed cannot, be separated. Psychological ideas are part of a larger totality.

The underlying theme of this book is that a more valid understanding of psychological ideas requires a broader and more *critical* attitude in regard to the theory and practice of traditional psychology. My critical approach can be characterized as historical and self-consciously value-laden, rather than ahistorical and supposedly value-free. Such an approach involves a contextual analysis of certain psychological theories and ideas—an analysis that penetrates to the underlying values and image of humanity that are presupposed and reinforced. Such a critical approach goes beyond the mere surface appearance of ideas and concepts, and unearths their social and historical content. In this way, it is possible to evaluate the validity of psychological ideas according to criteria other than those derived from a blind empiricism.

This book will be of particular interest to those who are beginning to feel some tension and disillusionment in regard to traditional psychology. It should prove stimulating to those who are seeking a broader understanding of the social and cultural context of psychological ideas. It should also be most appropriate for history and theory of psychology courses, as well for developmental and social psychology courses at the upper undergraduate and graduate levels.

I should like to thank the Social Sciences and Humanities Research Council of Canada (Research Grants S74-1376 and 410-78-0006) for their continuous support over the past few years.

A. R. Buss

A Dialectical Psychology

Chapter 1

The Structure of Psychological Revolutions

In 1962 Thomas S. Kuhn published *The Structure of Scientific Revolutions*, thereby setting into motion revolutionary waves within the seas of philosophy and the history of science. It is not very often that the kind of reception one's work receives serves to support the thesis itself. Such is the fortune of Kuhn's little paperback. Its short history is part of Kuhn's view of history. *The Structure of Scientific Revolutions* has itself become a revolutionary "paradigm" for many natural scientists, social scientists, philosophers, and historians of science who have found its framework for the reconstruction of the growth of knowledge much more satisfying than received doctrine.

Kuhn's view of the structure of scientific revolutions has been discussed and criticized[1] as well as defended and extended.[2] With respect to the applicability of Kuhn's ideas to the discipline of psychology, Kuhn himself initially[3] considered psychology (as well as other social sciences) to be preparadigmatic, since there was no one single paradigm which was generally accepted within the discipline, and much debate and energy was still being spent on trying to resolve fundamentals.

Recently, Kuhn has elaborated further on his concept of paradigms, and has proposed identifying them according to sociological criteria. Thus "A paradigm governs . . . not a subject matter but rather a group of practitioners."[4] In addition, a paradigm is thought to involve specific or

The author would like to thank Baruch Fischoff for his comments on an earlier draft of this article. Reprinted with permission from the *Journal of the History of the Behavioral Sciences* 14 (1978): 57–64.

unique kinds of solutions to particular puzzles, called "exemplars," as
well as shared values, metaphors, and metaphysical assumptions, which
make up a "disciplinary matrix." Thus, according to the Kuhn of 1970,
psychology need not have one single paradigm at any one time in order
to be considered a science.[5]

Perhaps there is more which can be said and done in characterizing
the nature of psychological revolutions than simply applying, in a
mechanical way, Kuhn's revised concept of, and criteria for, different
paradigms. Kuhn's characterization of the growth of science was illustrated and defended within the history of the natural sciences. One
might well ask: Is the structure of the growth of knowledge in the human
sciences, and psychology in particular, the same as that in the natural
sciences? I believe that the answer to this question must be in the
negative, and that by adopting a particular perspective (to be shortly
explicated), one can detect a *submerged pattern in the coming and going
of psychological revolutions*. Thus, while I believe that a Kuhnian
analysis (i.e., Kuhn as of 1970) is applicable to psychology, such an
analysis needs to be supplemented by an important dynamic structural
property. In this way, one can attempt to arrive at a more analytic
interpretation and reconstruction of psychology's history.

It is the purpose of this brief article to abstract and articulate in a
very simple manner certain structural changes characterizing past and
present paradigmatic changes within psychology—structural changes *not*
indigenous to the natural sciences, but very much *intrinsic* and *unique* to
psychology. In focusing on the endogenous, abstract structural basis of
psychological revolutions, I bracket the important question as to the role
of concrete forces exogenous to the discipline (e.g., social, political, and
economic) in helping to bring about paradigmatic change.[6] And, to the
extent that sister social science disciplines (such as sociology and political
science) have had, and continue to share, some of psychology's major
paradigms (e.g., behaviorism), then the thesis developed below may
have generality beyond the discipline with which I am most familiar.
Since the transformative method of Ludwig Feuerbach is the major
conceptual tool to be used for revealing the abstract commonality of
psychological revolutions, it will be of value to briefly consider the
historical origins of this method.

Ludwig Feuerbach and the Transformative Method

Ludwig Feuerbach (1804–1872) and his transformative method are
probably unknown to most psychologists. Feuerbach was a member of

that post-Hegelian group of German intellectuals variously known as the Young or Left Hegelians. The Young Hegelians sought to engage themselves in a vigorous campaign of criticizing extant religious and political institutions, claiming that the Master had not made explicit, and perhaps even suppressed, the revolutionary implications of his philosophy. Feuerbach himself was concerned throughout his life with issues related to religion, and, more specifically, with gaining a greater understanding of the psychological basis for religious practice and beliefs. It was in the arena of religion, then, where Feuerbach first developed and applied his transformative method. He later used it in criticizing Hegel's idealistic philosophy, and as a result of that success, the method was quickly adopted and expanded into an even more powerful critical tool by another, more famous Young Hegelian—Karl Marx.

Feuerbach's contribution, and his influence upon the intellectual development of Marx, have been reviewed and discussed in detail in several places.[7] For present purposes, it will suffice to briefly sketch the outlines of his transformative method. The essence of the method can be readily conveyed by transforming the statement "God created humanity in his/her own image," to "Humanity created God in its own image." While the idea revealed by this particular subject-object transformation may now seem rather simple, at the time, Feuerbach's insight was quite profound and had a tremendous liberating effect upon the minds of the Young Hegelians. According to Sidney Hook,[8] all of German philosophy and culture during the 1840s was under the shadow of Feuerbach. And, in the words of another Young Hegelian, with "Feuerbach's *Essence of Christianity* . . . The spell was broken. The 'system' (Hegel's) was exploded and cast aside . . . Enthusiasm was general; we all became at once Feuerbachians. How enthusiastically Marx greeted the new conception."[9]

What was all the excitement about? How had Feuerbach captured the attention of the leading German philosophers, intellectuals, and critics at this time? What Feuerbach had done was to open up a new dimension for viewing human nature and social reality. According to Feuerbach, religion involved unconsciously projecting or conferring desirable human qualities onto a nonhuman or supernatural being, and then worshipping such a being. The latter, in turn, made humanity derivative, or an object, of the subject "God."

The fetishlike tendencies involved in religion served to create a condition of human alienation insofar as humanity was deprived of, and divorced from, its true nature. In Feuerbach's words, "The more empty life is, the fuller, the more concrete is God. The impoverishing of the real world, and the enriching of God, is one act. Only the poor man has a rich God."[10] God represented the perfection of all that was truly human, and such a fetish arises, according to Feuerbach, because humanity has not as yet realized its own possibilities. Thus, the mystical nature of religion was exposed as having a very human basis. What needed to be done was to realize that it is humanity which is the subject, and God the object, and in this way, humanity can recover its primacy in the natural order.

Feuerbach also applied his transformative method to Hegel's philosophy, and believed that by reversing the subject and object of that system, one could get closer to the truth. In Hegel's idealism, the subject was *Geist*, Spirit, or abstract reason or thought, and the object was humanity, or real human beings in a real world. Feuerbach turned Hegel upside down, and postulated humanity as the subject, and thought as the object. According to Feuerbach, real, active, concrete people should be the starting point for any philosophy. By making people the subject, humanity could be liberated from alienating forces (e.g., *Geist*) which have in fact been created by, or are the objects of, human minds. Thus, Feuerbach's materialism and humanism was an outcome of a move which at once demystified that which was once mystical, and placed humanity in an active, rather than passive, role. Feuerbach's transformative method was truly revolutionary in that, like political revolutions, it reversed the subject-object relationship with respect to power, primacy, and influence.

PSYCHOLOGY, PARADIGMS, AND THE SUBJECT-OBJECT TRANSFORMATION

The way is now clear to consider the common structural basis of the emergence of new psychological paradigms. As the reader may have inferred by now, the attempt will be made to generalize Feuerbach's transformative method, and to characterize psychological revolutions in terms of a transformation of the subject-object relationship. Such a characterization of revolutionary paradigms within psychology is unique to the human of social sciences since they are reflexive studies.[11] The objects of study in the social sciences (people) are also subjects. They can therefore reflect upon their objectivity, and subsequently change it in light of previous research findings and new information. This largely unacknowledged subject-object contradiction has played havoc in the history of psychology's paradigms, where the unresolved tension had led to two separate structural "solutions," each of which, it is subsequently noted, is unsatisfactory in itself.

Two prototype statements are used below for characterizing the underlying structure of psychological paradigms. These are (a) *Person Constructs Reality* and (b) *Reality Constructs Person*. Psychological revolutions involve a shift from either (a) to (b), or from (b) to (a). Different paradigms involve grafting specific theoretical content onto one of the structural models, thereby offering a unique interpretation of such a model. Let us now consider what have probably been the three major paradigms within mainstream experimental psychology, as well as two additional ones which have had, and continue to have, a number of adherents outside of the mainstream. I believe that there would be a general consensus that the major forces and counterforces within psychology have been structuralism, behaviorism, the cognitive approach, psychoanalysis, and humanistic psychology. Of course, the above broad categories do not preclude differences of view, or competing theories, within a particular paradigm.

From Structuralism to Behaviorism

From: Person Constructs Reality.
To: Reality Constructs Person.

The early structuralism developed by Wilhelm Wundt has been considered to be the first truly experimental psychology. Traditional historical treatments of Wundt and his work[12] consider him to be a precursor to behaviorism insofar as his ideas, concepts, and methodology are seen as consistent with many of the basics of behaviorism. However, Wundt's place in history is currently undergoing a reinterpretation. According to Arthur Blumenthal,[13] Wundt's structuralism bears a much closer affinity to a cognitive than to a behavioristic orientation insofar as "Wundt's studies of volition . . . amounted to an elaborate analysis of selective and constructive attentional processes (often summarized under the term *apperception*)."[14] Blumenthal has argued very persuasively that Wundt's system anticipated many of the current cognitive topics in psychology, and that the influence of German idealism served to make his psychology one which stressed an active subject as the object of study—a subject which selected and very much constructed reality. Wundt's primary method, namely, introspection, demands the notion of an active subject reflecting and operating on his/her experience of the real world.

Behaviorism replaced structuralism as the paradigm in mainstream psychology, and there can be no doubt that the transition was revolutionary. While behaviorism would be considered by many to have been a progressive stage in the development of psychology, it is also true that it had certain regressive aspects. Thus, Wundt's rather enlightened view of an active, determining, and conceptive subject was replaced by the behavioristic view of a passive, determined, and receptive object. Wundt's idealism became transformed into John B. Watson's materialism. What had been the subject became the object, and vice versa.

From Behaviorism to Cognitive Psychology

From: Reality Constructs Person.
To: Person Constructs Reality.
Behaviorism, of course, came and comes in several varieties—from the radical behaviorism of Watson, which has been continued by B.F. Skinner, to the more liberal theories of Clark Hull and Edward Tolman, who did not hesitate to talk about theoretical constructs which referred to what was *in* the organism. However, behaviorism in its various forms denied the experimental "subject" the status of being a true subject, and recent cognitive approaches have transformed the subject-object relation of behaviorism back to Person Constructs Reality. The recent cognitive revolution is too well-known to warrant review in detail.[10] In emphasizing the creativity or open-endedness of language, as well as rules, attention, selection, construction, and information-processing ideas, the individual is once again considered to be a true subject. Let us now consider two revolutions lying outside of the mainstream.

The Psychoanalytic Revolution

From: Person Constructs Reality.
To: Reality Constructs Person.
With Freud there emerged a revolutionary conception of the nature of the individual and his relation to reality. Previous to Freud, rationality and consciousness were emphasized, where the individual was considered to behave in accordance with the notion of what a "reasonable person" would do. This pre-Freudian view clearly conferred subject status onto the individual. Freud and his biological theories of motivation undermined and transformed that dominant view. For Freud, irrational and unconscious psychological forces were what governed behavior. The latter, in turn, largely stemmed from the interaction of certain instinctive

drives and past experiences. Thus, Freud considered the individual to be a consequent of reality (biological drives plus environmental experiences), rather than an antecedent.

The Humanistic Revolution

From: Reality Constructs Person.
To: Person Constructs Reality.

As noted by Maslow,[16] hmanistic or third force psychology was a reaction to both psychoanalysis and behaviorism. It should not be surprising, therefore, that humanistic psychology has a structural form opposite to both. Humanistic psychology emphasizes *Self*-development, where the individual is seen as in control of his own destiny, and therefore responsible for actively striving towards "self-actualization." Within humanistic psychology, the individual is considered to be potentially free, creative, and spontaneous. In short, the person is considered a subject.

CONCLUSION: THE REVOLUTION TO END REVOLUTIONARY SUBJECT-OBJECT TRANSFORMATIONS

Thus far it has been argued that psychological revolutions can be characterized in terms of a transformation of the subject-object relation, where such a transformation profoundly changes the conception of the individual and his relation to reality. Any paradigm which is based upon only one of the two structural models discussed above is likely to eventually lead to an antithetical revolutionary paradigm, which, in turn, will lead to counterrevolutionary forces to try and reestablish the prerevolutionary subject-object relation.

In characterizing mainstream experimental psychology's brief history in terms of three major paradigms (structuralism, behaviorism, and the cognitive approach), it should be apparent that, structurally speaking, the cognitive paradigm can be viewed as a reactionary movement calling for a return to the subject-object relationship of Wundt's structuralism. Indeed, Blumenthal notes that "Strange as it may seem, Wundt may be more easily understood today that he could have been just a few years ago."[17] Blumenthal's observation is not so strange once it is realized that the paradigms of both Wundt and current mainstream psychology share an identical subject-object structure.

Different paradigms sharing an identical subject-object structure may also account for the facility of translating one theory into another. To

take one well-known example, the present analysis implies that the
reason that John Dollard and Neal Miller[18] were able to effect a
translation of psychoanalytic concepts and processes into "modern"
learning theory (I bracket the issue of the value of this work) was that
these two paradigms share an identical structure of the subject-object
relation. In other words, psychoanalysis and behaviorism share the same
deep structure (Reality Constructs Person), although each has a different
surface structure (unique theoretical terms). What the latter implies is
that, when dealing with psychological paradigms, there is need for,
reason to, and criteria for distinguishing between two levels of paradigm
incommensurability. And, in order to establish whether a paradigm
change has in fact been *truly* revolutionary, as defined here, one must
examine the deep structure of each.

At this point one might well wonder what the future holds for
psychology—can we expect a paradigm based upon the transformation of
the subject-object relation as it now exists within cognitive psychology?
Let us hope not! By now it can be seen that the circular "progress" of
transforming the subject-object relation could go on indefinitely. A
discipline not sufficiently appreciative or self-conscious of its history is
cursed to repeat the "errors" in its history. What the present analysis
implies is that there is a need for a paradigm which accommodates the
structure of *both* Person Constructs Reality and Reality Constructs
Person. Each of these separate structural models captures an important
but *single* dimension of the nature of the person-reality relation. Each
model is inadequate if it becomes totalized.

The way out of the vicious subject-object revolutionary circle is to
effect a revolution to end revolutions. Such a revolution is within our
grasp today. The new paradigm would embrace the idea that the subject-
object relation is two-dimensional, rather than one-dimensional. Such a
paradigm would transcend the limited perspectives of the various
partialist paradigms. The paradigm to end structural revolutions involving the subject-object transformation is a dialectical one. A *dialectical*
paradigm emphasizes the *reciprocal, interactive* relationship between
the person and reality such that each may serve as both subject and
object.[19]

While a dialectical paradigm may initially appear to be a bold and
exciting thrust into the future, and a useful way for conceptualizing the
subject-object relation within psychology, a consultation of Bo Ekehammer's[20] historical review article on interactionism should prove sobering.
Ekehammer's article reveals that others (i.e., organismic psychologists)
have been here before. In fact, the view presently being described can
be traced back to one of the Young Hegelians who wrote:

The materialist doctrine that men are products of circumstances and upbringing and that, therefore, changed men are products of other circumstances and changed upbringing forgets that circumstances are changed precisely by men and that the educator must himself be educated.[21]

The above quote is Thesis 3 on Feuerbach in which Marx is criticizing mechanistic-materialistic views which leave no room for an active, constructing individual. Equally was Marx opposed to an exclusive idealist position which, although stressing the active role of thought and reason, did so in an obscure and perverted manner by not placing this process within a real, material world which affects real, active people. Marx proposed a view which he called naturalism or humanism, where "naturalism or humanism distinguishes itself both from idealism and materialism, constituting at the same time the unifying truth of both."[22] In other words, Marx's view as to the subject-object relation was dialectical, where each aspect is "merely" one side of the same process. This is not to make the subject-object distinction superfluous, or collapse one category into the other, but, rather, this is to make the subject and object part of a *dialectical* unity. In adopting a dialectical paradigm in regard to the subject-object relation, psychologists can complete the revolution to end revolutions.[23]

Of course, no claim is being made here that with a dialectical paradigm the history of psychology comes to an abrupt end. One dialectician (Hegel) making that kind of mistake is enough. Rather, *with respect to the subject-object relation,* a dialectical perspective puts an end to the vicious circle of psychological revolutions having their basis in Feuerbach's transformative method. Let there indeed be future revolutions in psychology. One should certainly endorse the Popperian view of "revolutions in permanence" (Trotskyism at its best—a comparison which Popper would not appreciate!). However, let such future revolutions involve matters other than transforming the subject-object relation. The latter should end with the dialectical revolution—the revolution to end the need for revolutionary subject-object transformations and, in the spirit of Marx, a truly liberating revolution.[24]

Notes

1. See, for example, the collection edited by Irme Lakatos and Alan Musgrave, *Criticism and the Growth of Knowledge* (Cambridge: Cambridge University Press, 1970).

2.   Thomas S. Kuhn, "Logic of Discovery or Psychology of Research?" in Lakatos and Musgrave, *Growth of Knowledge*, pp. 1–23; "Postscript-1969," in *The Structure of Scientific Revolutions* (Chicago: University of Chicago Press, 1970); "Reflections on my Critics," in Lakatos and Musgrave, *Growth of Knowledge*, pp. 231–278; and "Second Thoughts on Paradigms," in *The Structure of Scientific Theories*, ed. Frederick Suppe (Urbana, Illinois: University of Illinois Press, 1974)

3.   Thomas K. Kuhn, *The Structure of Scientific Revolutions* (Chicago: University of Chicago Press, 1962), p. viii.

4.   Kuhn, "Postscript-1969," p. 180.

5.   For the view that mainstream experimental psychology has passed through three *major* paradigms (structuralism, behaviorism, and the cognitive view) and thus two *major* revolutions in its short history, see David S. Palermo, "Is a Scientific Revolution Taking Place in Psychology?" *Science Studies 1* (1971): 135–155, and Walter B. Weimer and David S. Palermo, "Paradigms and Normal Science in Psychology," *Science Studies 3* (1973) 211–244. For what seem to the author unconvincing arguments opposed to conferring paradigmatic status to psychology, see L. B. Briskman, "Is a Kuhnian Analysis Applicable to Psychology?" *Science Studies 2* (1972): 87–97; Mark W. Lipsey, "Psychology: Preparadigmatic, Postparadigmatic, or Misparadigmatic?" *Science Studies 4* (1974): 406–410; Brian D. Mackenzie, "Behaviorism and Positivism," *Journal of the History of the Behavioral Sciences 8* (1972): 222–231; and Neil Warren, "Is a Scientific Revolution Taking Place in Psychology?—Doubts and Reservations," *Science Studies I* (1971): 407–413.

6.   See, for example, my "Galton and the Birth of Differential Psychology and Eugenics: Social, Political, and Economic Forces," *Journal of the History of the Behavioral Sciences 12* (1976): 47–58; "The Emerging Field of the Sociology of Psychological Knowledge," *American Psychologist 30* (1975): 988–1002; and an edited volume, *Psychology in Social Context* (New York: Irvington, 1979). See also Klaus F. Riegel, "Influence of Economic and Political Ideologies on the Development of Developmental Psychology," *Psychological Bulletin 78* (1972): 129–141, and Susan Buck-Morss, "Socio-Economic Bias in Piaget's Theory and Its Implications for Cross-Cultural Studies," *Human Development 18* (1975): 35–49.

7.   For example, Sydney Hook, *From Hegel to Marx: Studies in the Intellectual Development of Karl Marx* (Ann Arbor: University of Michigan Press, 1962); Eugene Kamenka, *The Philosophy of Ludwig Feuerbach* (New York: Praeger, 1969); and David McLellan, *The Young Hegelians and Karl Marx* (London: Macmillan, 1969).

8.   Hook, *Hegel to Marx*, p. 220.

9.   Frederick Engels, *Ludwig Feuerbach* (first published in 1888. New York: International Publishers, 1941), p. 18.

10.   Feuerbach, 1841, quoted in Hook, *Hegel to Marx*, p. 247.

11. See, for example, Robert W. Friedrichs, *A Sociology of Sociology* (New York: Free Press, 1970); Howard Gadlin and Grant Ingle, "Through the One-Way Mirror: The Limits of Experimental Self-Reflection," *American Psychologist* 30 (1975): 1003–1009; Kenneth J. Gergan, "Social Psychology as History," *Journal of Personality and Social Psychology* 26 (1973): 309–320; and Alvin W. Gouldner, *The Coming Crisis of Western Sociology* (New York: Basic Books, 1970).

12. For example, Edwin G. Boring, *A History of Experimental Psychology* (New York: Appleton-Century-Crofts, 1950).

13. Arthur L. Blumenthal, "A Reappraisal of Wilhelm Wundt," *American Psychologist* 30 (1975): 1081–1088.

14. Ibid., p. 1083, original emphasis.

15. The cognitive revolution has been discussed by Erwin W. Segal and Roy Lachman, "Complex Behavior or Higher Mental Process: Is There a Paradigm Schift?" *American Psychologist* 27 (1972): 46–55, in terms of internal and external disciplinary forces of change. It has also been described from a more personal perspective by some of those who have lived through it and changed sides. See, for example, James Deese, "Behavior and Fact," *American Psychologist* 24 (1969): 515–522; James J. Jenkins, "Remember That Old Theory of Memory? Well, Forget It!" *American Psychologist* 29 (1974): 785–795; and Palermo, "Scientific Revolution."

16. Abraham H. Maslow, *Toward a Psychology of Being* (New York: Van Nostrand-Reinhold, 1968).

17. Blumenthal, "Wilhelm Wundt," p. 1087.

18. John Dollard and Neal E. Miller, *Personality and Psychotherapy* (New York: McGraw-Hill, 1950).

19. For a discussion of a dialectical versus nondialectical conception of interaction in the trait-situation controversy, see my "The Trait Versus Situation Controversy and the Concept of Interaction," *Personality and Social Psychology Bulletin* 3 (1977): 196–201. For a discussion of operationalizing dialectical ideas within the context of developmental methodology, see my "Methodological Issues in Life-Span Developmental Psychology from a Dialectical Perspective," *International Journal of Aging and Human Development* (in press).

20. Bo Ekehammer, "Interactionism in Personality from a Historical Perspective," *Psychological Bulletin* 81 (1974): 1026–1048.

21. Karl Marx, "Theses on Feuerbach" (written in 1845), in Engels, *Ludwig Feuerbach*, p. 82.

22. Karl Marx, *Economic and Philosophical Manuscripts* (written in 1844), in *The Marx-Engels Reader*, ed. Robert C. Tucker (New York: Norton, 1972), p. 93.

23. For a statement of the recent dialectical movement within psychology, see Klaus F. Riegel, "The Dialectics of Human Development," *American Psychologist* 31 (1976): 689–700.

24. Since writing this article I have come across Robert E. Lana's *The Foundations of Psychological Theory* (Hillsdale, N.J.: Erlbaum, 1976). Lana looks at the history of psychological ideas within the framework of the subject-object distinction, and I would consider his book to be consistent with the ideas presented in this article.

Chapter 2

The Fact-Theory Relationship and Marx's Epistemology

During the 1920s and 1930s, English-speaking social scientists largely adopted, uncritically, a view of the fact-theory relationship which came out of the philosophy of science. In retrospect, one can judge whether this community of scholars made what has been called an error to whatever extent that other and more appropriate options did in fact exist. It may indeed be argued that during the period when social scientists embraced a philosophy for the natural sciences, there did in fact exist an alternative and more appropriate epistemological basis for viewing the fact-theory relationship in their discipline. If this is so, the rush to imitate the natural sciences in terms of concepts, methods, and philosophy of science may be considered to have been a regressive event in the history of the social sciences.

Today, rather than the exclusive relationship in which the natural sciences have exerted a powerful and nonreciprocal influence on the foundational base of the social sciences, the social sciences are beginning to have an effect on the philosophy of science, by which is still understood natural science. In this process, the philosophy of natural science is beginning to arrive at an image of science and a view of the fact-theory relationship which existed well over a hundred years ago in rudimentary form (although not accessible in print), and over fifty years ago in a relatively sophisticated form. Since the "new" look in the

Reprinted with permission from the *Journal of the History of the Behavioral Sciences 13* (1977): 252–260; original title, "In Defense of a Critical-Presentist Historiography: The Fact-Theory Relationship and Marx's Epistemology."

philosophy of science on the fact-theory relationship places great
importance upon the notion of science as a distinctly human enterprise,
it is not surprising that the more enlightened epistemic view was first
espoused by individuals interested in the human, cultural, or what we
now know as the social sciences.

In determining whether certain events within the history of ideas
are historical "errors," one brings to bear upon such evaluative interpretations current knowledge, theories, beliefs, values, and ideologies.
Judging past events in the context of their present rather than trying to
understand them in their historical context forms the basis of what has
been called a presentist approach to historiography. Presentism has been
criticized from the vantage point of history in general by Butterfield [1] and
from the history of the behavioral sciences in particular by Stocking [2] and
criticized concretely as an approach within the history of psychology in
general by Weimar [3] and of social psychology in particular by Samelson. [4]
According to its critics, a presentist historical account abstracts from (and
therefore misrepresents) the historical complexity in such a way that
history is written as a glorification of the present—where the precursors
of current ideas are lauded and deviant or foreign ideas, vis-à-vis the
present, are treated as degenerate "mistakes" or "errors." Presentist
history has been described as linear, progressive, continuous, justificationist, or, in short, whiggish [5]—failing to concentrate upon understanding the past in its true historical context. Since those writing the history
of the natural sciences have adopted a presentist perspective as just
described, it is not surprising that historiography within the behavioral
sciences has also carried this stamp—given the dominance of a unified
science perspective and the drive to imitate the methodology of the
natural sciences so characteristic of North American social or behavioral
scientists.

In light of the serious criticisms which have been leveled against a
presentist historiography, and since the following argument adopts a
type of presentism insofar as the past is evaluated and interpreted in
light of the present, some concluding remarks attempt to justify a certain
kind of presentism. Important in this analysis is the distinction between
a naive "justification presentism" and an emancipatory and self-conscious
"critical presentism." The latter argument draws upon some of the ideas
of that body of thought which has come to be called the Frankfurt
School.

CRITICISMS OF THE RECEIVED VIEW OF FACTS AND THEORY

That the philosophy of natural science which was developed during the 1920s and 1930s exerted a powerful influence on the social sciences is no secret, and is too well known to review in detail. A philosophy of science which was based upon a long tradition of naive empiricism, and later joined with positivism and operationalism, was at first enthusiastically adopted by mainstream psychologists, later by sociologists, and most recently by political scientists in their quest for professional identity, status, and respect vis-à-vis the more established natural sciences. Such a philosophy of science stressed a strict separation between subject and object, and the possibility and desirability of studying a phenomenon in a disinterested and objective manner. Thus, in political science a movement arose during the 1950s which proclaimed the "end of ideology" [6] in their field insofar as it recommended the adoption of the "objective" procedures of behaviorism for studying political behavior—procedures which had proved so "successful" in psychology and sociology for establishing their "scientific" status. Indeed, the impact of behaviorism on the social sciences has been so strong that the term "behavioral sciences" is now well entrenched in the literature and is fighting a winning battle to replace the less epistemologically narrow and less excessive term "social sciences." This is a most unfortunate state of affairs.

While the philosophy of science which arose during the 1920s and 1930s was by no means a system of thought that was well integrated and without controversy, it is also true that there were some core ideas which were generally accepted and served to color this emerging view with a definite perspective. Especially pervasive was the notion that scientific theories should involve formalized axioms, where the strict separation between one's observational language and theoretical language was to be bridged by correspondence rules. The important point, then, was that observation and the establishment of facts were thought not to presuppose a particular theoretical perspective. Theoretically neutral facts were to be explained by one's theory, the implication being that different or opposing theories tried to explain the *same* facts. This view, now widely known as *The Received View on Theories*, [7] has been so dominant that "virtually every significant result obtained in philosophy of science between the 1920s and 1950 either employed or tacitly assumed the received view." [8]

As is well known to readers, this received view has come under increasing criticism such that it is now apparent that it cannot remain intact. While the nature of this criticism has spanned several issues, the notion in the received view that facts are theoretically neutral because they are expressed in a neutral observational language has not fared well under close scrutiny. One of the earliest attacks on the independence of both one's observational language and the expression of facts from one's theoretical language is that of Popper.[9] Popper dissented from traditional positivism and empiricism on many issues in his classic 1935 book, and he most certainly paved the way for later elaborations on the notion of theory-impregnated facts by such individuals as Hanson,[10] Feyerabend,[11] Naess,[12] and Kuhn.[13]

THE MARXIAN TRADITION AND THE FACT-THEORY RELATIONSHIP

There is now a veritable stampede of philosophers and historians of science who are rushing to the conclusion that all observation and facts are theory-laden, and that there is no such thing as hard-core, indubitable facts which are invariant across different theoretical explanations. This more enlightened view as to the theory-laden nature of all facts was actually cogently expressed by the Hungarian Marxian scholar Georg Lukacs in his book *History and Class Consciousness*, which was first published in the year 1923. Consider the contemporary ring of the following quoted paragraph:

The blinkered empiricist will of course deny that facts can only become facts within the framework of a system—which will vary with the knowledge desired. He believes that every piece of data from economic life, every statistic, every raw event already constitutes an important fact. In so doing he forgets that however simple an enumeration of "facts" may be, however lacking in commentary, it already implies an "interpretation." Already at this stage the facts have been comprehended by a theory, a method; they have been wrenched from their living context and fitted into a theory.[14]

Statements such as that quoted above agree in essence with certain aspects of the more recent views of such philosophers and historians of science as Feyerabend, Hanson, Kuhn, Naess, Popper, and others, and indeed, it would seem that we could be quoting any of the latter here on the fact-theory issue.[15]

Although Marx himself paid decreasing attention to philosophic issues as he progressed in elaborating his social, historical, and economic views,[16] there is an implicit epistemology in his writings which Lukacs detected and made explicit in terms of the modern issue of the relationship between facts and theory. It is interesting to note that Lukacs's view of theory-laden facts was based upon a Hegelian reading of Marx—a reading which recovered the, until then, lost idealist dimension of Marx's dialectic. Such an interpretation stressed an active, constructing subject [17] in opposition to the Marxist-Leninist one-way deterministic, materialistic, undialectical, positivistic "copy" theory of knowledge. Lukacs's view was developed at a time before some of the most important of Marx's early writings were made available in published form—works which were later to substantiate his insightful interpretation of Marx. Especially important in this respect were the early *Economic and Philosophic Manuscripts* which were written in 1944, although not published until 1927 in Russian and later in German in 1932. In these manuscripts Marx hints at an epistemology where nature is revealed as "humanized nature"; where the individual's needs play heavily in what he/she observes. This point is nicely illustrated in the following quotes:

The needy man, burdened with cares, has no appreciation of the most beautiful spectacle. The dealer in minerals sees only their commercial value, not their beauty or their particular characteristics.[18]

The eye has become a *human eye* when its *object* has become a *human*, social object, created by man and destined for him. The senses have therefore become directly *theoreticians* in practice. . . . the thing itself is an *objective human* relation to itself and to man, and vice versa.[19]

The point that Marx was making here is rather simple in essence yet profound in implication, and he adopts a tactic which more recent philosophers of science were to use over one hundred years later. Marx is arguing that what one perceives as the facts depends upon the context of the total situation, and, more specifically, the psychological determinants within an active, constructing subject. Thus all facts involve an interpretation. In the words of Kolakowski, the implications of such an epistemology for science is that "scientific thinking is a kind of human creation (not imitation), since both the linguistic and the scientific division of the world into particular objects arises from man's practical needs."[20]

The effect on perception of organismic properties, or what is "in" the organism (needs, beliefs, and, one might add, theoretical perspectives), was a central notion of the new look in perceptual research during the 1950s. Such kinds of psychological evidence were advanced by

Hanson, Kuhn, and Naess in developing their arguments concerning the impossibility of a neutral observational language and the necessary theory-laden nature of all facts. However, we have seen that Marx well anticipated such thinkers as Hanson, Kuhn, and Naess with respect to the argument that individual differences in organismic variables affect observation, and Marx's insights occurred well before there was even a field of experimental perception within psychology. Marx's epistemology, then, stressed the notion that what one perceives is highly context-dependent in terms of what the individual brings to the situation, and if we consider two different individuals holding radically different and possibly even contradictory theories, their explication of the facts will therefore be quite different.

Marx considered humanity's needs to be historical since humanity produces products and social relationships and thereby produces itself and new needs. It follows that cognitive categories, and, therefore, what is observed and considered as fact, will undergo historical change, since "The cultivation of the five senses is the work of all previous history." [21] The historicity of cognition implied by Marx's epistemology is at variance with the trans-situational and ahistorical approach of the received view of scientific knowledge which mainstream behavioral scientists have adopted. Explicitly protesting the universalist assumptions of the received view within the social sciences, and implicitly reaffirming Marx's epistemology, is a recent article written in the USA on the epistemological basis of social psychology. Thus Gergen [22] has persuasively argued that social psychology is an historical inquiry, and, therefore, it is impossible in principle to arrive at transhistorical or universal theories in this area. [23]

In addition to relying upon psychological and historical arguments in characterizing the context dependency of all observation and facts, Marx also furthered the latter view by laying down the foundations for the discipline of the sociology of knowledge; that is, the intimate relation between the underlying social, political, and economic structure and, broadly speaking, cognitive structure or knowledge structures. Thus, what one considers to be the facts, and the theoretical interpretation of such facts (especially with respect to social reality), was thought by Marx to be heavily influenced by sociohistorical background variables. Whereas Marx stressed the class structure in terms of identifying distinct groups with distinct ideologies or "distorted" views of social reality, latter-day sociologists such as Weber [24] and Mannheim [25] expanded on two issues: (1) The notion of ideology was enlarged to include Marxist theory itself; and (2) In addition to distinct groups based upon class structure, the possibility of relating particular theories or views of social reality to additional groups was considered, such as religious, age, occupational, and political groups—the former of special interest to Weber and the latter of special interest to Mannheim.

The point in alluding above to some of those individuals who explicitly recognized the sociohistorical nature of the dialectic between facts and their theoretical interpretation is to emphasize that, at the time when social scientists were committing themselves to the received view on foundational issues, there existed in the 1920s and 1930s alternative conceptions of the epistemological status of the fact-theory relationship. The views of such people as Marx, Lukacs, Weber and Mannheim explicitly recognized the theory-laden nature of all facts and, even further, expounded on the important relationship between social factors and one's interpretation or "theory" of social reality. It is a sad, but telling, commentary on the majority of social scientists, yet nonetheless probably true that, since philosophers of natural science have all but abandoned naive empiricism and positivism, and have endorsed some important Marxian epistemic ideas, can mainstream social scientists be far behind?

CONCLUDING COMMENTS: TOWARDS A "CRITICAL PRESENTISM"

During the crucial formative years of the social sciences, if social scientists had opted for the *epistemological* position (not necessarily the accompanying substantive theory) as set out by Marx and later elaborated by others, then they would not have adopted a regressive position on the fact-theory issue. The early insights of Marx and certain scholars in the Marxian tradition [26] are finally appearing in recent discussions of the history and philosophy of the natural sciences. The crisis in the received view of the philosophy of science, which led to more adequate conceptions of the fact-theory relationship, was generated by the "rediscovery" of the importance of psychological, sociological, and historical variables in formulating an adequate conception of the nature, structure, and growth of science. The latter image of science recovers the important human dimension, as well as the dialectic between facts and theory, science and society, all of which Marx stressed so well.

It should be noted that the modern heir to Marx's and Lukacs's more enlightened view on the fact-theory relationship was the neo-Marxian perspective known as the *critical theory of society*. [27] Critical theory explicitly recognizes that, in the social sciences, different theories explain different facts. Therefore, according to critical theory, paradigm resolution in this area should proceed on the basis of evaluating the underlying image of humanity that a certain theoretical position assumes and affirms. Critical theory attempts to go beyond the facts, beyond mere appearances, and penetrate to the underlying values and theoretical assumptions of a position. That theory which leads to greater human emancipation is the one to be endorsed according to critical theory.

The critical theory of the Frankfurt School developed rapidly during the 1930s and after under its key spokesmen—Adorno, Horkheimer, and Marcuse. It is unfortunate that its criticisms of naive empiricism and positivism within the social sciences did not have a more profound effect on the theory and practice of North American social scientists. Part (and not all) of the problem was the unavailability of much of this work in English. Fortunately, however, over the last five years much of the early work of the Frankfurt School has appeared in English translation.[28]

In addition to drawing the reader's attention to critical theory for purposes of demonstrating the existence of a more enlightened philosophy for the social sciences at a time when the Vienna Circle was beginning to have an impact upon English-speaking social scientists, there is another point this school of thought can help make. That is to say, critical theory provides the conceptual machinery for engaging in an enlightened or "critical presentism" in reconstructing the intellectual past, thereby drawing the methodological tack adopted in this article under its theoretical umbrella. Committed to the dual Marxian legacy of a genuine historical approach (an approach which attempts to understand historical events in their social, political, and economic context),[29] as well as simultaneously engaging in a radical criticism (interpreting and judging the past in its historical context from the vantage point of the present),[30] critical theory combines the very best of both understanding *and* judgment. In this way, critical theory provides the concept methodology for realizing the dialectic which Stocking posed in the last sentence of his editorial concerning the limits of both presentism and historicism,[31] namely, "By suspending judgment as to present utility, we make that judgment ultimately possible."[32]

However, it should be noted that Stocking's recommendation can flounder without due "critical" reflection. Thus, in suspending judgment of the past *now* for the sake of that cherished but ever elusive judgment in the *future*, one may lose sight of the "ultimate" goal and transform the means (temporary suspension of judgment of the past in light of the present) into an end (permanent suspension of judgment of the past in light of the present). In this way, by alluding to some "ultimate" goal, there is the real danger and likelihood of neutralizing the critical dimension of presentism. In robbing presentism of its critical cutting edge by withholding current judgment in the past in the context of the present (and judgment of the present in light of the past), the result is a kind of impotent historicism which Stocking attempted to transcend.

In spite of the above important cautionary note regarding Stocking's recommendation, the spirit of his essay is towards the development of what has been called here a "critical presentism." As such, it is part of a growing self-consciousness on the part of historians committed to the *explicit* introduction of values into historiography. Thus, in an essay on history in the "critical spirit," Zinn argued that "Historical writing is most true when it is appropriate simultaneously to what was in the past, to the conditions of the present, and to what should be in the future." [33] This brand of presentism, critical in intent, is traced by Zinn back to the philosophy of history of Carl Becker, who, in 1912, defined presentism as "the imperative command that knowledge shall serve purpose, and learning be applied to the problem of human life." [34] In fact, and as implied earlier, presentism in the critical sense constituted the very core of Marx's historiography. [35] To read Marx any other way is to misunderstand him. Thus, current criticisms of socially irrelevant historicism and naive or "justificationist presentism" [36] may be seen as attempts to reclaim orthodox presentism in the true Marxian critical spirit.

In light of the recent attempts to revive and retrieve orthodox presentism in the critical tradition, Butterfield's revisionism as to the nature and meaning of presentism may now be seen to be misguided. Butterfield justly singles out the fallacy of an historiography based upon a Whig interpretation of the past, but then, unfortunately, generalizes to condemn *any* interpretation of the past in light of the present. [37] His valid critique of a "justification presentism" leads him not to embrace orthodox or critical presentism, but, rather, to a position which attempts to eschew all value judgments from historical inquiry. [38] Thus Butterfield drives values underground, thereby obscuring, but not lessening, their effect. In this way, his historiography robs history of its critical function, transforming it into an inconsequential, erudite historicism which, because it studies the past for its own sake, ignores the present. [39] By default, Butterfield's historiography is paradoxically justificationist vis-à-vis the present. In penetrating beyond the appearance of his critique of the Whig interpretation of history, it can be seen that the underlying values and theoretical roots of his argument are firmly planted in whiggish soil. Butterfield's surface critique is at bottom a cleverly disguised capitulation, and he affirms that which he denies. The message should be clear—critics of "justificationist presentism" inadvertently support that very position to the extent they advocate a naive historicism rather than a "critical presentism."

In conclusion, it should be noted that in this chapter I have attempted to demonstrate the contemporary nature of Marx's epistemology with respect to current philosophy of science, and have then sought to defend my historiography by again calling upon the genius of Marx and his legacy.

Notes

1.   Herbert Butterfield, *The Whig Interpretation of History* (London: G. Bell and Sons, 1931).

2.   George W. Stocking, Jr., "On the Limits of 'Presentism' and 'Historicism' in the Historiography of the Behavioral Sciences," *Journal of the History of the Behavioral Sciences 1* (1965): 211–218.

3.   Walter B. Weimer, "The History of Psychology and its Retrieval from Historiography: I. The Problematic Nature of History," *Science Studies 4* (1974): 235–258, and "The History of Psychology and its Retrieval from Historiography II: Some Lessons for the Methodology of Scientific Research," *Science Studies 4* (1974): 367–396.

4.   Franz Samelson, "History, Origin Myth, and Ideology: Comte's 'Discovery' of Social Psychology," *Journal for the Theory of Social Behavior 4* (1974): 217–231,

5.   "The whig historian stands on the summit of the 20th century, and organizes his scheme of history from the point of view of his own day" (Butterfield, p. 13).

6.   See, for example, M. Rejai, ed., *Decline of Ideology?* (Chicago: Aldine-Atherton, 1971).

7.   First so designated by H. Putnam, "What Theories Are Not," in *Logic, Methodology, and Philosophy of Science,* ed. E. Nagel, P. Suppes, and A. Tarski (Stanford: Stanford University Press, 1962).

8.   F. Suppe, "The Search for Philosophic Understanding of Scientific Theories," in *The Structure of Scientific Theories,* ed. F. Suppe (Urbana: University of Illinois Press, 1974), p.3.

9.   Karl R. Popper, *The Logic of Scientific Discovery* (New York: Basic Books, 1959), which is the English translation of *Logik der Forschung* (Vienna: Springer, 1935).

10.   Norwood R. Hanson, *Patterns of Discovery* (Cambridge: Cambridge University Press, 1958).

11.   Most recent of Paul K. Feyerabend's *Against Method* (London: New Left Review Books, 1975).

12.   Arne Naess, *The Pluralist and Possibilist Aspect of the Scientific Enterprise* (London: Allen & Unwin, 1972).

13. Thomas S. Kuhn, *The Structure of Scientific Revolutions* (Chicago: University of Chicago Press, 1962). See also "Logic of Discovery or Psychology of Research?" and "Reflections on My Critics," both in *Criticism and the Growth of Knowledge,* eds. Imre Lakatos and Alan Musgrave (Cambridge: Cambridge University Press, 1970), as well as "Postscript—1969," in the 1970 edition of *The Structure of Scientific Revolutions,* and "Second Thoughts on Paradigms," in Suppe, *The Structure of Scientific Theories.*

14. George Lukacs, *History and Class Consciousness* (Cambridge: MIT Press, 1971), p. 5.

15. Readers who are familiar with Popper's *The Open Society and its Enemies* (Princeton, N.J.: Princeton University Press, Vols. 1 and 2, 5th edition, 1966) and *The Poverty of Historicism* (London: Routledge & Kegan Paul, 1960, 2nd edition), which contain his biting attacks on Plato, Hegel, Marx, and historicism (defined in this debate as the belief that there are general laws of historical development that render the course of history inevitable and predictable), will appreciate the irony beginning to unfold and which becomes readily apparent subsequently. Popper, Marx, and neo-Marxists in the Hegelian tradition all share nontrivial similarities in regard to their emphasis placed upon the idealist dimension of an active, constructing subject. The latter forms the theoretical basis for the more enlightened view of the fact-theory relationship. Thus, one could argue that Popper's views owe much to Hegel and Marx, and "conjecture" that, in his early critical reading of Hegel and Marx on historicism, Popper assimilated some key Hegelian-Marxist ideas.

16. "The philosophers have *interpreted* the world in various ways: the point however is to *change* it," from Karl Marx, "Theses on Feuerbach" (written in 1845), in Frederick Engels, *Ludwig Feuerbach* (New York: International Publishers, 1941), p. 84.

17. But not to the exclusion of the materialist aspect of the dialectic.

18. Karl Marx, "Economic and Philosophical Manuscripts" (written in 1844), in *Marx's Concept of Man,* ed. Erich Fromm (New York: Ungar, 1966), p. 134.

19. Ibid., p. 132.

20. Leszek Kolakowski, *Toward a Marxist Humanism* (New York: Grove Press, 1968), p. 48.

21. Marx, "Economic and Philosophical Manuscripts," p. 134.

22. Kenneth J. Gergen, "Social Psychology as History," *Journal of Personality and Social Psychology, 26* (1973): 309–320.

23. It should be noted, however, that the historicity of social psychological concepts and processes was previously explored by the Soviet psychologist B. Porshnev in *Social Psychology and History* (Moscow: Progress Publishers, 1970), who may be considered as part of a long tradition of Soviet interest in the historicity of cognition (e.g., see Alexander K. Luria's discussion of I.S. Vygotskii's contribution in the 1920s to this topic in "Towards the Problem of the Historical Nature of Psychological Processes," *International Journal of Psychology 6* [1971]:259–272.

24. In Max Weber's classical essay "'Objectivity' in Social Science," in *The Methodology of the Social Sciences*, eds. Edward A. Shils and Henry A. Finch (Glencoe, Illinois: Free Press, 1949), the focus is primarily upon the fact-value distinction. While Weber held fast to the logical separation between facts and values, he certainly maintained that values affect observation and the theoretical interpretation of social reality ("All knowledge of cultural reality, as may be seen, is always knowledge from *particular points of view*," Weber, p. 81). Thus, according to this view, theoretical perspectives, which are intimately connected to underlying values and metaphysical assumptions, affect the selection and interpretation of the facts. The latter statement implies a distinction between "value" and "theory" insofar as it would seem values per se are prescriptive, ontological commitments without an explanatory function, while theories carry both prescriptive baggage and explanatory power. While the focus of the present article is upon the fact-theory relationship, values must be acknowledged in passing (also see below the discussion of values and critical theory) since they are deeply embedded in any theoretical interpretation of the facts, especially of social facts. An extended discussion of the distinction between facts, values, and theories is beyond the scope of the present article. For an introduction to the literature on the fact-value issue, see Gresham Riley, ed., *Values, Objectivity, and the Social Sciences*, (Reading, Mass.: Addison-Wesley, 1974), and the selected bibliography.

25. Karl Mannheim, *Ideology and Utopia* (New York: Harcourt, Brace & World, 1936). The longer German version was first published in 1929.

26. I exclude here, naturally, the hard-line, positivistic, undialectical, and non-Hegelian interpreters of Marx.

27. See, for example, Max Horkheimer's *Critical Theory* (New York: Herder & Herder, 1972).

28. The output of the Frankfurt School is substantial, and the novice to this area should consult what is probably the single best comprehensive introduction to this literature, Martin Jay's *The Dialectical Imagination: A History of the Frankfurt School and the Institute of Social Research 1923–1950* (London, Heinemann, 1973), which also includes a very useful bibliography of the publications of the members of the Frankfurt Institute of Social Research, as well as publications related to their work. Articles on the Frankfurt School and their members frequently appear in such journals as *New Left Review, Philosophy of the Social Sciences, Social Research*, and especially *Telos*.

29. Admittedly I have not developed this theme here with respect to placing the fact-theory issue in its historical context, but have elsewhere in reconstructing psychology's history. See, for example, my "The Emerging Field of the Sociology of Psychological Knowledge," *American Psychologist 30* (1975): 988–1002 (and a reply by Hans J. Eysenck "Ideology Run Wild," *American Psychologist 31* (1976): 311–312; and my counter-reply "Buss Replies," *American Psychologist 31* (1976): 312, as well as "Counter-Culture and Counter-Psychology: The Interface of the Youth Movement and Humanistic Psychology,"

Interpersonal Development 5 (1975): 223–233; "Galton and the Birth of Differential Psychology and Eugenics; Social, Political, and Economic Factors," *Journal of the History of the Behavioral Sciences 12* (1976): 47–58;; "Galton and Sex Differences," *Journal of the History of the Behavioral Sciences 12* (1976): 283–285; and "Development of Dialectics and Development of Humanistic Psychology," *Human Development 19* (1976): 248–260.

30.   It should be noted that critical theory is conceptually more sophisticated than to be only equipped to judge the past from the perspective of the present. Thus by "critical presentism" I therefore mean the dialectic involving the critical evaluation of the past in light of the present, and the critical evaluation of the present in light of the past. Pursuing the complexity here for a moment, a complete critical approach would focus upon the dialectical interface of the past, present, and future in arriving at critical analyses, and, therefore, in addition to the past-present dialectic, accommodate the past-future and present-future dialectics and combinations thereof.

31   Stocking, p. 212, defines historicism as "the essential quality of the commitment to understanding the past for its own sake." For present purposes I adopt this meaning in subsequent occurrences of this term.

32.   Ibid., p. 217.

33.   Howard Zinn, "History as Private Enterprise," in *The Critical Spirit: Essays in Honor of Herbert Marcuse,* ed. Kurt H. Wolff and Barrington Moore, Jr. (Boston: Beacon Press, 1967, p. 181.

34.   Quoted in, but unfortunately not documented by, Zinn, p. 174.

35.   Of course Marx also introduced the third dimension of the future into his critical theory of society.

36.   "Justificationist presentism" may be considered as viewing the past in light of the present for purposes of justifying present reality rather than for purposes of radically transforming that reality.

37.   "The study of the past with one eye, so to speak, upon the present is the source of all sins and sophistries in history" (Butterfield, p. 31).

38.   "Above all it is not the role of the historian to come to what might be called judgments of value" (ibid., p. 73).

39.   "The value of history lies in the richness of its recovery of the concrete life of the past" (ibid., p. 68).

Chapter 3

The Historical Context of Differential Psychology and Eugenics

In writing the history of their discipline, psychologists as a general rule have tended to parade one theory, school, or person's ideas after the other, focusing almost exclusively on the internal conflicts, disputes, and controversies. Such being the case, psychology would seem to be no different than "The separate disciplines, such as philosophy, the sciences, or political theory, [which] insofar as they study their past ideas tend to do so unhistorically, treating them substantively and as if they arose in a vacuum" (Stromberg, 1968, p.2). The development of ideas in general, however, is intimately connected to the underlying social fabric of a society, and psychological ideas, it would seem, are not immune to social influences. An adequate understanding of the historical development of any set of ideas requires an appreciation of the sociohistorical conditions (which serve as a background or context) which in no small way condition or help to give shape to intellectual ideas. Professional historians concerned with the history of ideas are coming to realize that to exclude a consideration of the underlying social conditions in any discussion of the development of intellectual ideas is a grave sin. The recent discipline of intellectual history is dedicated to the task of assessing the many factors (both internal and external) which bear upon the development of intellectual ideas. The concerns of intellectual history as an academic discipline have been well expressed by Strom-

Reprinted with permission from the *Journal of the History of the Behavioral Sciences 12* (1976): 47–58; original title, "Galton and the Birth of Differential Psychology and Eugenics: Social, Political, and Economic Forces."

berg: "The interaction of historically important ideas with the social milieu from which they emerge and which they in turn influence—this is, broadly, the domain of intellectual history" (1968, p.2). It should be noted that the study of intellectual history does not deny the importance of internal factors in the shaping of intellectual ideas, but, rather, compliments such considerations with an equal emphasis upon the social context (e.g., political, economic, etc.) from which ideas spring.

Although psychologists have in the past been negligent in considering the sociohistorical context of their ideas (e.g., Boring's 1950 classical work on the history of psychology), there are recent rumblings which would seem to indicate that this state of affairs may soon be corrected. Thus Gergen (1973) has recently argued that social psychology is an historical inquiry, where current theories in this area reflect current cultural values, norms, and ideologies. As the latter change, our social psychological theories must change in profound ways, thereby precluding the attainment of general laws of social behavior which are transhistorical. Sympathetic with Gergen's thesis, yet more inclusive, is what I have called elsewhere (Buss, 1979) the emerging field of the sociology of psychological knowledge. The latter takes as its goal to try and apply a sociohistorical analysis to psychological models, theories, or paradigms, in an attempt to appreciate the social context from which psychological ideas develop.

The spirit of the present chapter is within a sociology of psychological knowledge inquiry, or, an intellectual historical approach to psychological ideas. More specifically, the purpose of the present chapter is to explore the sociohistorical relationship between normative and existential thinking concerning the individual at the time when the fields of differential psychology and eugenics were launched in Britain by Sir Francis Galton. It will be argued that the social, political, and economic forces operative at this time served to give rise to a specific normative conception of the individual which, in turn, conditioned the birth of the scientific study of individual differences and the field of eugenics. That is to say, the normative doctrine of individualism, which was embedded in the social infrastructure, served to focus scientific attention to the study of individual differences as well as influence the substantive interpretation of such differences. In this process, it will be further argued, the original normative view of the individual at this time became transformed into its dialectical opposite—a feat which Galton unwittingly accomplished by pursuing his scientific substantive interpretation of individual differences to its logical conclusion. After briefly outlining the rise of liberalism, democracy, and capitalism in nineteenth century Britain, Galton's ideas, then, will be examined in their social context.

THE RISE OF MODERN INDIVIDUALISM IN BRITAIN

The rise of modern individualism as a normative doctrine in Europe was closely tied to the social, political, and economic changes which occurred from the sixteenth century onward. While individualism was being espoused by British, German, and French social thinkers by the nineteenth century, the particular brand of individualism differed somewhat from country to country. It was in nineteenth century Britain, however, that liberalism, democracy, and capitalism were all in ascendance and thus paved the way for the development of an integrated doctrine of individualism that permeated and served as a higher order integrator of diverse social spheres.

As outlined by Smith (1968), classical liberalism refers to the unique experience of Britain, where Britain achieved through peaceful means (i.e., the greater freedom for the individual) what the Continent had tried to achieve through revolution. Based upon a dislike for arbitrary authority and a belief in the desirability of the free expression of the individual personality, liberalism in Britain brought into being political reforms that increasingly placed the individual above the state. By the seventeenth century significant constitutional gains had been made allowing for such political rights as the right of opposition, the rule of law, and the separation of powers. The Reformation and the attendant Protestant religion helped to give rise to a new spirit of individualism and anti-institutionalism where each individual could now communicate directly with God and was solely responsible for his own salvation. The demand for religious freedom and the tolerance of diverse beliefs were aspects of a more general attitude which may be characterized as enlightened, rational, pragmatic experimentalism. Progress in all aspects of society was encouraged, and by the nineteenth century, liberalism looked favorably upon advances made in science, technology, and economics at the expense of a decline in religious beliefs (for a characterization of the Victorian mind as a curious mixture of optimism, critical spirit, rigidity, and enthusiasm, see Houghton, 1957). The rise of capitalism was producing a broad middle class base which emphasized individual responsibility and individual enterprise. Thus the liberal gains made in the political arena were paralleled by the theory and practice of economic liberty.

That classical liberalism was an integrated doctrine encompassing social, political, and economic aspects of individualism is partly due to the forces which gave rise to it. Girvetz, for example, states that "classical liberalism cannot be understood unless one is aware of [at least] two factors which profoundly influenced its formation: the impact of the physical sciences on the thinking of the seventeenth and eighteenth centuries, and the aspirations of the new capitalist class" (1963, p. 23). The successful methods of the physical sciences, which emphasized mathematical laws, measurement, quantification, and atomism, were applied to man and society, and helped give rise, for example, to a hedonistic calculus (see below). With respect to the growing capitalist class, the classical economists, under the leadership of Adam Smith (1723–1790), stressed a laissez-faire approach, calling for a self-regulating market which was to be unrestricted either by monopoly or political intervention. John Stuart Mill (1806–1873) formulated the political doctrine which was necessary to protect individual freedom within a laissez-faire approach to capitalism. In his autobiography he writes, "I was as much as ever a radical and a democrat . . . I thought the predominance of the aristocratic classes . . . an evil worth any struggle to get rid of" (Mill, 1969, p. 103). By broadening and democratizing the values of liberalism, that is, drawing the growing commercial middle class under its umbrella, the classical economists thereby strengthened liberalism and helped to make it a total ideology. It was the English utilitarians, Jeremy Bentham (1748–1832) and Mill, who completed the latter task by uniting liberal politics and liberal economics with the concepts of utility and market. Thus, just as a capitalist was accountable in a free market, those who govern in politics were accountable to those governed. Armed with their hedonistic calculus and the principle of equality, they argued for "the greatest good for the greatest number." Politicans were to now survive in the political market by drafting laws which would provide for a maximum of free choice and practical liberty within the constraint of the general utilitarian maxim. Mill's views on individual liberty were set down in his classical essay, *On Liberty*, where "The object of this Essay is to assert one very simple principle . . . that the only purpose for which power can be rightfully exercised over any other member of a civilized community, against his will, is to prevent harm to others" (Mill, 1969, p. 359). This philosophy paved the way for legislation which encouraged more universal education, free speech, inclusive representation, and an expanded suffrage—all of which provided for constitutional security and good government. Thus Bentham and Mill formulated a theory of positive political action by effectively joining constitutional democracy, economic liberalism, and utilitarianism.

Up until the mid-nineteenth century, liberalism in Britain had provided only the aristocrats and bourgeoisie with the rights they needed, and after the revolts on the continent in 1848, it became increasingly necessary that more positive action be taken by the state to guarantee the rights of the expanding proletariat. Thus, as argued by Girvetz (1963) and Stromberg (1968), liberalism came to abandon its old belief that that government which governed least was best, and turned instead to the idea of the affirmative state, thereby accommodating itself to democratic, nationalistic, and socialistic sentiment. The industrial revolution had by now produced a complex society requiring greater and greater bureaucracy to administer, and it became increasingly apparent that a laissez-faire society meant that one man's freedom entailed the oppression of another. Liberalism during this period retained its goal of the autonomous individual, but needed to change its means in the face of changing social conditions. The previous laissez-faire attitude gradually gave way to an emphasis on collective participation where the state was invoked in order to safeguard the rights of individuals and disadvantaged groups. Opponents of this new liberalism, which embraced democratic and socialistic principles, did exist. Thus Herbert Spencer (1820–1903) clung to the principle of nonintervention backed up by his theory of Social Darwinism, but his particular brand of liberalism, which of necessity became a conservative ideology in the face of changing social conditions, did not have any significant impact upon social policy.

In any case, by the late 1800s liberalism itself began to decline in importance as a political ideology, mainly because of its contradictory nature. As pointed out by Hutchison, "The paradoxical mission of nineteenth-century liberalism was to create both the free-market economy and the democracy that was to destroy it" (1966, p. 13). The successive democratic reform bills of 1832, 1867, and 1884 ultimately resulted in the transfer of political power to the masses, and their political demands were at variance with economic inequality, the latter a necessary consequence of liberal economics. The contradictions within liberalism were apparent to Mill, who expended some energy in an attempt to resolve them (e.g., Himmelfarb, 1974).

In summary then, by the nineteenth century the growth of liberalism in Britain had given rise to a normative view of the individual which stressed freedom and opportunity which in turn made explicit recognition of and sanctioned the existence of a pluralistic view of man. Individuals were to be equal before the law but have the freedom to develop their potential in diverse directions. Indeed, the promotion of the diversity of individuals was a necessary step in maintaining the growth of a capitalistic economy in an industrial state which had by now become so complex that specialization of human talent was required to keep the machinery running smoothly.

GALTON, INDIVIDUAL DIFFERENCES, AND INDIVIDUALISM

Sir Francis Galton (1822–1911) lived and wrote at a time when the British Empire under Queen Victoria was at its peak—a time when modern democracy, liberalism, capitalism, and industrialization were all more advanced in Britain as compared to continental Europe or North America. It was a time when extreme optimism in the perfectibility of society and the individual permeated all aspects of social life. Galton was a noted statistician, anthropologist, geographer, and world traveller, as well as being the founder of the scientific study of individual differences and the field of eugenics. This genius (Terman estimated his IQ to be 200) had the good fortune of becoming independently wealthy at the age of 22 when his father, a banker, died and left Galton sufficient means to live for the rest of his natural life. At this point Galton promptly dropped out of medical school and elected to become a gentleman scholar.

"Galton the man" has been recorded in Galton's (1908) autobiography, as well as extensively documented by his friend and biographer Karl Pearson (1857–1936) in four separate volumes (Pearson, 1914, 1924, 1930A, 1930B), and more recently by Blacker (1952). Besides Pearson and Blacker, reviews of Galton's contributions to statistics and psychology have appeared by Sir Cyril Burt (1883–1971), who knew Galton as a boy (Burt, 1961, 1962), Boring (1950), who has assessed Galton's work within the framework of the history of psychological thought, and Cowan (1972), who has argued that Galton's statistical contributions were motivated by a concern to put eugenics on a firm scientific basis. Galton's major ideas are contained in four separate volumes, *Hereditary Genius* (1869), *English Men of Science, their Nature and Nurture* (1874), *Inquiries into Human Faculty* (1883), and *Natural Inheritance* (1889). For a bibliography of Galton's 227 publications, see Blacker (1952). Galton's ideas were undoubtedly influenced in a major way by other nineteenth century thinkers, but his ideas were also, in part, embedded in the prevailing social, political, and economic forces operative in nineteenth century Britain, and his perspective of reality may be traced, in part, to the social infrastructure of his time.

Probably the most important thinker to affect Galton's views on individual differences was his half-cousin Charles Darwin (1809–1882). As noted by Pearson, "Galton had read and assimilated Darwin's *Origin of Species*, and in Galton's own words that book had formed 'a real crisis in my life' and had driven away 'the constraint of my old superstition as if it had been a nightmare, and was the first to give me freedom of thought'" (1924, pp. 4–5). The idea that the evolution of man occurred according to principles amenable to scientific understanding took the study of man and his being out of a supernatural context and placed it squarely within natural processes. Galton took over Darwin's ideas of variation, the inheritance of physical traits, and natural selection, and applied them to the area of mental traits. The idea of specialization of physical structures and their functions was able to make a smooth transition to the notion of specialization of mental structures and functions· which have survival value, and was quite compatible with a capitalistic economy which required specialized talent. The growing division of labor and specialization of occupations may be seen as a social phenomenon crying out for a scientific explanation as to the basis of individual differences. That such social conditions had an impact upon Galton's thinking is illustrated by his comment that "Peculiar gifts, moreover, afford an especial justification for division of labour, each man doing what he can do best."[1] In capitalistic British society there were great group or class differences in the extent to which the different careers and vocations required different levels of intelligence and specialized training. How was one to explain and justify the hierarchically structured occupational groups and attendant social inequalities other than by the principle of inherited individual differences in mental abilities? Indeed, the prevailing democratic liberalism, which stressed freedom for individual development, would have been inconsistent with a primarily environmental interpretation of individual differences in intelligence given the gross class differences characteristic of capitalistic Britain. Thus all people theoretically had the opportunity and freedom to develop their potential, and the existent class structure therefore must represent inherited individual differences in ability. Liberal individualism was still secure and thereby conditioned the scientific interpretation of individual differences.

The above interpretation of liberal individualism conditioning the interpretation of individual differences would be strengthened to the extent that Galton's personal political views reflected the prevailing capitalistic liberal individualism of this time. Galton was indeed a bourgeois liberal thinker, valuing personal and political freedom and exhibiting these values in his actions and writings. In regard to liberal laissez-faire economics, Galton writes in *Hereditary Genius* that "Life in general may be looked upon as a republic where the individuals are for the most part unconscious that *while they are working for themselves they are also working for the public good*" (Galton, 1907, p. 195, emphasis added). His interpretation as to the moral value of the evolution of inborn qualities for adaptation to the environment is clearly compatible with Bentham's hedonism, insofar as he states that "if we cease to dwell on the miscarriages of individual lives or of single generations, we shall plainly perceive that the actual tenantry of the world progresses in a direction that may in some sense be described as *the greatest happiness of the greatest number*" (Galton, 1907, p. 195, emphasis added).

At a more personal level Galton's extensive early travels around the globe gave expression to his own belief in the personal freedom to carry out one's desires as well as served to introduce him to an interest in the psychological and social processes which either hinder or nurture freedom (as stimulated by his contact with the African peoples and their culture). As Blacker (1952, pp. 72–80) has argued, Galton had a deep ethical commitment to individual freedom and was much opposed to tyranny, paternalism, and authority. He had a strong conviction in the perfectibility of man, and indeed it was towards this end that he felt that the theory and practice of eugenics could significantly contribute. These two threads of thought, the normative belief in the freedom and opportunity for full development of each individual and, on the other hand, the scientific study of individual differences or the existential question, are tightly interwoven in Galton's ideas, especially his eugenics program, which will be examined subsequently.

In order to more fully appreciate that Galton's scientific ideas were indeed influenced by the prevailing social and political conditions at the time, it may be instructive to consider some additional thoughts he had on democracy and liberalism. In *Hereditary Genius* he stated that "I cannot think of any claim to respect . . . a peer on the ground of descent, who has neither been nobly educated, nor has any eminent kinsman" (1962, p. 126). Here we see Galton lashing out at the existing social practice of inherited privilege per se. Towards the end of the book his views on freedom and class mobility are clearly stated: "The best form of civilization in respect to the improvement of race would be one . . . where incomes were chiefly derived from professional sources, and not much through inheritance; where every lad had a chance of showing his abilities, and, if highly-gifted, was enabled to achieve a first-class education and entrance into professional life" (p. 415). In this passage we get a glimpse of a man committed to equal opportunity, but the standard for individual participation in society is always the same—innate intelligence. This fusion of individual freedom and a genetic interpretation of individual differences in ability lead Galton to qualify his views on democracy in later life. Thus in 1873 he stated:

As regards the democratic feeling, its assertion of equality is deserving of the highest admiration in so far as it demands equal consideration for the feelings of all, just in the same way as their rights are equally maintained by the law. But it goes further than this, for it asserts that men are of equal value as social units, equally capable of voting, and the rest. This feeling is undeniably wrong.

Passages such as the above led Pearson to conclude that:

Galton was an ardent democrat, if such means to refuse birth any privilege if birth be not accompanied by mental superiority; he was a through-going aristocrat, if such be involved in a denial of the equality of all men; he would have graded mankind by their natural aptitudes, and *have done his best to check the reproduction of the lower classes*. (1924, p. 85, emphasis added)

The paradox in Galton's thinking is beginning to show. His normative belief in individual freedom seems to be negated when coupled with his genetic interpretation of individual differences in mental ability and his "adoration of ability" (Pearson, 1924, p. 94). This aspect of Galton's thinking reached a climax in his utopia *Kantsaywhere* (see below).

Galton had a love for measurement and quantification as well as some mechanical aptitude, the latter revealing itself in the design of experimental apparatus. Riegel (1972) has recently, in part, traced the development of the mechanistic model of human development, which implies a view of continuous growth, to a capitalistic orientation as represented in Britain and North America. The measurement and quantification of individual differences may also be viewed in the context of reflecting capitalistic values, where measurement and quantification play such an important role in determining salaries, prices, losses, profits, markets, etc. Just as it is possible to measure and quantify man's products, it is possible to measure and quantify man himself. It was to this end that Galton set up his Anthropometric Laboratory in 1884 at the International Health Exhibition (later moved to the South Kensington Museum in London) and subsequently in 1904, the Galton Laboratory which was established at the University of London. Thus the emphasis upon measurement, quantification, and science and technology, which was intimately bound up to the growth of capitalism, made nineteenth century Britain the natural birthplace for the scientific study of individual differences to take place.

The more complex the society the greater the need for specialization of human talent. By the nineteenth century the forces of democracy and capitalism in Britain had created a specialization of occupations and a large governmental bureaucracy to oversee the administration of the Empire and all its activities. Specialization and bureaucracy came to characterize all aspects of social life—including business, government, science, the arts, religion, etc. Capitalism as an economic system was making Britain wealthy. The basic idea of efficiently producing a surplus of products and exchanging them on the open national and international market yielded good returns to both the private sector and government and permitted the growth of science, technology, additional markets, specialization, etc. In short, a capitalistic society created individual differences in the sense of demanding previously unheard of specialization of human talent. Capitalism at this time had produced mainly two large classes—the bourgeoisie and proletariat. Within each of these separate classes, however, there was a high degree of occupational diversity. *Genotypic* individual differences served as a necessary prerequisite for the development of the modern differentiated state, but once the latter process was well underway, the capitalistic structure fed back to the pool of human talent, thereby developing, encouraging, and promoting even greater *phenotypic* individual differences than had previously been the case. Phenotypic individual differences became manifested in all aspects of social life. The days of the "universal man" were over.

In summary then, democratic, liberal, capitalistic individualism conditioned the birth of the scientific study of individual differences as founded by Galton in at least three important ways. First, the rise of the modern capitalistic state depended upon and fostered the growth of the division of labor and occupational specialization of human talent. The spread of substantive rationalism to all sectors of society (government, science, economics, art, religion, etc.) had produced a highly advanced and differentiated society requiring a professional bureaucratic machinery based upon formal rationalism to maintain coordination. For the first time in the history of man phenotypic individual differences ran rampant. Second, the measurement, quantification, and description of individual differences was closely associated with an economic society which depended upon and developed the measurement and quantification of its material products. The rise of a capitalistic economy was producing a new image of man which paved the way for the measurement and quantification of psychological characteristics. Science and technology had been highly successful in the material world. Might not these principles and techniques be successfully applied to the realm of mental phenomena? Third, having observed and described individual differences, Galton's exclusively genetic interpretation was demanded by the prevailing doctrine of bourgeois, liberal, democratic individualism. Given the belief that each individual did indeed have the freedom and opportunity to fulfill his potential, it naturally followed that the existent hierarchical class structure reflected innate differences in mental ability.

GALTON, EUGENICS, AND KANTSAYWHERE

English and English (1958) define eugenics as "the attempt to improve in inborn qualities of a race or breed, especially of men. . . . Though sometimes called a science, eugenics is properly an application of the science of genetics." As argued subsequently, Galton, the founder of eugenics, was responsible for forging eugenics into a total ideology.

In 1883 Galton's book *Inquiries into Human Faculty and its Development* was first published and has been considered (e.g., Boring, 1950) as marking the beginning of the scientific study of individual differences. It was in this book that Galton first introduced the concept of eugenics, where the book was "to touch on various topics more or less connected with that of the cultivation of race, or, as we might call it, with 'eugenic' questions" (Galton, 1907, p. 17). Thus Galton's description and measurement of individual differences in mental ability, his genetic interpretation of such differences, and his statistical contributions were all based upon furthering the improvement of race through encouraging the propagation of those individuals having desirable traits (positive eugenics) and discouraging those with undesirable traits (negative eugenics). The view that Galton's eugenic concerns underlay most of his other scholarly contributions has been expressed by Pearson, as well as more recently by Cowan (1972). Thus Pearson has stated that "the inheritance of mental and moral characters in man was the fundamental concept in Galton's life and work. It led him to all his later quantitative investigations on heredity" (1924, p. 82). What were Galton's views on eugenics, an outgrowth of his interpretation of individual differences, and what relationship did they have to the social, political, and economic forces operative in nineteenth century Britain?

As already noted, Galton's views on eugenics were significantly influenced from his reading Darwin's *The Origin of Species*, first published in 1859. This book had a tremendous effect on Galton's personal view of religion, wherein he felt that he was purged of the oppressive feeling of original sin and subscribed to the view that man's nature was the result of the orderly process of nature. Galton did not give up the idea of religion, but substituted human defect for original sin and felt that religion should concern itself with the improvement of the human species through intelligent selection. Thus, as argued by Blacker (1952, pp. 81–123), Galton's eugenics encompassed three distinct aspects which he believed were inseparable: it was to be a science, a religion, and a platform for social policy and change—in other words, a total ideology.

Lest there by any doubt that Galton indeed embraced eugenics as a religion, the following passages should make clear his position:

Man has already furthered evolution very considerably, half unconsciously, and for his own personal advantages, but he has not yet risen to the conviction that it is his *religious duty* to do so deliberately and systematically. (Galton, 1907, p. 198, emphasis added)

The chief result of these inquiries has been to elicit the *religious significance of the doctrine of evolution*. It suggests an alteration in our mental attitude, and imposes a new *moral duty*. (Galton, 1907, p. 220, emphasis added)

The direction of the emotions and desires towards the furtherance of human evolution, recognized as rightly paramount over all objects of selfish desire, justly merits the name of a *religion*. (Galton, 1894, p. 758, emphasis added)

Concluding his autobiography, Galton notes:

I take Eugenics very seriously, feeling that its principles ought to become one of the dominant motives in a civilized nation, much as if they were one of its *religious* tenets. I have *often* expressed myself in this sense. (Galton, 1908, p. 232, emphasis added)

In the above passages it is clear that Galton has combined both existential and normative statements to give birth to a total ideology; what "is" the case (inherited individual differences in mental ability) has been linked to what "ought to be" the case (the improvement of race).

How did Galton's eugenic program fare in his own lifetime? It has already been argued that his scientific ideas were to a large extent conditioned by the prevailing social, political, and economic forces. Were these same forces, which helped to give birth to eugenics, compatible with its acceptance? In order for Galton's eugenics program to be successful, the general public had to be informed and educated as to the merits of this new science. In his own lifetime, Galton's eugenics as a social policy was not enthusiastically endorsed to the extent he had hoped. This was probably due in no small measure to the contradictory nature of Galton's eugenic program with respect to the prevailing liberal individualism at the time. For example, Galton (1907, pp. 208–216) believed that in the near future eugenic certificates should be issued, and went so far as to draft a preliminary form which he circulated privately (reproduced in Pearson, 1930A, pp. 292–295). He believed that eugenically favored people should be encouraged to marry early and that marriage laws and customs be changed to be consistent with a total social policy of eugenics. Such ideas certainly seemed to put the state before the individual, and implied a corroding of individual freedom and liberties. Thus, it would seem that Galton's science of eugenics, which was to serve as a new religion and the basis for social action, was indeed a total ideology, the *acceptance* of which was both out of tune with the current social infrastructure of democratic liberalism and individualism and also has not thus far become realized or established as an acceptable general social policy to the extent Galton had hoped.

In the last year of his life Galton wrote a utopia entitled *Kantsaywhere*, which was really an ideological treatise. Although it was submitted but rejected for publication, some of it has been reproduced in Pearson (1930A, pp. 414–424). In *Kantsaywhere* the number of children that a couple could have was to be strictly determined by their joint eugenics score. *Personae non gratae* were to be encouraged to emigrate and, failing this, they were to be subject to surveillance. Those individuals who were insane or mentally defective were to be segregated for life, while the power of the state was to be in the hands of a eugenic *corps d' élite* or caste. A system of competitive examinations were to determine one's social status.

To what extent were Galton's ideas as expressed in *Kantsaywhere* meant to be taken as a serious proposal for a new social order? Although Galton had decided to destroy the manuscript twenty-four days before his death, Blacker concludes that "Nevertheless we are justified in thinking that the intuitions Galton described reflected the general trend of his thought" (1952, p. 122). We see in *Kantsaywhere* an ideological doctrine of eugenics that was a distortion of reality vis-à-vis British nineteenth century liberal individualism. Although Galton was a liberal bourgeois and reflected humanistic concerns in some of his writing and thinking, these aspects of Galton's value system were transformed into their dialectical opposite when they were juxtaposed with his exclusive genetic interpretation of individual differences and the entailing eugenics policies.

In *Kantsaywhere* the political system would seem to be totalitarian, where a select group of people formed the senate and were to lay down the rules of human conduct in an unopposed manner. This hierarchical, genetically based caste system bears striking resemblance to Plato's totalitarian ideal state as described in the *Republic*, where the individual is always subordinate to the state. Plato's ideal state was to be composed of rulers, auxiliaries, and workers—each class being determined by innate individual differences; that is, "no two people are born exactly

alike. There are innate differences which fit them for different occupations" (*The Republic of Plato* as translated by Cornford, 1941, p. 56). As
argued by Popper (1950), Plato's ideal state was premised upon a
collectivism that was anti-individualism; that is, the rights of human
individuals were to be superseded by the interests of the state, a state
composed of a rigid class structure apparently having its basis in innate
individual differences. Thus Galton's eugenic ideology implied a modern
version of Plato's totalitarian ideal state which served to transform
(unknowingly and possibly inadvertently) his liberal bourgeois individualism into its dialectical opposite, collective totalitarianism.

SUMMARY AND CONCLUSION

It has been the purpose of this chapter to trace the social, political,
and economic influences which gave rise to a normative view of the
individual which in turn helped to condition the birth of the scientific
study of individual differences and the field of eugenics. Thus, although
there may be a sharp logical distinction between questions of value and
questions of fact, these two types of knowledge may both be intimately
related and form an ideology having its basis in the extant infrastructure
of a particular society. Although it has been argued that liberal
individualism helped condition the birth of the scientific study of
individual differences and the entailing field of eugenics, the same social
conditions prevented the acceptance of eugenics as a social policy. The
latter was due in no small way to the negation of Galton's liberal views
when juxtaposed to his emphasis upon a genetic interpretation of
individual differences in mental ability. The critical point, then, is that
Galton did not embrace one crucial aspect of liberal thinking, an aspect
illustrated in the following somewhat long sentence quoted from Mill's
(1969) autobiography:

I have long felt that the prevailing tendency to regard all the marked distinctions
of human character as innate, and in the main indelible, and to ignore the
irresistible proofs that by far the greater part of those differences, whether
between individuals, races, or sexes, are such as not only might but naturally
would be *produced by differences in circumstances*, is one of the chief
hindrances to the rational treatment of great social questions, and one of the
greatest stumbling blocks to human improvement. (p. 162, emphasis added)

Had Galton accepted liberalism *in toto*, then there would have been no
possibility of him giving birth to the field of innate individual differences
and the entailing eugenics ideology. In being influenced by the

prevailing social, political, and economic forces, as summarized by the term democratic, liberal, capitalistic individualism (except for the above-mentioned aspect of liberal thought), he gave rise to an ideology at variance with those same forces. That which nurtured the birth of Galton's eugenic ideology prevented it from being accepted.

Notes

1. Quoted in Pearson, 1924, p. 385, from an article written by Galton in 1890 entitled *Anthropometric Laboratory, Notes and Memoirs,* printed privately.

References

Blacker, C.P. *Eugenics: Galton and After* (London: Duckworth, 1952).

Boring, E.G. *A History of Experimental Psychology* (New York: Appleton-Century-Crofts, 1950).

Burt, C. "Galton's Contribution to Psychology." *Bulletin of the British Psychological Society 45:* 10–21(1961).

"Francis Galton and His Contributions to Psychology." *British Journal of Statistical Psychology 15:* 1–49 (1962).

Buss, A.R. "The Emerging Field of the Sociology of Psychological Knowledge." *American Psychologist,* 1975, *30,* 988–1002.

Buss, A.R. ed. *Psychology in Social Context* (New York: Irvington Publishers, Inc., 1979).

Cornford, F.M. *The Republic of Plato* (London: Oxford University Press, 1941).

Cowan, R.S. "Francis Galton's Statistical Ideas: The Influence of Eugenics." *Isis 63:* 509–528 (1972).

English, H.B. & English, A.C. *A Comprehensive Dictionary of Psychological and Psychoanalytical Terms* (New York: McKay, 1958).

Galton, F. "Hereditary Improvement." *Frazer's Magazine 8:* 116–130 (1873).

Galton, F. *English Men of Science, Their Nature and Nurture* (London: Macmillan, 1874).

Galton, F. *Natural Inheritance* (London: Macmillan, 1889).

Galton, F. "The Part of Religion in Human Evolution." *The National Review,* August 1894, 755–765.

Galton, F. *Inquiries into Human Faculty and Its Development* (London: Dent, 1907, (first published in 1883).

Galton, F. *Memories of My Life* (London: Methuen, 1908).

Galton, F. *Hereditary Genius* (Cleveland: World, 1962, first published in 1869).

Gergen, K.J. "Social Psychology as History." *Journal of Personality and Social Psychology 26:* 309–320 (1973).

Girvetz, H.K. *The Evolution of Liberalism* (New York: Collier, 1963).

Himmelfarb, G. *On Liberty and Liberalism: The Case of John Stuart Mill* (New York: Knopf, 1974).

Houghton, W.H. *The Victorian Frame of Mind* (New Haven: Yale University Press, 1957).

Hutchison, K. *The Decline and Fall of British Capitalism* (Hamden, Conn.: Archon, 1966).

Mill, J.S. *Autobiography and Other Writings*, J. Stillinger, ed. (Boston: Houghton Mifflin, 1969).

Pearson, K. *The Life, Letters and Labours of Francis Galton* (Cambridge: Cambridge University Press, Vol. I, 1914; Vol. II, 1924; Vol. IIIA and IIIB, 1930).

Popper, K.R. *The Open Society and Its Enemies* (Princeton, N.J.: Princeton University Press, 1950).

Riegel, K.F. "Influence of Economic and Political Ideologies on the Development of Developmental Psychology." *Psychological Bulletin 78:* 129–141 (1972).

Smith, D.G. Liberalism. *International Encyclopedia of the Social Sciences 9:* 276–282 (1968).

Stromberg, R.N. *European Intellectual History Since 1789* (New York: Appleton-Centuy-Crofts, 1968).

Chapter 4

Psychology's Future Development as Predicted from Generation Theory

Long-term prediction and planning has become so important in today's society because of the rapidity of technological and cultural change that planning as a profession has become firmly established. Today's futurists take as their maxim that in order to control the present tomorrow, it is first necessary to anticipate the future. By predicting the future, man can increase the control over his own destiny by initiating forces of change (or stability) in the present that either increase or decrease the probability that some later state of affairs will obtain. That long-term prediction is at best a risky business is continually borne out by comparing yesterday's predictions with today's actualities. In spite of the inaccuracy of long-term prediction, it can serve to foster the development of an important derivative or secondary function to society—it can promote reflective thought in society's decision-makers concerning the general effects of today's policies on future generations. Thus concerning some present policy, it is not always necessary to know *exactly* when and how chaos will arrive in order to implement a change. In other words, if it is obvious that a certain course of action can only eventuate in disaster, it may be too late to reverse such a trend if one waits until enough "facts" are in order to make precise predictions as to when and how impending doom will occur.

The above comments concerning long-term prediction may be considered with advantage in the context of predicting the future of psychology as an academic discipline. In predicting psychology's future,

Reprinted with permission from *Human Development* 17: 449–455 (Karger, Basel, 1975).

I am not concerned here with anticipating the specific methodological and/or theoretical paradigms that eventually will win the day (e.g., Foa and Turner, 1970). Rather, I have focused upon some present social conditions which, *if* continued long enough, will have in general a serious negative impact upon the development of psychology as a whole regardless of the specific direction psychology will (might have?) take (taken). In other words, I wish to play the role of a prophet of doom with respect to the future development of psychology, where it is not necessary to make precise predictions as to when and how impending doom will occur, but to simply know that it is coming *if* present trends continue. Knowing this, one will then be in a position to possibly avert disaster.

SOCIAL CONDITIONS

What exactly are the current social conditions which, if continued on a long-term basis, will seriously retard the development of a vigorous and responsive psychology? We are all aware of them, and simply stated, they involve all of the following interrelated aspects: declining enrollments; a curtailment of research funds; a questioning of the role of universities; and a tightening academic job market. It is the latter situation as it relates to the future of psychology which is the focus of attention in this article.

That there are more qualified Ph.D.s being produced than can be absorbed into academic settings has been well-documented of late (e.g., Buss, 1975c; and see the special issue of the *American Psychologist* devoted to psychology's manpower, May 1972). Although there is evidence that there are a sufficient number of jobs for recent psychology graduates, these jobs are in the main not to be found in society's institutions of higher learning in the numbers they were during "the good old days" (the sixties). What will be the consequences for psychology departments if present trends continue for a significant number of years? As time passes, the academicians will certainly not become any younger. As the mean age of the professional staff increases there will be a decrease in the proportion of assistant and associate professors and an increase in full professors. It may turn out that to be an academician is synonymous with being a full professor! What will be the consequences of the lack of "new blood" being injected into the academic mainstream? Will psychology be moving on at a new-found speed of advancement because the knowledge seekers will now have the significantly greater experience, knowledge, expertise, and wisdom that accompanies the rank of full professor? I think not. In fact, I would make the opposite prediction: psychology as a discipline will become unduly inflexible, unresponsive, and conservative. Such characteristics will cut across particular content areas and theoretical approaches. The net effect of such characteristics upon the discipline as a whole will surely be undesirable, and steps should be considered to avoid the realization of such a prediction. But what is the basis for forecasting the general decline of psychology given that current social conditions discussed above will continue unabated into the future? Although it may be possible to offer different rationales couched in various frameworks for making the above disquieting prediction, there is one particular interpretation of today's social conditions vis-à-vis psychology that I find compelling. It involves viewing the development, continuity, and transitions of psychology as a discipline within the perspective of generation theory.

GENERATION THEORY AND THE DEVELOPMENT OF PSYCHOLOGY

The concept of generation has been fundamental in accounting for the continuity and structural changes in society. Sociology has given much emphasis to the generation concept as the unit of analysis in accounting for social stability and change (Ryder, 1965). Developmental psychology has also been concerned with generational analysis as reflected by a concern with intergenerational relationships, socialization, and continuities and discontinuities across generations (for reviews, see Bengtson and Black, 1973; Neugarten and Datan, 1973). Recently there have been some methodological developments (Baltes, 1968; Buss, 1973, 1975a,b; Cattell, 1970; Labouvie, 1975; Schaie, 1965) which in part center around the controversy of attempting to disentangle ontogenic (age-related) changes and cohort (generation-related) differences, where a cohort may be defined as an aggregate of individuals who are born at roughly the same point in time and who are therefore the same age and experience historical events at the same period in their individual development.

Mannheim's Theory of Generations and Social Change. One of the more important thinkers who developed a theory of generations was the German sociologist Karl Mannheim. In Mannheim's view, there are several important properties to consider in any society where there is not just one generation that lives on forever (1952). Thus in a society where there is both a continuous emergence of new participants and a disappearance of former participants in the cultural process, cultural creation and cultural accumulation are not carried out by the same individuals at the same time. Each new generation of cohorts makes "fresh contact" with the accumulated heritage handed down by older generations, thereby altering or transforming that heritage to some degree by selecting and emphasizing certain aspects. The latter process occurs since the new generation comes into contact with the cultural heritage without the years of commitment to the existent ideology, and in the process of assimilating the cultural material will alter the interpretation of the legacy of older generations. The idea of "fresh contact" of each new generation thus provides the vehicle for social and cultural *change*, where each generation may reevaluate the existent cultural heritage and selectively emphasize certain aspects. If there were not a continuous process of succeeding generations, the existent social pattern would be perpetuated largely unaltered. If the latter were the case, the social structure would not provide for either adaptive additions or deleterious deletions.

The members of each generation in a given culture experience historical events at the same age or point in development. Since they have a common experiential base in development they may participate as an integrated group. Although different generations may experience the same historical event at the same time, because of age and previous experiential differences the historical event will have differential effects on different generations. Older generations will tend to assimilate and interpret reality in terms of previously well-formed structures and categories of experience, while youth's interpretation of reality will be quite different.

Those values, beliefs, theories, etc. which continue to prove their worth to a society in new situations are transmitted to incoming generations, while those aspects of the culture which are not of value fade out of existence along with the outgoing generations. The transmission of the cultural heritage is not strictly a one-way process from older to younger generations since intergenerational interaction provides for the opportunity of the old to learn from the young as well. In this way the accumulated cultural heritage is constantly being transformed and thus modified to some degree.

According to Mannheim, whether a particular generation will play the role of mediating social change by participating as an integrated group depends upon the trigger action of specific historical events (1952). Thus it is the unique historical event which serves as a catalyst in creating a distinct generational style or "entelechy." For example the recent technical advances in the field of birth control have created the possibility for a new morality which can be more readily assimilated by younger generations. In this situation we may speak of the realization of the potential for implementing change that is inherent in each generation. Thus the biological given that we have a continuous succession of incoming generations does not guarantee the implementation of change, but merely provides for the possibility of change. There are several cultural groups that have successive generations and yet have little social change because of the lack of acceleration in tempo of social and cultural transformations. Thus any generational group may set in motion forces of social change, but it will be the incoming younger generations which will be readily able to assimilate such change and thereby transform the cultural heritage.

It will be useful to consider the implications of Mannheim's theory for the future development of psychology given that psychology departments will be recruiting few junior staff for some years to come. In applying generational theory to the development of psychology, use will be made of the idea of changes in models, theories, interpretations, and approaches in academic psychology rather than exclusively social changes *per se*. The latter will also be relevant, however, to the extent that psychology is sensitive to different social conditions. For example, Riegel (1972a) has recently traced two major developmental traditions (quantitative and qualitative growth models) to two different socioeconomic systems (capitalistic and mercantilistic-socialistic, respectively). That generational theory may be applied to an academic discipline is strengthened by the observation that Mannheim actually presented his theory in the context of a sociology of knowledge. In the present framework the focus of attention is upon the specialist knowledge-seekers rather than upon the knowledge or interpretation of reality arrived at by society's members in general. In other words, the question being considered here is the following: What will be the general effect upon the discipline of psychology, as predicted from Mannheim's generation theory, given that there will be a lack of incoming young academicians for a significant number of years?

Implications for Psychology's Development. Several predictions follow from the interface of Mannheim's theory and the lack of continuously emerging new generations of academicians within the discipline of psychology. (1) In order to have a psychology that is adaptive to both external changing social conditions and internal theoretical advances, it is necessary to have a constant input of new generations of academicians that make "fresh contact" with the discipline. If there are no participants entering academic psychology for a number of years, the existent models, theories, orientations, *and controversies* would tend to be perpetuated largely unaltered. (2) Since eventually psychology's academicians will be composed of generations more similar in time location than different, they will tend to assimilate new material in terms of the same well-established categories. There will be an undesirable within-generational reinforcement of existent models, theories, and controversies. (3) To the extent that there is a lack of incoming young academicians into psychology, there will not be the full range of intergenerational interaction. Thus the psychological heritage that will *eventually* be transmitted to younger academic generations will be of necessity lacking in the changes and transformations denied and lost forever by the lack of continuous "fresh contact" with younger generations. (4) If there is a lack of continuous inflow of younger academic psychologists, when the incoming generation finally does make its appearance on the academic scene there will be no intermediary generations. The result of this large "generation gap" will be such that there will be sufficient intergenerational conflict to produce a revolution within psychology. In this situation we would have a scientific revolution brought about by the necessity of a shift in scientific paradigm (Kuhn, 1962) and triggered by intergenerational conflict.

Some further comment is required in order to appreciate fully the validity of the above predictions. While it is true that psychologists of varying ages and generations can and do initiate considerable change in theoretical orientation within a given area, any major redirection in psychology largely becomes assimilated, evaluated, transformed, and implemented by incoming new generations. The latter are more likely to pick up and extend new approaches within psychology because they lack the commitment to previous orientations. Thus important creative breakthroughs must be made, of course, at the micro level by individuals who may be of varying ages,[1] but one must turn to a macro level of analysis in order to appreciate how such changes become incorporated into the accepted body of knowledge. It is at the generation level that new paradigms may be easily accommodated since individuals as a rule are much more limited in accommodating to change the more advanced they are in age. At the individual level, each person attempts to maintain a continuity and be disturbed as little as possible by structuring new inputs in terms of previously formed categories. The possibility for major transformations is quite limited since the individual strives to maintain continuity through time. Throughout development the individual makes choices that progressively reduce his degrees of freedom. He develops a growing commitment to a particular line of activity.

Exceptions to the general process described above with respect to the development of the individual academician exist, and Riegel has recently considered two psychologists (Piaget and Wundt) as exhibiting multi-paradigmatic progressions in their development (1975). Thus it is Riegel's view that it is the exceptional individual that is able to break out of a previous and into a new paradigm; and in order to have some impact upon the field, one can add that in general it will be the incoming new generation that will need to endorse the new paradigm. Thus in considering the new generation of academicians as the vehicle for implementing change, it will be the new paradigm as initiated by the exceptional individual which will serve as the unique historical event that triggers the establishment of a new generational consciousness, style, or "entelechy."

It is possible to further consider the intimate relationship between the changing, developing, or aging academician and the changing, developing, or aging discipline of psychology. Riegel has recently pointed out the dialectical relationship that exists between the changing individual and a changing society (1972b), and more recently the dialectical relationship between the development of the scientist and his discipline (1975). Thus there is mutual determination between the developing academician and the development of psychology as a discipline. When contradictions, conflicts, or crises appear in this process of mutual influence, new paradigms emerge to resolve or synthesize them at higher levels of analysis. This dialectical relationship between a changing psychology and a changing psychologist may be considered within the context of generation theory. To the extent that there is a lack of incoming young psychologists in academia, there will be a tendency for less change at both the individual level (because of the increasing limitation for change associated with aging) and at the level of psychology as a discipline (because of the lack of "fresh contact" to assimilate and transform the new paradigms). In other words, if there is a restricted number of incoming young psychologists into academia, the dialectical relationship between psychology and psychologist will be much less "active" than might otherwise be the case.

CONCLUSION

In concluding the thesis of this chapter a few cautionary comments are in order. First, the adverse prediction made here concerning the future development of psychology is predicated on the assumption that there will be insufficient new generations of psychologists entering academia. To the extent that this social phenomenon is not realized in the future then the adverse predictions made here may be averted.

Secondly, it is not the intent of this chapter to denigrate one age-group of academicians (senior) and revere another (junior). The full age-strata of academicians is necessary, of course, and various age-groups serve different functions in the total developmental process of psychology. Thus it has been emphasized that creative breakthroughs will probably be initiated by the more senior academician, but in order for the new paradigm to have a somewhat lasting impact upon the field, it is necessary that it be picked up and extended by the incoming new generation.

Notes

1. In fact it is not the incoming new generation of academicians that will necessarily be most creative. Lehman has collected data on creative people in various disciplines and found that the age for maximum quality of production varies for different fields—being in the early thirties for chemists and mathemeticians and in the late thirties and early forties for philosophers (1953). Psychologists probably come somewhere in between.

References

Baltes, P. B.: "Longitudinal and Cross-sectional Sequences in the Study of Age and Generation Effects." *Human Development 11:* 145–171 (1968).

Bengston, V. L. & Black, K. D.: "Intergenerational Relations and Continuities in Socialization." In *Life-span Developmental Psychology: Personality and Socialization* Baltes & Schaie, eds. (New York: Academic Press, 1973).

Buss, A. R.: "An Extension of Developmental Models That Separate Ontogenetic Changes and Cohort Differences." *Psychological Bulletin 80:* 466–479 (1973).

Buss, A. R.: "Generational Analysis: Description, Explanation, and Theory." *Journal of Social Issues 30 (2):* 55–71 (1975a).

Buss, A. R.: "More on the Age X Cohort Developmental Model: A Reply to Labouvie." *Psychological Bulletin 82:* 170–173 (1975b).

Buss, A. R.: "Systems Theory, Generation Theory, and the University: Some Predictions." *Higher Education, (4:* 429–445 (1975c).

Cattell, R. B.: "Separating Endogenous, Exogenous, Ecogenic, and Epogenic Component Curves in Developmental Data." *Developmental Psychology 3:* 151–162 (1970).

Foa, U. G. & Turner, J. L.: "Psychology in the Year 2000: Going Structural." *American Psychologist* 25: 244–247 (1970).

Kuhn, T. S.: *The Structure of Scientific Revolutions* (Chicago: University of Chicago Press, 1962).

Labouvie, E. W.: "An Extension of Developmental Models: A Reply to Buss." *Psychological Bulletin* 82: 165–169 (1975).

Lehman, H. C.: *Age and Achievement* (Princeton University Press, Princeton 1953).

Mannheim, K.: "The Problem of Generations." In Mannheim, *Essays on the Sociology of Knowledge* (London: Routledge & Kegan, 1952).

Neugarten, B. L. & Datan, N.: "Sociological Perspectives on the LIfe Cycle." In *Life-span Developmental Psychology: Personality and Socialization*, Baltes & Schaie, eds. (New York: Academic Press, 1973).

Riegel, K. F.: "Influence of Economic and Political Ideologies on the Development of Developmental Psychology." *Psychological Bulletin* 78: 129-141 (1972a).

Riegel, K. F.: "Time and Change in the Development of the Individual and Society." In *Advances in Child Development and Behavior*, Reese & Lipsitt, eds. vol. 7 (New York: Academic Press, 1972b).

Riegel, K. F.: "Adult Life Crises: A Dialectic Interpretation of Development." In *Life-span Developmental Psychology: Normative Life-Crises*, Datan & Ginsberg, eds. (New York: Academic Press, 1975).

Ryder, N. B.: "The Cohort as a Concept in the Study of Social Change." *Sociological Review* 30: 843–861 (1965).

Schaie, K. W.: "A General Model for the Study of Developmental Problems." *Psychological Bulletin* 64: 92–107 (1965).

Chapter 5

The Historical Roots of the Individual-Society Dialectic

INTRODUCTION

Dialectical concepts and thinking have a long history. Like many ideas, those of dialectics can be traced back to the early Greeks. Recently there has been an attempt to incorporate dialectics into psychology. The prime movers of this recent interest in psychology and dialectics have been Joseph F. Rychlak and the late Klaus F. Riegel. Rychlak's book *A Philosophy for Personality Theory* (1968) first introduced psychologists to the intellectual history of dialectics and its relevance to understanding the works of Freud and Jung. Riegel, beginning with a series of articles and chapters in the early 1970s (e.g., 1972a, 1972b, 1973, 1975), emphasized the value of dialectics for developmental psychology, including the idea of a dialectic between the changing or developing individual and the changing or evolving society. It is the latter idea on which I will focus here.

In spite of the recent concern for the individual-society dialectic within developmental psychology, it would appear that there has been little conceptual progress beyond earlier efforts to deal with this issue. Part of the explanation for the apparent lack of significant theoretical and conceptual advancement concerning the issue of the individual-society dialectic is the inherent difficulty of the task. An additional factor, I believe, is that important past efforts have been forgotten. In recent psychological treatments, there has generally been no historical appreciation of the idea of an individual-society dialectic as constituting a real problem. That is to say, there is a history to the idea of the individual-society dialectic, and to make theoretical progress on this issue requires one to take cognizance of its history.

The history to which I allude is itself part of an ongoing social as well as intellectual dialectical process. The changes and transformations the idea of an individual-society dialectic has undergone are based on concrete sociopolitical events,·and on the failure of previous theoretical efforts to accommodate the new social realities.

It is not my purpose here to review recent contributions to a dialectical psychology. Rather, my intent is to try and recover a bit of recent history for those life-span developmental psychologists interested in the idea of the individual-society dialectic. In so doing, we may at least clear the way for moving beyond past and present theoretical efforts to deal with the individual-society dialectic. Thus, the present chapter is propaedeutic to a major coup in this area—nothing more, but certainly nothing less.

THE HISTORICAL PROBLEM

The Failure of Orthodox Marxism

Historically speaking, it was Marx who gave modern expression to the dialectical nature of the relationship between the individual and society:

Men make their own history, but do not make it just as they please; they do not make it under circumstances chosen by themselves, but under circumstances directly encountered, given and transmitted from the past. (Marx, quoted in McLellan, 1971, p. 125)

However, Marx did not supply the needed social psychological theory to explain the individual-society dialectic. The pressure for a more analytical treatment of the idea of a changing or developing individual in a changing or evolving society goes back to the failure of social revolution in the West just after World War I. The proletariat's refusal to rise up against the bourgeoisie and seize control over its own destiny in post-World War I Europe was contradictory to Marx's prediction of the collapse of capitalism due to its inherent contradictions. The revolution that did materialize in 1917 occurred in what was really a feudalistic rather than a capitalistic society, and it did not produce the democratic and emancipated social order Marx had envisioned as arising out of the ashes of bourgeois capitalism. Orthodox Marxism had failed; and during the aftermath of the Great War and the Russian Revolution there were three major attempts to supplement and rework its core in order to make the theory at least compatible with events, and thereby transform it into a more valid theory of social and historical change.

One attempt to revise Marx was Marxism-Leninism (also known as vulgar Marxism by its critics—see below). This solution to the failure of orthodox Marxism was based on Lenin's theory of the Party. According to Lenin, the revolution should be directed from the top by a small revolutionary elite, rather than emerging spontaneously from the rank and file, or bottom. Lenin was quite successful in bringing into being a new social order based upon the power of the Party. That society, however, did not conform to Marx's emphasis on emancipation, democracy, and freedom (e.g., see Buss, 1977). Lenin emphasized a hierarchical, one-way boss relationship in both the political and scientific arenas. Marxism-Leninism, and dialectical materialism, were based upon an authoritarian, unidirectional view of the relationship between the Party and the masses, and between nature and ideas, respectively.

A second attempt to "update" Marx became known as revisionism. Revisionists sacrificed the iron cage of economic determinism, and thus dialectical materialism, for a more subjective, idealistic, or free-will approach to achieving the socialist state based upon ethical considerations. Led by Bernstein in Germany, the revisionists formed the Social Democratic Party and advocated democratic and peaceful means for transforming society into a socialist state.

A third group steered a dialectical course by bringing together the materialist and idealist dimensions of Marxism. The major figures in this neo-Marxist group included the Hungarian Georg Lukacs, the Italian Antonio Gramsci, and the German Karl Korsch. Although different in many respects, during the 1920s all three attempted to emphasize the Hegelian foundations of Marxism. They thus stressed the active subject within the context of a concrete or objective historical reality before the discovery and publication of Marx's *Economic and Philosophic Manuscripts* of 1844. The latter works actually confirmed the various Hegelian interpretations of Marx's thinking, and supported neither the objective one-way economic determinism of dialectical materialism nor the subjective one-way determinism of Bernstein's revisionism. Rather, they presented a truly dialectical conception of base and superstructure, social structure and cognitive structure, sociology and psychology, society and the individual. Lukacs, Gramsci, and Korsch all emphasized the view that consciousness and ideology were not merely the "reflection" of the social and economic relations of production, but rather constituted separate and independent forces of history. Of course, ideas, the collective consciousness, or ideologies were still seen as connected to the material base, but they also had a life over and above that base. In other words, they were *dialectically* connected to the material base.

In spite of the important insights of the early Hegelian interpreters of Marx, none of them produced a social psychological theory that accounted for the mediation between the objective material base and the subjective psychological superstructure. More specifically, they did not explain the concrete or specific form of bourgeois ideology that served to prevent the postwar proletariat from seizing its historical opportunity for successful revolution. According to all objective measures the moment was ripe, yet the proletariat failed to keep its appointment with destiny and to achieve social, political, and economic emancipation. Korsch was at least aware of the need for such a social psychological theory during the period (1918–1922) when he was interpreting the failure of the socialist revolution as being due to psychological or ideological factors:

In the fateful months after November 1918, when the organized political power of the bourgeoisie was smashed and outwardly there was nothing else in the way of the transition from capitalism to socialism, the great chance was never seized because the *socio-psychological* preconditions for its seizure were lacking. For there was nowhere to be found any decisive *belief* in the immediate realizability of a socialist economic system which could have swept the masses along with it and provided a clear knowledge of the nature of the first steps to be taken. (Korsch, 1970, p. 10, original emphasis)

Thus, the failure of orthodox Marxism was due to its ignoring the psychological importance of bourgeois ideology in reducing the revolutionary potential of the proletariat. What was needed now was a social psychological theory to explain the hidden, covert, or subjective forms of domination that had emerged. In other words, overt repression and exploitation had been replaced by more subtle mechanisms of psychological control brought about by the internalization of capitalist irrationality. The exploited now accepted the exploiters and their own exploitation! What was required was theoretical analysis, and an even more powerful and radical critique of class consciousness than Marxism was able to provide.

During the 1920s and 1930s, Western neo-Marxists turned to a study of psychoanalysis in the hope of flushing out in a more concrete fashion the individual side of the individual-society dialectic. In this way they sought to achieve a theoretical understanding of the psychological mechanisms that served to reproduce and support social reality, however alienating that social reality might be. Consistent with the emphasis upon the dialectic between theory and practice, such theoretical effort was considered to be a requisite for undermining false consciousness and negating the integration of the individual into an irrational society.

The Failure of Orthodox Psychoanalysis

While neo-Marxists were scurrying around looking for a powerful psychological theory, there was also pressure to provide a more adequate analysis of the individual-society relationship from the other side. That is to say, post-Freudians were attempting to supplement psychoanalysis with social, cultural, and historical considerations. The importance of Freud and psychoanalysis within the history of ideas has been well documented by others, and thus there is no need to repeat it here. Rather, I wish to focus very briefly upon some aspects of psychoanalysis that are relevant to the idea of the individual-society dialectic. In this way we will be in a position to appreciate just what post-Freudians were reacting to vis-à-vis the idea of the individual-society dialectic.

While the conceptual shortcomings of orthodox Marxism were related to its not taking sufficient account of the psychological side of the individual-society dialectic, that of orthodox psychoanalysis was the converse; it ignored the social, cultural, and historical side. Those who were to later attempt a synthesis of Marxism and psychoanalysis had an important insight: Each alone was reductionistic insofar as it committed the error of sociologism and psychologism, respectively, yet together their individual truths could flourish by complementing one another.

The criticism that Freud ignored the role of social and cultural factors in affecting the psyche is a well-worn saw. In Freud's view, there was an endless repetition from generation to generation of the same developmental sequence. Although it is true that Freud advanced a theory of psychological development which he believed to be universal, it is also true that his theory contained some important ideas vis-à-vis the individual-society dialectic. For one thing, the individual-society relationship in psychoanalysis was considered to be fraught with conflict. Society, or civilization, was a mixed blessing, since it is achieved at the unavoidable price of harnessing, inhibiting, and repressing many of the individual's most basic and powerful life drives and instincts. Thus, psychologically speaking, the achievement of civilization cripples and scars the individual.

A second idea of Freud's relevant to the idea of the relationship between individual and society is his theory of the origin of society and its symbolic repetition within each family. Briefly, Freud adopted

Darwin's theory of the Primal Horde, which was really a sort of myth as to how society began. According to that myth, the primal father of the clan threatened all other males with castration if they had sexual contact with any of the women. Eventually the primal father was killed by the other males of the clan, and the idea of the nuclear family became established to avoid such problems in the future. Freud supplemented this theory with some ideas from Greek mythology, and thereby advanced his notions concerning the Oedipus conflict and the development of the superego. There is no need to become tangled in the details of this rich theory; the important point for present purposes relates to the structure of Freud's developmental theory and its relationship to history. That is to say, in Freud's view individual development within the family was a reenactment, in symbolic form, of the history of the species. In other words, Freud subscribed to the notion that individual development repeated species development, or that ontogeny recapitulated phylogeny.

Post-Freudians were to expand and modify the idea of ontogeny recapitulating phylogeny, as well as Freud's view that the unavoidable conflict characteristic of the individual-society relationship was rooted in the unchanging, essential, universal human psyche. Freud's pessimistic, deterministic, ahistorical theory of the individual and society was an expression of an age that had seen the end of the high tide of optimism so characteristic of much of the nineteenth century. Freud's time was one that held out little hope. The evidence was mounting against the historical idea of continual progress in the human condition. In a sense, Freud arrived at a conclusion for the development of the human psyche similar to that of Hegel for history in general: human development (or history) had reached the end of the line. Post-Freudians, however, were also to become sensitive to the rapidly changing world around them, and to the growing interest in cross-cultural questions. To them and to their generation, history was very much on the move; and along with it came new possibilities for the changing, developing individual psyche.

In summary, then, the theoretical failure of both classical Marxism and psychoanalysis can be seen as due to a model of the individual-society relationship inadequate in light of the new social realities. Marxism was heavy on the side of society and short on the individual, whereas psychoanalysis had the opposite emphasis. Some attempts were made to salvage the truth content of both Marxism and psychoanalysis by bringing them together (e.g., Reich, Horkheimer, Fromm; see below). These attempts can be contrasted with those of post-Freudians whose sociohistorical approach was not Marxist-inspired (e.g., Erikson; see below). In both cases, however, the overriding concern was with formulating a model or theory that would provide a more valid interpretation of the individual-society relationship in light of the new sociohistorical realities. Let us now examine these various theoretical attempts to avoid the errors of both sociologism and psychologism.

PROPOSED SOLUTIONS

Reich

In looking back at the various attempts to achieve greater theoretical understanding of the individual-society dialectic, one cannot help but be struck by their developmental orientation, an orientation that stems from a single major underlying theme. The various attempts to synthesize individual and social development focused on the role of the *family* in reproducing an alienating and irrational society through its child-rearing habits. Thus, according to several neo-Marxists of the 1930s, the new enemy of exploitation and domination was the patterns of psychological development that the family executed with great efficiency, rather than individual capitalists per se. It was the deep structure of society, the family, that produced an individual character susceptible to manipulation and submission.

In Wilhelm Reich's *The Mass Psychology of Facism*, (1933) we find a bold attempt to account for the mass movement of facism in terms of the family—the chief social agent responsible for the creation of the authoritarian personality. In his words:

The authoritarian state gains an enormous interest in the authoritarian family: *It becomes the factory in which the state's structure and ideology are molded.* (Reich, 1970, p. 3, original emphasis)

Most important for our purposes is to note Reich's appreciation of the dialectic between the individual and society within the contest of the family's role in reproducing a conservative, traditional—or, more accurately, outdated—character structure, one that comes into conflict with changed socioeconomic relations:

The basic traits of the character structures corresponding to a definite historical situation are formed in early childhood, and are far more conservative than the forces of technical production. It results from this that, as time goes on, *the psychic structures lag behind the rapid changes of social conditions from which they derive, and later come into conflict with new forms of life.* This is the basic trait of the nature of so-called tradition, i.e., of the contradiction between the old and the new social situation. (Reich, 1970, pp. 18–19, original emphasis)

In this passage we see that, in contrast to an orthodox Marxist view, the motor of history was not merely changes in the means and relations of production. The latter was certainly an important and necessary factor, but it comprised only one side of the dialectic. The internalization of the social structure into the character structure, the transformation of social categories into psychological categories, the conversion of social relations into ideology—in short, the subjective or psychological element—comprised the other side of the dialectic of history.

In common with Freud, then, Reich stressed the *conflict* between the individual and society, although he added the important historical dimension to this process. For Reich, the individual-society conflict had its basis in the contradiction between an older sociohistorical reality, as represented in the character structure of the adult, and the newer reality in which the adult functioned. The development of character structure in childhood was thereby seen to be a process that was historical to its very core. This very important insight of Reich's set him apart from Freud. For Freud, the invariant nature of humanity from generation to generation carried with it no provision for any changes or transformations in the basic rhythm of the developmental process. Reich's emphasis on the historicity of childhood implies that the very concepts we use to describe development are historical, and that therefore we cannot understand the developing individual divorced from his or her sociohistorical context. Thus, Reich's approach may be seen as an important precursor of the current fervor with which the childhood-history dialectic is studied (e.g., de Mause, 1976; Gillis, 1974).

Fromm and the Frankfurt School

Perhaps the most systematic and concentrated attempt to better understand the failure of revolution in the West—to provide a social psychology that mediated between base and superstructure, society and individual—was that of the Frankfurt School. The Frankfurt Institute for Social Research, established in 1923, was committed to a critical social theory of society and the individual based on an interest in human emancipation. During the 1930s, under its most eminent director, Max Horkheimer, the institute flourished and produced some of its more important critical studies of Marxism and psychoanalysis. Characteristic of the contributions of its members at this time—Horkheimer, Fromm, Marcuse, and Adorno—was the union of Freud and Marx for better understanding the new internalized forms of dominance and repression. In the five-year project *Studies on Authority and Family* (published in 1936), the institute's members explored, as did Reich at the same time, the role of the family in the service of producing an authoritarian character structure.

In the theoretical section of the 900-page *Studies*, Fromm developed the thesis that Freud's strictly biological and psychological account of authority had to be supplemented, perhaps even replaced, by a historical approach that emphasized socioeconomic factors. Fromm later developed this idea in a more systematic and comprehensive way in his *Escape from Freedom* (1941). In this book Fromm echoed many of the same concerns and impressions as Reich concerning the family, society, and authority. *Escape from Freedom* was based upon the importance of ideas and ideologies as independent forces in history. In addition, of course, there was the specific socioeconomic context in which such ideas arise. The link—the cement holding society together at any particular historical moment—was thought to be psychological.

Adopting Reich's term "character structure," Fromm rejected Freud's ahistorical view of human nature and placed the nature of humanity, the "*social* character structure," squarely *in* history: "We look upon human nature as essentially historically conditioned" (p. 290). Thus, according to Fromm, needs arise and form a unique social character structure in the context of new socioeconomic conditions. In fulfilling these needs, individuals satisfy their individual or psychological requirements, but in addition, they serve the interests of the particular society. In Fromm's words, "The social character internalizes necessities and thus harnesses human energy for the task of a given economic and social system" (p. 284). Critical in this whole process is the family, which is "considered to be the psychological agent of society" (p. 284). And it is in the structure and dynamics of the family that the contradictions, conflicts, and crises between the individual and society are manufactured.

Thus, the social character structure inculcated in childhood represents the internalization of a historically unique set of social and economic relations. When the child becomes an adult, his or her character structure may be inconsistent with the new social and economic realities. Conflict thus develops between psychological interests and social interests. According to Fromm, the mismatch between current character or psychological structure (past social structure that has been internalized) and current social structure is the breeding ground for aberrant ways of satisfying psychological needs. It is within this theoretical context that Fromm explains the authoritarian personality, the sadomasochistic character structure, and the rise of Nazism and Fascism as mass movements.

Fromm's attempt to integrate history, sociology, and psychology may be viewed as lying within the tradition of a Hegelianized Marxism, with the important addition of a social psychology that mediated between base and superstructure. The locus for that social psychology, the glue that held together psychological and social interests under conditions of little socioeconomic change, was the *inter*development of ideas, psychological structure, and social structure within a dialectical unity. This important methodological commitment can be especially appreciated in the following statement:

Economic forces are effective, but they must be understood not as psychological motivations but as objective conditions: psychological forces are effective, but they must be understood as historically conditioned in themselves; ideas are effective, but they must be understood as being rooted in the whole of the character structure of members of a social group. In spite of this interdependence of economic, psychological, and ideological forces, however, each of them has also a certain independence. (Fromm, 1941, p. 298)

In addition to historicizing Freud's idea of an individual-society conflict, Fromm went beyond Freud in another important aspect of the individual-society dialectic. He adopted the structural model of ontogeny recapitulating phylogeny, but grafted new ideational meat upon those bones. For Fromm, the important story to be told about humanity's past concerned the rise of the idea of the individual, and the accompanying gains of greater self-consciousness and freedom. That is to say, the history of humanity has been one of breaking the "primary ties," mastering nature, and achieving a sense of separateness and greater self-consciousness. "Freedom from" the primary ties prepares society for the next important stage—"freedom to" actualize human possibilities and to chart a course of social development consistent with the values of reason and liberty. The important point to note in the present context is that, in Fromm's view, individual development involved the same pattern as historical or species development. That is to say, the breaking of the primary ties (the family), the mastery of nature, the sense of separateness, the achievement of self-consciousness, and the growth of reason and freedom all were characteristic of both history and ontogeny. The same hurdles and setbacks that may plague social development can also occur at the individual level. That is to say, one can choose to escape the burdens and responsibilities that accompany freedom by giving up critical reason and individuality, thereby achieving a state of false security. The latter involves uncritically committing oneself to an idea, ideology, or group that, although irrational, nonetheless relieves one of the pain of choice, freedom, and individuality.

Horkheimer's opening theoretical essay for *Studies on Authority and Family* contained many of the major methodological points that Fromm later employed in *Escape from Freedom*. Horkheimer's essay has been translated into English and appears in his *Critical Theory* (1972). In the section dealing with the family, Horkheimer weaves back and forth between the critical and negative view of the family Marx developed and the more positive interpretation Hegel provided. He points out in a dialectical way that the importance of the family in the new age was precisely due to its decline in importance as an agent of society. The previously positive aspects of the authority structure of the family for socializing the young were now no more; certain social forces have led to the usurping of the father's authority by extrafamilial institutions. In other words, the previously rational authority structure of the family (for that historical point in time) had been undermined, and the void was filled by the sometimes irrational authoritarian figures within society. Here Horkheimer was relying upon the theoretical argument previously discussed in connection with Reich and Fromm—the mismatch between the current character structure (based upon the internalization of outdated socioeconomic relations), and the new historical realities.

A more thorough treatment of the contributions of the Frankfurt School in relation to the idea of a changing individual in a changing society is beyond the scope of this chapter. Most important our purposes here is to note that its members wrestled with the historical failure of Marxism in the West after World War I, and in the process transformed both classical psychoanalysis and classical Marxism. In so doing, they carved out the beginnings of a social developmental psychology. That social developmental psychology is certainly not similar to what may go under that banner today. It is really a thoroughly dialectical, historical, and critical developmental social psychology. Thus, for example, the role of the family in the *mis*-developmental process vis-à-vis current social reality is a function of the rapidity of socioeconomic change. Authority within the family becomes increasingly irrational due to certain social structural changes. Recovery of the positive function of the family lies in social transformation.

Erikson

Some post-Freudians considered themselves faithful to the essential ideas of Freud, although they stressed the ego rather than the unconscious, as well as sociocultural considerations. Neo-Freudians such as Horney, Sullivan, and Erikson attempted to correct the ahistorical view of human nature within classical psychoanalysis by emphasizing the social and cultural determinants of personality development. Their concern for social factors affecting individual development was part of a more general *Zeitgeist* tied in to the rapid development of the disciplines of sociology and anthropology during the 1920s and 1930s. However, the neo-Freudian concern for society, culture, and history did not stem directly from an interest in Marxism and its failure. Rather, in contrast to post-Freudian neo-Marxists such as Reich and Fromm, the neo-Freudians approached the individual-society dialectic from an initial position that emphasized the individual, or psychology. Their reworking of that dialectic did not, in general, contain the social dimension characteristic of the neo-Marxists.

A partial exception to this rule is the work of Erik Erikson, whose psychological theory of ego development did contain some social criticism. Erikson, more than any of the other neo-Freudians, was also genuinely interested in historical and sociocultural issues for their own sake, rather than simply regarding them as subordinate to the concerns of psychology. His treatment of the individual-society dialectic was much more analytical and substantial than other neo-Freudian efforts. Erikson's appreciation for the interpenetration of psychology and history is evident in his placing of Freud's theory, as well as his own, within a historical context. Thus, in Erikson's view, Freud's theory of psychosexual development cannot be understood unless one appreciates the Victorian society from which it sprang. A society in which there was real sexual repression produced psychoanalysis, which was to provide the appropriate antidote. It was through a psychoanalytical understanding of sexual repression, inhibition, and conflict that critical self-consciousness, or emancipation, was to be won.

The society in which Erikson formed his developmental theory was quite different from Freud's. Erikson, the very successfully converted American, was struggling with unique sociohistorical realities that demanded significant revision of psychoanalysis. He desexualized psychoanalysis and replaced Freud's emphasis on the unconscious with a concern for the ego. The new historical problem to be explained for a developmental psychology in postindustrial, technologically advanced America was ego diffusion and the loss of ego identity. Thus, in contrasting his own patients with Freud's, Erikson states:

The patient of today suffers most under the problem of what he should believe in and who he should—or, indeed, might—be or become; while the patient of early psychoanalysis suffered most under inhibitions which prevent him from being what and who he thought he knew he was. (1963, p. 279)

Erikson developed his psychosocial theory of ego development and ego identity in response to the new historical realities confronting the developing individual: "We begin to conceptualize matters of identity at the very time in history when they become a problem" (p. 282). Ego identity for Erikson was a lifelong process, and thus he proposed a life-span developmental theory consisting of eight distinct ego stages. First set out in *Childhood and Society* in 1950, and later elaborated in *Identity and the Life Cycle* in 1959, Erikson's view of development was two-dimensional. Paralleling, yet also interpenetrating each other, were the development of the individual (ontogeny) and the social evolution of society (history). Corresponding to eight stages of individual development were eight stages of social development. For Erikson, ontogeny also recapitulated history.

Figure 1 shows Erikson's psychosocial stage theory of ego development. At each of the biological stage divisions there is a psychological crisis that is resolved in one of two ways. The outcome is carried forward, for better or for worse, into the next stage. Not indicated in Figure 1 are the corresponding social stages of development. Thus, the social counterpart of the individual's sense of trust is the institution of religion; of autonomy and self-control, the institution of law and order; of initiative, economics; of industry, a culture's technology; of identity, some kind of ideology; of intimacy, ethics; of generativity, education, art, and science; and of integrity, all the great cultural institutions including economics, politics, philosophy, and religion. It is in this last stage that the beginning and end of the life cycle come together, insofar as the development of trust in the young child depends upon the integrity of the parents.

Admittedly, Erikson did not develop the sociohistorical stages as well as he did the psychological stages. One is never certain of the exact relationship between the two developmental processes, except that society plays a crucial role in the individual outcome of the various stages. In contrast to Freud, who viewed the relationship of individual and society to be fundamentally one of conflict, Erikson saw society mainly in a supportive role. Individual development was facilitated by society's institutions, and in achieving individual goals the person was simultaneously advancing society, and vice versa. Thus, the interface of the individual and society, of psychology and history, was generally one of compatibility, nonconflict, integration. The noncritical interpretation of the role of society vis-à-vis individual development has led some (e.g., Jacoby, 1974; Roazen, 1976) to charge Erikson with having given us a bourgeois theory that is conformist in nature and supportive of the status quo. However, no simple judgment can be made on this issue, since Erikson has certainly been critical of much of society. His theory must be viewed as containing both conformist and critical dimensions. The critical content of Erikson's theory was present even in 1950, when he lashed out at the adverse effects of industrialization and technology on development:

This idea of a self-made ego was . . . reinforced and yet modified by industrialization and by class stratification. Industrialization, for example, brought with it mechanical child training. It was as if this new man-made world of machines . . . offered its mastery only to those who would become like it. . . . Thus, a movement in child training began which tended to adjust the human organisim from the very start to clocklike punctuality in order to make it a standardized appendix of the industrial world. (pp. 294–295).

In this passage we get a strong impression of a psychologist looking at development in its historical context for the purpose of criticizing alienating and repressive social forces. The passage is not an isolated one; in several places Erikson is critical of social institutions and structures that hinder ego development and the achievement of freedom. At the same time, his ambivalence toward American society is revealed in his sometimes naive and accepting attitude toward the family. In sharp contrast to Reich, Fromm, and Horkheimer, Erikson considered the family to be the breeding ground for the *democratic* rather than the authoritarian personality! Consider the following:

The American family . . . tends to guard the right of the individual member— parents included—not to be dominated. . . . [there is a] give-and-take [that] cuts down . . . the division of the family into unequal partners. . . . The family becomes a training ground in tolerance of different *interests*—not of different *beings* . . . [there is] an automatic prevention of autocracy and inequality. (pp. 316–318)

	1	2	3	4	5	6	7	8
VIII MATURITY								EGO INTEGRITY VERSUS DESPAIR
VII ADULTHOOD							GENERATIVITY VERSUS STAGNATION	
VI YOUNG ADULTHOOD						INTIMACY VERSUS ISOLATION		
V PUBERTY AND ADOLESCENCE					IDENTITY VERSUS ROLE CONFUSION			
IV LATENCY				INDUSTRY VERSUS INFERIORITY				
III LOCOMOTOR-GENITAL			INITIATIVE VERSUS GUILT					
II MUSCULAR-ANAL		AUTONOMY VERSUS SHAME, DOUBT						
I ORAL SENSORY	BASIC TRUST VERSUS MISTRUST							

Figure 1. Erikson's psychosocial stage model of ego development (From Erikson, 1963).

Erikson's model was the American rather than the European family, and yet such a positive, uncritical description is suspicious from a dialectical-critical standpoint. The family, for Erikson, represents all that is good in the American political system, where "The analogy . . . to the two-party system is clear" with its "checks and balances" (p. 318). The problem of authority and the family does not exist in the American family, according to Erikson: "The adolescent swings of American youth do not overtly concern the father, nor the matter of authority, but focus rather on his peers" (p. 318). It is one's peers rather than the structure of the family that is the source of youth's conflict and rebellion.

It would appear that, for Erikson, the family belongs in the same category as applie pie and motherhood. Or does it? In marked contrast to some of his positive musings on the American family, we can find the opposite view as well. Consider this passage:

This long childhood exposes adults to the temptation of thoughtlessly and often cruelly exploiting the child's dependence by making him pay for the psychological debts owed to us by others. . . . We have learned not to stunt a child's growing body with child labor, we must now learn not to break his growing spirit by making him the victim of our anxieties. (p. 100)

Characteristically, Erikson the radical critic of the family betrays that position in the very next sentence, when he states: "If we will only learn to let live, the plan for growth is all there" (p. 100). The position expressed here is conformist and capitulatory; unfortunately, the critique is defused as soon as it is made.

Yet, in a noncritical sense (assuming that that makes sense!), Erikson does view the family dialectically. Thus, the developing child within the family is only one side of a more complex process. In Erikson's words:

It is as true to say that babies control and bring up their families as it is to say the converse. A family can bring up a baby only by being brought up by him. His growth consists of a series of challenges to them to serve his newly developing potentialities for social interaction. (1959, p. 55)

The relationship between children and parents is reciprocal and dialectical—each changes and is changed by the other through time.

Erikson's psychosocial theory of ego development is concerned with conflict, crises, and their successful resolution. The problem for each individual is to preserve a thread of continuity in the context of change and growth. Ego identity is achieved by the ego functions that integrate, synthesize, and resolve contradictions. However, maintaining a sense of continuity and sameness through time requires that the individual's development be consistent with the major trends of history. For Erikson, psychological growth and health is possible only to the extent that the individual is not out of step with society. At times, integration of individual and society seems for Erikson to supersede justified confrontation, conflict, and alienation. The price of continuity, synthesis, and integration may be the achieving of *false* continuities, syntheses, and integrations.

We may reach this conclusion in yet another way. Mastery of one's environment and of one's experience is a theme that appears often in Erikson's writings. Although he is concerned with individual mastery through development, he would seem to be satisfied with a *sense* of mastery rather than *real* mastery. Erikson is too much the subjectivist; he is too satisfied with a *sense* of mastery, continuity, and identity and does not critically examine the objective situation. Such a position once again leads him to conformist conclusions, as when he states:

The growing child must, at every step, derive a vitalizing sense of reality from the awareness that his individual way of mastering experience is a successful variant of the way others around him master experience and recognize such mastery. (Erikson, 1959, p. 89)

Another aspect of Erikson's theory that potentially leads to false continuities, resolutions, and integrations concerns the outcome of each of the eight developmental stages. I can imagine a society where the more valid reaction *is* shame and doubt rather than autonomy, guilt rather than initiative, identity diffusion rather than identity. The conflict and confusion that an individual experiences may represent a healthy response to a social reality that is psychologically (not to mention physically) repressive, alienating, and constricting. Integration of the individual into society is not an absolute to be unquestioningly sought after. Thus, I disagree with Erikson's view that the healthy individual in the eighth and final stage of life chooses integrity versus despair and disgust, where integrity is defined as follows:

It is the acceptance of one's own and only life cycle and of the people who have become significant to it as something that *had to be* and that, by necessity, permitted no substitutions. (Erikson, 1959, p. 98, emphasis added)

Unqualified acceptance of one's total life history, and by implication, the external forces that helped shape that life, is too heavy a price to pay for the comfort of integration.

In summary, then, Erikson's theory, like the others previously discussed, is an attempt to look at the individual-society dialectic in its sociohistorical context. The conflict in that dialectic is historical rather than absolute, and is based upon a mismatch between social structure and psychological structure. Resolving that conflict can involve altering the individual (capitulation to social reality), or altering that social reality (critique of social structure). Erikson is ambiguous as to which solution is most desirable. Finally, we can note that Erikson's model of individual development paralleling sociohistorical development is a closed rather than an open one. For Erikson, the structure of ego development is universal (his stage theory), although the psychological content of the various stage solutions is cultural and historical. Thus, in a real sense Erikson's attempt to historicize psychoanalysis falls somewhat short of the mark. The structure of his developmental theory is as absolute and rigid as Freud's, although that rigidity is not as apparent.

RETHINKING THE INDIVIDUAL-SOCIETY DIALECTIC

Thus far I have attempted to reveal some of the twists and turns that the idea of the individual-society dialectic has taken through history. The transformations and modifications of that idea have been a response to certain sociopolitical events, and the conceptual limitations of both classical Marxism and psychoanalysis for accommodating the new social realities. A key idea that emerged in later refinements of the individual-society dialectic was that individual development repeats the basic themes and stages of the history of the species. The implications of that idea for greater theoretical understanding of the individual-society dialectic have yet to be explored, but let us end by hinting at how such an exposition might begin.

There has been a lot of loose talk within the life-span developmental literature about the individual-society dialectic as involving mutual or reciprocal determination—each influences and is influenced by the other. Yet such a conception provides no rationale for understanding the concrete direction of both individual and historical development. That is to say, does the hypothesized mutual determination between the individual and society simply involve a random tradeoff of pushes and pulls? Or is it more than that? I believe that the way to make sense of the individual-society dialectic, and to inject some intellectual power into the idea as well, is to frame it in the context of ontogeny recapitulating phylogeny.

Freud's basic insight that, in symbolic form, individual psychologi-

cal development repeats the themes and crises of the social history of the
species is, I believe, an extremely valuable one. We can historicize the
model and provide for the changing nature of psychological development
by noting that the history of the species *continually* unfolds. Freud's
paradigm (as well as Erikson's) dealt with a history that was prematurely
cut off and dead, rather than one that was open and alive. If we view
development as fundamentally a teleological process, in which the telos
is ever more progress or advancement in terms of such things as reason,
the mastery of nature, and the humanization of social relations, then we
can begin to make sense out of both historical and individual development in terms of each other. One can read history through ontogeny,
since ontogeny contains, in code form, the history of the species.
Indeed, that is what Piaget has done insofar as he has attempted to
identify the historical counterpart of his individual developmental stages
(pre-operational, concrete operations, formal operations) in such areas as
the history of mathematical thinking. The important point, then, is that
ontogeny and history are structurally part of the same developmental
process. They belong to a single developmental totality. Each informs
and is informed by the other, and the structure of each is contained
within the other.

This model is appealing to the extent that it suggests various kinds of
developmental structural analyses, but it is necessary to push onward if
we are to grasp the truly dialectical aspect of the individual-society
dialectic. Consider the following final thought: The *social* development
of a property of an entire culture, (e.g., reason, freedom from the
primary ties, formal operations, individuation, self-consciousness) is
dependent upon, or conditional upon, like development at the *individual*
level (i.e., reason, freedom from the primary ties, formal operations,
individuation, or self-consciousness, respectively). Similarly, individual
development and the achievement of some more advanced state is
conditional upon the existence of a like developmental state at the social
level. In other words, one cannot have reached a given developmental
level at the social level *before* that same developmental level has been
reached by the majority of individual members of the society, and vice
versa.

The individual-society *dialectic* is not such because of such matters
as reciprocal causation, simultaneous antecedent-consequent status, and
the like. The latter attributes do not make the individual-society
relationship distinctly dialectical (though they might in fact be valid
attributes of that relationship). What makes the individual-society
dialectic a *dialectic* is that a given level of development on one side of the
relationship is dependent upon, *and at the same time* is a condition for,

that same level of development on the other side of the relationship. This fundamental paradox needs further analysis. Perhaps the reader may be able to push this idea further than I have been able to do.

SUMMARY

The individual-society relationship is a key idea for a life-span developmental psychology. An adequate conception of the changing or developing individual in a changing or evolving society must involve dialectical thinking. Part of such thinking is a historical appreciation of the origin of this idea and the reality that brought it into being. The recent history of the idea of an individual-society dialectic is rooted in two theoretical failures—failures in the sense of their not adequately accommodating the sociopolitical reality current when they were formulated. One of these was the failure of orthodox Marxism to account for the lack of social revolution in the West just after World War I. Neo-Marxists began to feel the need for a social-developmental theory to explain the psychologizing, or internalization, of various social forces of irrationality, repression, and alienation. Orthodox Marxism had not anticipated this phenomenon, and thus provided no social-developmental theory to explain it.

The second theoretical failure that contributed to a concern for the individual-society dialectic was that of psychoanalysis. The neo-Freudians attempted to supplement Freud's exclusively biological and historical theory of personality and personality development with sociocultural factors. Erikson was probably the most successful in offering a psychosocial theory of development that partially accommodated the historical dimension in the individual-society relationship. The post-Freudians supported such ideas as cross-cultural differences, historical change, the resurgence of a belief in the possibility of progress, and a renewed optimism founded on the notion of controlling and manipulating the human environment. These were new social experiences that could not be integrated within orthodox psychoanalysis.

Finally, I have undertaken a brief reconceptualization of the idea of an individual-society dialectic, more as a challenge to the reader than as a closed and finished model. I have proposed that the idea of an individual-society dialectic contains a contradiction—a puzzle that cannot be solved through clever mental gymnastics. It is *this* contradiction that makes the individual-society relationship a distinctly *dialectical* one.

References

Buss, A. R. "Marx and the Russian Revolution: Betrayal of the Promise." *Humanist in Canada 10:* 2–5 (1977).

de Mause, L. "The Evolution of Childhood." In *Varieties of Psychohistory*, G. M. Kren & L. H. Rappoport, eds. (New York: Springer, 1976).

Erikson, E. H. *Identity and the Life Cycle* (New York: International University Press, 1959).

Erikson, E. H. *Childhood and Society* (New York: Norton, 1963, first published in 1950).

Fromm, E. *Escape from Freedom* (New York: Holt, Rinehart and Winston, 1941).

Gillis, J. R. *Youth and History* (New York: Academic Press, 1974).

Horkheimer, M. *Critical Theory* (New York: Herder and Herder, 1972).

Jacoby, R. *Social Amnesia* (Boston: Beacon, 1975).

Korsch, K. *Marxism and Philosophy* (New York: Modern Reader, 1970).

McLellan, D. *The Thought of Karl Marx* (London: Macmillan, 1971).

Reich, W. *The Mass Psychology of Fascism* (New York: Farrar, Straus and Girous, 1970).

Riegel, K. F. "Influence of Economic and Political Ideologies on the Development of Developmental Psychology." *Psychological Bulletin 78:* 129–141 (1972a).

Riegel, K. F. "Time and Change in the Development of the Individual and Society. In *Advances in Child Development and Behavior* (Vol 7), H. Reese, ed. (New York: Academic Press, 1972b).

Riegel, K. F. "Developmental Psychology: Some Historical and Ethical Considerations." In *Life-span Developmental Psychology: Methodological Issues*, J. R. Nesselroade & H. W. Reese, eds. (New York: Academic Press, 1972).

Riegel, K. F. "Adult Life Crises: Toward a Dialectic Theory of Development." In *Life-span Developmental Psychology: Normative Life Crises*, N. Datan & L. H. Ginsberg, eds. (New York: Academic Press, 1975).

Roazen, P. *Erik H. Erikson* (New York: Free Press, 1976).

Chapter 6

Development of Dialectics and Development of Humanistic Psychology

The term "dialectic" is as old as Western philosophy—dating back to at least the Greek philosophers. Through the centuries, this word has taken on different meanings so that today it is neither possible, nor desirable, to attempt to stipulate *the* meaning of dialectic. There are several senses in which the term "dialectic" has been used that are worthy of mention. A useful discussion along these lines has been offered by Hook (1953) and Rychlak (1968, 1976). Hook distinguishes two broad or generic conceptions of dialectic, including (a) dialectic as an ontology or pattern of existential change, and (b) dialectic as a method of understanding change. Dialectic as a pattern of change in either society and/or nature emphasizes such notions as the negation of existing states, contradictions, and conflicts. Especially as applied to *process* and social *development*, dialectical *change* embodies the idea that conflict and struggle are necessary properties of change in order to achieve higher levels of social evolution. Another meaning of dialectic under the rubric of social and historical change involves the idea of the interaction between a changing individual in a changing society, where each is both cause and consequence of the other. In this way, the individual is both shaped by existing conditions and shapes his/her own nature and destiny by changing those conditions.

I would like to thank Susan Buck-Morss for her reading of and commentary on an earlier draft of this chapter. The standard, but important, disclaimer in this situation holds—namely, that I alone am responsible for any remaining deficiencies or errors of interpretation. Reprinted with permission from *Human Development 19*: 248–260 (Karger, Basel, 1976).

Dialectic as a method of understanding change holds that one may arrive at "truth" by employing dialectical techniques. Generically, dialectic as a method involves the notion of a *dialogue*, where "truth" is increasingly approximated through a clash of opinions, and conflict is resolved at higher levels of analysis. An essential property of a dialogue is its *critical* function, where the questioning and testing of ideas are part of its very nature. Although a dialogue is typically considered as an ongoing process involving two individuals, the true generality of the dialectic as a method becomes apparent once we broaden our notion of dialogue to include self-dialogue, interdisciplinary dialogue, and existential dialogue rooted in the very being of nature (Riegel, 1976).

One may be a methodological dialectician without endorsing the dialectic as an existential position. The latter position would state that, while changes in nature may not be inherently dialectical, dialectical thinking can help us understand nature. This position would be similar, for example, to using certain methodological data analysis models (e.g., linear) which are known not to reflect "true" reality yet are of some value in trying to understand or approximate that reality. On the other hand, one may hold a dialectical ontological position without subscribing to the dialectic as a method. However, for the methodological dialectician who also endorses dialectics as an ontology, dialectical concepts permit one to understand ongoing natural processes such that their true essence may be penetrated and revealed.

The purpose of the present chapter is to trace the development of the dialectic from Hegel to Marx with special reference to humanistic psychology. That is to say, it will be argued that Hegelian dialectics has much to offer in terms of an ontology and concept methodology for humanistic psychology, although it is necessary to *aufheben* (at the same time negate, affirm, and transcend) such a dialectic in order to further develop the foundational base of humanistic psychology. It is argued that Marxian dialectics provides a higher level of development for the conceptual basis of humanistic psychology. In this way, the dialectical (historical) development of the dialectic from Hegel to Marx furnishes one with a framework for a *critical* (i.e., dialectical) analysis of certain aspects of humanistic psychology, which, in turn, point the way towards the dialectical development of a truly humanistic psychology.

HEGEL'S DIALECTIC AND HUMANISTIC PSYCHOLOGY

The dialectic in the hands of Hegel is of primary significance insofar as he developed it as an all-encompassing logic and ontology. In Hegel's words: "But it is of the basic prejudices of traditional logic and of commonsense conception that contradiction is not such an essential and eminent determination as identity; indeed, if we were to consider a rank order and if both determinations were to be kept separated, contradiction would have to be accepted as deeper and more essential. For identity, in contrast to it, is only the recognition of the single immediate, the dead being; but contradiction is the source of all motion and vitality; only insofar as something contains contradiction does it move, has its drive and activity" (as translated by Riegel, 1973, p. 348).

Marcuse has outlined some of the kernel ideas of Hegel as well: "To know what a thing really is, we have to get beyond its immediately given state (S is S) and follow out the process in which it turns into something other than itself (P). In the process of becoming P, however, S still remains S. Its reality is the entire dynamic of its turning into something else and unifying itself with its 'other.' The dialectical pattern represents, and is thus 'the truth of,' a world permeated by negativity, a world in which everything is something other than it *really* is, and in which opposition and contradiction constitute the laws of progress" (1954, p. 49).

The above passages touch upon several important points. For Hegel, all Being is characterized by an essential contradiction and negativity, where in the process of Becoming, a thing becomes other than what it now is. In this view, what "is" the case, the facts, are not to be the ultimate criterion of truth, since truth is achieved only in the process of Becoming and the realization of a "thing's" potential. Whereas positivism fosters a conservative and affirmative attitude by dealing with existing states, a dialectical perspective emphasizes not only the possibility but the necessity of change and progress through negation. "As Hegel shows, in a world where facts do not present what reality can and ought to be, positivism amounts to giving up the real possibilities of mankind for a false and alien world" (Marcuse, 1954, p. 113). Present reality is not ultimate reality, and an epistemology which emphasizes the realization of truth through Becoming and the negation of what "is" the case is better able to appreciate what can be, what could be, and what should be the case. "Something is true if it is what it can be, fulfilling all of its objective possibilities" (p. 25). According to Hegel, for a thing to become what it "really" is, it must become what it is not. The essence of a thing's "ideal" contradicts what its state of existence is at any particular point in time. Being must be construed in terms of a process of Becoming, a process which is based upon the principle of the "negation of the negation" (e.g. Lobkowicz, 1972). Hegel's ontology involves a dynamic process in which the essential negativity of existence is a condition of, and the source for, development, Becoming, and the realization of a thing's potential.

Hegel's radical ontology requires a radical logic since traditional or formal logic does not accommodate the negative and contradictory nature of reality. In formal logic, contradictions are to be avoided, and since, according to Hegel, contradictions exist in reality, formal logic is unable to reveal the true nature of reality. Dialectical logic embraces contradictions and is therefore a superior method for getting at the inherent contradictory nature of reality.[1]

To understand something dialectically it must be understood in terms of what qualities it both does and does not have, where the true essence of a thing is ultimately defined in terms of an endless set of relations. "Everything has to be understood in relation to other things, so that these relations become the very being of that thing" (Marcuse, 1954, p. 68). Hegel was absolutely opposed to the notion of there being little autonomic "facts" which can somehow be added together in order to achieve some understanding of totalities. Equally was he opposed to a simple notion of the dialectic involving the well-known sequence: thesis, antithesis, synthesis. Hegel emphasized the totality of relations and contradictions of a thing, and to force his position into the simple notion of thesis, antithesis, synthesis is to fail to capture the complexity of his ontology. As noted by Kaufmann (1966) and Bernstein (1971), respectively:

"Fichte introduced into German philosophy the three-step of thesis, antithesis, and synthesis, using these three terms. Schelling took up this terminology; Hegel did not. He never once used these three terms together to designate three stages in an argument or account in any of his books. And they do not help us understand his *Phenomenology*, his *Logic*, or his philosophy of history; they impede any open-minded comprehension of what he does by forcing it into a schema which was available to him and which he deliberately spurned" (Kaufmann, 1966, p. 154).

"There has been a lot of loose talk about Hegel's dialectic being a movement from thesis to antithesis to synthesis. Not only do these concepts play an insignificant role in Hegel's philosophy, they are essentially static concepts and completely misrepresent what Hegel means by "dialectic." The dialectic . . . is essentially a dynamic and organic process. One "moment" of a dialectical process, when it is fully developed or understood, gives rise to its own negation; it is not mechanically confronted by an antithesis" (Bernstein, 1971, p. 20).

Hegel was a monist in his view of reality, and more specifically, an idealist. Reason, mind, "spirit," or "God" was the stuff of existence, and

Being and Becoming involved an unfolding and realization of reason.[2] In emphasizing reason, Hegel was in fact establishing the beginnings of a critical philosophy—a philosophy which did not trust the existing order—a philosophy which employed reason as a critical tool—and a philosophy which he himself ultimately rejected (see below). To the extent that the given reality falls short of potential reality, then the former must be acted upon to bring about its realization or actuality. Realization of reality is the realization of reason. Objective reality realized is the realization of the subject. Thought is the superstructure of reality.

One of the more important ideals to be attained for Hegel was freedom. As an idealist, he believed that freedom could be attained in the mind and this would of logical necessity correspond to the realization of freedom in reality. For Hegel, freedom is a necessary condition for the actualization of reason, and by implication, the realization of reality's potential or "true reality." By freedom Hegel means that the realization of reason, the self, or mind, is a process which occurs independently of external forces. Bringing into being true reality involves Becoming or the self-realization of the subject—free from external influence. A knowing and self-conscious subject who is aware of his own possibilities and that of the world can achieve self-realization and thereby can bring into being a true reality. "True reality . . . must be understood as the realization of a knowing *subject*" (Marcuse, 1954, p. 154).

While there are problems in Hegel's dialectic, the general flavor of his ontology is congenial in several ways to a humanistic psychology. In order to see this compatibility, we should briefly note some general characteristics of humanistic psychology. Humanistic psychology encompasses diverse theoretical views and may be considered as reflecting more of a general perspective, frame of reference, or world view rather than representing a systematic and integrated body of knowledge. Humanistic psychology has come to be closely identified with the work of such leaders in the field as Allport, Bugental, Fromm, Giorgi, Jourard, Lyons, Maslow, Matson, and Rogers to name but a few. Proponents of this new perspective in psychology are united in a concerted rejection of a positivistic behavioristic psychology, and indeed, it is the existence of a common adversary which has given this new force some cohesion and has served as the major impetus in pursuing a new image of humanity and society. Thus humanistic psychology has taken its cue from the positivistic, mechanistic, deterministic view of psychology and seeks to negate these adjectives which modify the noun "psychology." In brief, a humanistic psychology emphasizes all of the following: the individual as a subject in the world rather than an object; the freedom and dignity of the individual rather than the individual as determined and dehumanized; the whole person rather than a fractionated being; and the person's inherent potential for self-fulfillment, actualization, initiative action, and creativity rather than the individual as a merely passive respondent to his/her environment.

Both Hegelian dialectics and humanistic psychology emphasize the attempt to look at things in their context—the interrelatedness of things—the totality of reality. Both place a premium upon the individual as a subject—a subject capable of initiating change and action in the real world. Both emphasize that Being involves Becoming—that truth is realized in the process of an individual achieving his/her potential. Both emphasize the necessity for change and development. Humanistic psychology places great importance upon self-actualization—the realization of the subject's potentiality. Dialectics provides the ontology of such a position, where in order for an individual to become what he/she really is, he/she must become other than what he/she now is. Being is defined in terms of Becoming, and Becoming involves negating one's present state. Humanity's inherent negativity is the source for its development, where those contradictions which result in crises and which are resolved lead to higher levels of Being. The latter statement does not imply that all conflicts, crises, and resolutions lead to higher levels of Being, but, rather, the former are a necessary, though not sufficient, condition for the latter.

Hegelian dialectics is able to go some distance in providing a concept methodology and ontology for humanistic psychology. But there are problems. Hegel's philosophy was one of arriving at the understanding of things *after* they happened. In his metaphysics, whatever is real is the unfolding of reason. Whatever "is" is reasonable in the sense that whatever "is" is part of the actualization of reason and therefore necessary in the actualization of reason. Hence in Hegel "all explanation *is* justification" (Hook, 1962, p. 23), and his impractical philosophy had the very practical effect of justifying existing real conditions. For Hegel, what did happen ought to have happened. His idealism, with its emphasis upon reason, is a betrayal to reason, *if* by reason we mean critically evaluating reality and making prescriptive statements, and then acting on the basis of reason in order to change the real existential conditions as need be.

Hegel had made the assumption that history had ended with the establishment of the secular state based upon rational law. In his own time, absolute truth had been achieved by the completion of the real dialectic. "It is only 'at the end of time' that a Wise Man (who happened to be named Hegel) can give up the dialectical *method*—that is, . . . a 'critique' of the given—and limit himself to describing the given" (Kojeve, 1969, p. 191). By placing the Prussian state at the end of the dialectical process of history, Hegel's philosophy and phenomenology thereby forfeited any critical function. Truth had arrived, and it remained for Hegel to describe this truth, thereby making his system a defense of the status quo. Hegel had paradoxically abandoned critical reason: "If man is truly satisfied by what *is*, he no longer desires anything real and therefore no longer changes reality, and thus he himself ceases really to change" (Kojeve, 1969, p. 192).[3]

The above criticisms of Hegel are important with respect to a humanistic psychology to the extent that there is in both cases an implicit justification of the existing social conditions. In the latter case, this occurs because of an emphasis upon the actualization of the individual's mind, reason, spirit, or psyche without due recognition of his/her *real* conditions. Too often, it would seem, humanistic and existential psychologists' stress upon self-actualization, development, and Becoming is carried out as if the individual did not live in a real society with real social, political, and economic conditions. Can the individual reach his/her potential in pure reason, regardless of the real social and material relationships which envelop him/her? Glass' observations on this point are worth quoting: "Psychologists must remember that man is inescapably a *social* being; he becomes human only through interaction with others and the world he finds himself in. This is the flaw of 'pure' existentialism and of *intra*personal psychology, which considers man in a vacuum, the individual apart from the society he lives in. To believe that the individual can achieve fulfillment as an isolated person is sheer folly, but some humanistic psychologists appear to take this view" (1972, p. 170).

When the social context and the real factors which make up a person's reality are considered in the quest for self-actualization, they are too often taken as "given" in an uncritical manner—much as Hegel's system would have it. In order for the individual to Become and actualize his/her potential, therapists even within a humanistic orientation stress the adjustment of the person to existing reality, rather than entertaining the possibility that for this person to reach his/her potential, it is society which must do the accommodating. In Beit-Hallahmi's words: "What we are all interested in, or, that is, what we say we are interested in, is the maximal actualization of human potential. The question before us is whether such an actualization is possible without a major transformation of society. Most psychologists today are committed to a viewpoint which sees self-actualization as totally dependent on the individual and are totally satisfied with a role definition which demands that we leave society intact, while changing only the individual" (1974, p. 128).

What much of humanistic psychology is guilty of is the failure to realize that the realization of the individual's potential is conditional upon certain social conditions. *A humanistic psychology is conditional upon a humanistic society*. As Marx clearly saw, Hegel must be turned rightside up, for the dialectic is played out, not in pure reason and derivatively in the real world, but, rather, in the interaction between reason or thought and the real material conditions and social relationships thus entailed.

MARX'S DIALECTIC AND HUMANISTIC PSYCHOLOGY

Marx was heavily influenced by Hegel and adopted what he interpreted as Hegel's dialectical method but rejected his system. What may be called Hegel's dialectical method, especially the important principle of negativity as being the source for development and change, was stripped of its mystical form by Marx. He accomplished the latter by adopting Feuerbach's transformative method. Ludwig Feuerbach (1804–1872) was also a young Hegelian who was critical of Hegel's idealism and whose humanistic and materialist ideas had a great effect upon Marx in his early development. Feuerbach's transformative method involved reversing the subject-predicate relation posited by Hegel. As argued by Feuerbach and adopted by Marx, Hegel had things upside down, since "*Reason* is not a subject; it is not a source of agency. It is a predicate, the result of real, active, subjects" (Bernstein, 1971, p. 38). As Marx himself says: "Instead of treating self-consciousness as the self-consciousness of real men, living in a real, objective world and conditioned by it, Hegel transforms man into an attribute of self-consciousness. He turns the world upside down" (quoted in Hook, 1962, p. 32).

By giving conceptual priority to real people acting in a real material world and which influences reason, mind, or ideas rather than vice versa, Marx was objecting to the conservative and static social implications of Hegel's system. Whereas Hegel's view sanctified past and present socio-historical events, Marx's theory provided for understanding, criticizing, and changing social reality according to certain humanistic criteria. As employed by Marx, the dialectic became a very practical instrument in that it permitted the understanding of social reality, which in turn implied a certain course of action for changing that reality. In this way, theory and the practice of people are intimately connected.

The desire to unite theory and practice forms a central idea in Marxist thought, as illustrated in the following excerpts from Marx's theses on Feuerbach written in 1845 and reproduced in Engels: "Social life is essentially *practical*. All mysteries which mislead theory to mysticism find their rational solution in human practice and in the comprehension of this practice" (1934, p. 72). "The philosophers have only *interpreted* the world in various ways; the point, however, is to *change* it" (p. 75). For Marx, theory was an aid in bringing into being a more human world in which the practice of people would involve freedom, dignity, and self-actualization. According to Marx, theory which cannot find expression in the practical affairs of society is of little value, and the test for the value of theory is the extent to which it permits changing the practice of society's individuals for the better.

Related to the dialectic between theory and practice is the merging in Marxism of two kinds of knowledge which Kant considered logically distinct. According to Kant, there is a sharp logical distinction between what "is" the case, or the cognitive or epistemic question, and what "ought to be" the case, or the prescriptive question. One cannot derive knowledge of one from the other. In Marxism, these two types of knowledge are intimately connected and form a synthetic whole, where in this system of thought, what "is" the case implies what "ought to be" the case and vice versa. In Hook's words, "the 'ought to be' is never identical with 'what is.' But yet it is a temporal function of 'what is.'" (1962, p. 53). The real practice of people (what "is" the case) gives rise to certain theory specifying how people's practice should be changed (what "ought to be" the case) in accordance with Marx's humanistic values. The actual practice of people (e.g. scientific practice, social practice, work, etc.) does have implications for changing the material basis upon which that practice depends. Marxism is a theory of action which epitomizes the merging of theory and practice, fact and value, knowing and doing.

Marxism embodies an epistemology which adopts a criterion for truth which is quite different from positivism. Whereas the latter emphasized explanation and understanding the laws of the objective world as based upon the epistemic properties of factual confirmability and intersubjective unanimity, a Marxian dialectical materialism adopts a criterion for truth based upon the practice of people. In practice, or *praxis*, people must verify their theory and knowledge. *Praxis*, as a technical concept, occurs much more frequently in Marx's early writings—his more humanistic period—than in his later work.[4] Praxis is closely linked to Marx's underlying epistemology, the latter characterized by Kolakowski (1969) as hinging upon people's practical needs and practice. Knowledge arises out of social practice and is tested in social practice. Expanding people's consciousness, and more specifically, their self-consciousness, was thought by Marx to be the aim of social theory. To the extent that people can be made aware of their own situation within society, then there exists the possibility for implementing social change to better their situation. From interpreting reality and humanity's practice to making humanity self-conscious of that reality to changing that reality through praxis—this was the goal of Marx. Thus praxis for Marx referred to "the activity of Man which aims at transforming the world as well as aiding his own self-development" (Janousek, 1972).

The dialectic for Marx permitted one to grasp the basic contradictions in a capitalistic society. Alienation, relations of production, means of production, ideology, etc., were all technical concepts employed by Marx in relentless criticism of the contradictory state of society. Working out these contradictions was to lead to higher levels of social development. Rather than leave the working out of society's contradictions to reason, as Hegel would have it, Marx believed that it was necessary for people to intervene on their own behalf,[5] negate existing reality, and build a new social order. Humanity could make its own history armed with what others later referred to as the theory of historical materialism.

An important concept in Marx's dialectical view of history was the notion of a changing individual in a changing society, where each affects and is affected by the other. Once again, Marx's theses on Feuerbach contain this important view: "The materialist doctrine that men are products of circumstances and upbringing and that, therefore, changed men are products of other circumstances and changed upbringing, forgets that circumstances are changed precisely by men" (Marx, 1945, reproduced in Engels, 1934, p. 74).

In the above thesis on Feuerbach, Marx is criticizing a simple materialist position which regards ideas as merely the reflection of material reality. In other words, Marx rejected both "pure" materialism and "pure" idealism and opted for what he called *naturalism*, that is, both mind and matter are part of nature and can be studied scientifically. For Marx, naturalism "distinguishes itself both from idealism and materialism, constituting at the same time the unifying truth of both" (Marx, 1844, p. 93). Thus Marx was neither a simple dualist, monistic materialist, nor monistic idealist—he was a "naturalist"—believing in the interaction between the spiritual and material world. "[For Marx] Human consciousness is conditioned in dialectical interplay between subject and object, in which man actively shapes the world he lives in at the same time as it shapes him" (Giddens, 1971, p. 21). For Marx, the dialectic was neither in mind nor matter, but in the interaction between humanity and nature, the subject and object, the individual and society.

What are the implications of Marx's dialectic for humanistic psychology? One of the most important Marxian concepts for a humanistic psychology is that of *Praxis*. In *Praxis* humanity must verify its theories of humanity. Humanistic psychological theories and knowledge should be evaluated according to an epistemic criterion involving the *changing of the practice of people for the better*. Humanistic psychologists should take greater account of the individual as a social being, and formulate *social* theories of humanity which accommodate the dialectical relationship between the individual and society. Humanistic psychologists should begin to realize that self-actualization, Becoming, and the realization of one's potential is *conditional upon* a certain social reality. Humanistic psychologists should begin to consider the kind of really social conditions which will permit the maximization of individual development, richness of inner experience, expansion of consciousness, etc. Humanistic psychologists should adopt a *radical criticism* of existing dehumanizing social conditions, and thereby help bring into being a humanistic society. Humanistic psychologists should unite their emphasis upon human values with an equal emphasis upon human action in order to realize humanistic values on a large scale.

To the extent the above prescriptions are not carried out, humanistic psychology will remain a class psychology—relevant to those who "have" (i.e., achieved sufficient economic wealth) and completely irrelevant to those who are the "have-nots" (i.e., in Maslow's terms [1968], those too busy concerning themselves with lower-level needs rather than higher-level needs such as self-actualization). Herein lies the contradiction in the practice of contemporary "humanistic" psychology— a contradiction which must be resolved in order for "humanistic" psychology to evolve into a truly *humanistic* psychology.

CONCLUSION

At this point in our social evolution we should voluntarily abandon the pursuit of a "humanistic" psychology as it presently exists, that is, as a bourgeois-class psychology for human growth. The establishment of a meaningful and valuable *humanistic* psychology—a psychology which can speak to the self-development of the majority of individuals—is conditional upon a humanistic society. We do not yet have a humanistic society. *Social* scientists should take seriously the adjective which modifies their discipline and take on the responsibility of considering the individual in his/her social context. It is social reality which must be emphasized, understood, criticized, and transformed if the individual is to have the opportunity for self-development and self-actualization.

The dialectic in this chapter has now been played out. In taking both *humanistic* psychology and dialectics seriously we must conclude that a nonclass *humanistic* psychology does not exist at this point in historical time. Contemporary "humanistic" psychology must be *aufheben*. In negating "humanistic" psychology in the manner described here, we are hopefully taking action which will help to bring into being a *humanistic* psychology. Extant "humanistic" psychology both is and is not a *humanistic* psychology. Dialectics as a methodology permits us to see and understand the contradiction (the ontological dimension), and it also provides us via its critical function with insights as to how to help bring into being a truly *humanistic* psychology.

Notes

1.   For a good discussion of the differences between formal logic and dialectical logic, see Comey (1972).

2.   I sidestep here the controversy surrounding the meaning of Hegel's term *Geist* (see, for example, Solomon, 1975).

3.   The above interpretation of Hegel's system *ultimately* ending or concluding with the absence of a dialectical and critical method is central to subsequent developments of this article. It should be noted, however, that other interpretations on this point exist, and, in particular, Marcuse (1972, p. 416) views the attainment of absolute knowledge in Hegel's system as resulting in a method ("In the final analysis, Hegelian dialectics eventually proves to be precisely what, at the outset, it did not seem to be, a method"). The latter interpretation rests on the idea that the eventual attainment of absolute knowledge involves "not any given content as such but the universal of its form, i.e. the method" (Hegel, quoted in Marcuse, 1972, p. 416). While Hegel's dialectic may be viewed as a critical method, it would seem that one can only arrive at this conclusion in the manner of Marx, that is, the end result of Hegel's dialectic should be *aufheben* rather than taken as given as Marcuse (1972) suggests.

4.   While students of Marx have been arguing over whether there is "one Marx or two" since publication of his early *Economic and Philosophic Manuscripts* for the first time in the 1930s, from my cursory look at this issue the general feeling seems to be: that there was really only "one Marx," that there is a basic continuity throughout his work, that his early humanistic terminology underwent some change but the ideas were retained in essence, and that even *Capital* can

be read as containing many ethical references to the idea of creating the humane social conditions that will permit the realization of each individual's potential. Those whom I am aware of who argue for a basic continuity in Marx's writings include Avineri (1968), Bernstein (1971), Bottomore and Rubel (1956), Fromm (1966), McLellan (1971), and Tucker (1972), while Althusser (1970) and Hook (1962), for example, have taken the opposite position, explicitly arguing that the discontinuities between the young Marx and the more mature Marx overbalance the continuities. It is true, however, that a careful reading of the young Marx may be more rewarding for humanistic psychologists insofar as it is more psychological than his later works. Tucker, for example, notes that Marx's early psychological conception of alienation later becomes transformed into a sociological one: "The war of self-alienated Marxian man with himself has become a class war across the battlefield of society" (1972, p. 146).

5. For a discussion of the unresolved tension in Marxian dialectics between the freedom of people to transform social reality and the historical necessity for such transformations, see Marcuse (1972).

References

Althusser, L. *For Marx* (New York: Vintage, 1970).

Avineri, S. *The Social and Political Thought of Karl Marx* (Cambridge, Eng.: Cambridge University Press, 1968).

Beit-Hallahmi, B. "Salvation and Its Vicissitudes: Clinical Psychology and Political Values." *American Psychologist 29:* 124–129 (1974).

Bernstein, R.J. *Praxis and Action* (Philadelphia: University of Pennsylvania Press, 1971).

Bottomore, T.B. & Rubel, M. (eds). *Karl Marx: Selected Writings in Sociology and Social Philosophy* (London: Watts, 1956).

Comey, D.D. "Logic." In Kernig, *Marxism, Communism and Western Society*, vol. 5 (New York: Herder & Herder, 1972).

Engels, F. *Ludwig Feuerbach* (London: Martin Lawrence, 1934).

Fromm, E. *Marx's Concept of Man* (New York: Ungar, 1966).

Giddens, A. *Capitalism and Modern Social Theory: An Analysis of the Writing of Marx, Durkheim, and Max Weber* (Cambridge, Eng.: Cambridge University Press, 1971).

Glass, J.F. "The Humanistic Challenge to Sociology." *Journal of Humanistic Psychology 11:* 170–183 (1971).

Hook, S. "Dialectic in Society and History." In Feigl and Brodbeck, *Readings in the Philosophy of Science* (New York: Appleton Century Crofts, 1953).

Hook, S. *From Hegel to Marx: Studies in the Intellectual Development of Karl Marx* (Ann Arbor: University of Michigan Press, 1962).

Janousek, J. "On the Marxian Concept of Praxis." In Israel and Taifel, *The Context of Social Psychology: A Critical Assessment* (New York: Academic Press, 1972).

Kaufmann, W. *Hegel: A Reinterpretation* (New York: Anchor, 1966).

Kojeve, A. *Introduction to the Reading of Hegel* (New York: Basic Books, 1969).

Kolakowski, L. *Marxism and Beyond,* translated by J. Z. Peel (London: Pall Mall Press, 1969).

Lobkowicz, N. "Negation of the Negation." In Kernig, *Marxism, Communism and Western Society,* vol. 6 (New York: Harder & Harder, 1972).

Marcuse, H. *Reason and Revolution: Hegel and the Rise of Social Theory* (London: Routledge & Kegan, Paul, 1954).

Marcuse, H. "Dialectics: The History of Dialectics." In Kernig, *Marxism, Communism and Western Society,* vol. 2 (New York: Harder & Harder, 1972).

Marx, K. "Economic and Philosophic Manuscripts (written in 1844)." In *The Marx-Engels Reader* (New York: Norton, 1972).

Maslow, A.H. *Toward a Psychology of Being* (New York: Van Nostrand, 1968).

McLellan, D. *The Thought of Karl Marx* (London: Macmillan, 1971).

Riegel, K.F. "Dialectical Operations: The Final Period of Cognitive Development." *Human Development 16:* 346–370 (1973).

Riegel, K.F. "From Traits and Equilibrium toward Developmental Dialectics." In *1974–1975 Nebraska Symposium on Motivation,* Arnold & Cole, eds. (Lincoln: University of Nebraska Press, 1976), pp. 349–407.

Rychlak, J.F. *A Philosophy of Science for Personality Theory* (Boston: Houghton Mifflin, 1968).

Rychlak, J.F. "The Multiple Meanings of 'Dialectic.'" In Rychlak, *Dialectic: Humanistic Rationale for Behavior and Development* (Basel: Karger, 1976).

Solomon, R.C. "Hegel's Concept of 'Geist.'" In *Hegel: A Collection of Critical Essays,* MacIntyre, ed. (New York: Anchor, 1975).

Tucker, R.C. *Philosophy and Myth in Karl Marx* (Cambridge, Eng.: Cambridge University Press, 1972).

Chapter 7

Counter-Culture and Counter-Psychology

The youth movement of the sixties in North America has been described, analyzed, and explained in various ways by numerous social observers and social scientists (e.g., Altbach and Laufer, 1972; Braungart, 1974; Flacks, 1971; Langman, 1971; Reich, 1970; Starr, 1974). A common theme running throughout most of the attempts to understand the first really *major* youth movements in the USA is that such a phenomenon had a social basis and social consequences. Not surprisingly, molar phenomena demand molar conceptualizations, and sociological models and theories have played heavily in the attempt to understand the sudden emergence of a vocal and visible age group of society which, in the USA, had traditionally been complacent and silent. The rise of the counterculture has served to transform much of society in terms of its underlying mores, attitudes, and life styles. As a result of these changes the youth movement has also had considerable impact on such institutions as family, marriage, school, government and occupational role.

In emphasizing the social, economic, and political significance of the youth movement of the sixties, there has been little if any explicit recognition of its possible influence in the shaping of science. While it is true that the concern of youth for *quality life* has undoubtedly served as an impetus for focusing scientific and technological know-how in combating such social problems as pollution, overpopulation, poverty,

Reprinted with permission from *Interpersonal Development* 5: 223–233 (Karger, Basel, 1974–75).

education, etc., it is also the case that in this instance science is influenced only insofar as its *existent* knowledge is routed or rerouted. The problems upon which science and technology focus may well have a social basis residing in part of the youth movement, but one may also wish to examine the impact of the counter-culture on basic scientific models, theories, conceptualizations, or—to use Kuhn's (1962) term— paradigms.

The purpose of this chapter is to examine the role of the youth movement in bringing into being a new psychological model of man. Within academic psychology this new paradigm has been termed "third force psychology" (contrasted with behaviorism and psychoanalysis), or, more descriptively, "humanistic psychology." After examining the philosophy of science underlying traditional experimental psychology, the argument to be presented involves viewing both the youth movement and the rise of humanistic psychology within the framework of Mannheim's (1952) theory of generations and social change. An important new subarea thus emerges in this analysis which I have labelled the *sociology of psychological knowledge*. A sociology of psychological knowledge seeks to establish the relationship between social transformations and the emergence of new psychological paradigms. Thus knowledge which is considered legitimate within psychology may in part be conditioned by the underlying social structure.

PSYCHOLOGY, POSITIVISM, AND IDEOLOGY

Academic psychology as practiced and developed within traditional psychology departments in North America was and is based largely upon a behavioristic, positivistic, and deterministic philosophy of science (Turner, 1967). While various theories were spawned, thrived, and eventually laid to rest (e.g., Boring, 1950), mainstream experimental psychology remained a united force to the extent that it was based on a philosophy of science borrowed from classical physics. It has now become apparent to some that the wholesale adoption by psychology of a philosophy of science for the natural sciences has not served psychology well (Wolman, 1971). Scientists working in the physical sciences and philosophers of science discarded traditional conceptions inherent in classical physics over 50 years ago, while psychologists continued to base their research on a model of man which rested upon an outworn mechanistic view of nature (Brandt, 1973).

A positivistic approach to social science has its roots in the early writings of Saint-Simon (1760–1825) and Comte (1798–1857). These early sociologists shared similar views in regard to science and society, partly because of Comte's adoption of Saint-Simon's ideas without due acknowledgement (Zeitlin, 1968). In any case, these thinkers developed their ideas in response to the *philosophes* of the French Revolution. They called for a *positive* philosophy which would preserve the existent social order in response to those who advocated a negative philosophy involving revolution and social transformation on a large scale. Science was to replace religion as a solidifying force in society, where the problems of the time could be solved by the application of scientific knowledge in a relatively straightforward manner. The scientists and industrialists were to serve as society's elite, dictating the application of science in order to preserve the status quo.

The positivism of Saint-Simon and Comte served as a philosophy of science which advocated the "disinterested" application of scientific principles in studying man and society. In actuality, implicit in such a view were some deeply held values and attitudes concerning what *ought* to be the case. Prescription, description, and explanation were all tightly interwoven. The basic acceptance of the existing social order, the acceptance of the individual as an object rather than as a subject, the emphasis upon order rather than change—all served to give positivism the status of denying individual freedom and dignity. Science was to serve and maintain those already in power.

What can we say today of the relationship between psychology's positivistic stance and political ideology? That mainstream psychology has served those in power and their underlying ideology rather than the needs of the individual has been argued by Looft (1971). Thus psychology has characteristically been a "psychology of more," based upon the capitalistic belief that unrestricted growth is necessarily good. In his own words:

The dominant "model of man," espoused either as theories of behavior by scientists or as common-sense notions of "human nature" by the populace in general, is one of competitiveness, acquisitiveness, and future orientation. . . . As a result of the reinforcement and maintenance of these acquisitive and competitive assumptions both by formal and informal agents of socialization, the psychology of more will remain especially resilient to change at the level of individual persons. (p. 564)

That science in general serves political power has been argued by Lasswell (1970):

The consequence for the subserviency of science to political power, or to other "practical" values, is evident. Those who, in effect, "have skill, will move" make themselves understood and available to the demands of decision-makers at every level. These are the mid-elite and rank and file of science and scholarship. From them are recruited the thousands who cement the interdependence of science and the established structure of society. In the aggregate they contribute more directly to the service of war and oligarchy than to world security and the welfare of the whole community. (p. 118)

That the basic values underlying even clinical psychology may serve to maintain the existent social structure has been argued by Beit-Hallahmi (1974). Thus psychological problems are seen as residing within the individual rather than in society, and, in this sense, much of clinical psychology shares the ideological aspects of positivism. According to this view, bringing about greater self-actualization involves changing the individual to be in concert with the existing social order rather than entertaining the possibility of changing an aberrent society. In Beit-Hallahmi's words:

What we are all interested in, or, that is, what we *say* [editor's italics] we are interested in, is the maximal actualization of human potential. The question before us is whether such an actualization is possible without a major transformation of society. Most psychologists today are committed to a viewpoint which sees self-actualization as totally dependent on the individual and are totally satisfied with a role definition which demands that we leave society intact, while changing only the individual. (p. 128)

Positivism in the social sciences was born out of a belief in the desirability of maintaining the status quo in a supposedly value-free, unbiased, objective approach to man and society. Unwittingly, those that gave shape to positivism within the social sciences did not realize the value-laden nature of this commitment. As Tyler (1970) has pointed out:

Psychology as a science was early formalized as an objective, nonmetaphysical, empirically based search for truth. As such it was conceived as being free from bias, purpose, judgments, or assumptions. As one looks at its development and present status it is self-evident that as a science it has borne fruit and is growing. Yet the very base on which it has rested has been eroded away until it seems barely existent. We can no longer assert that psychology is a totally objective, totally nonmetaphysical, totally empirically based, and totally impersonal search for the truth. (p. 224)

One might add here that in looking back in historical perspective, psychology was *never* "free from bias, purpose, judgments or assumptions." In attempting to eschew values from science, positivism inadvertently became committed to a value-laden view of man and society which emphasized mechanization, objectivity, and determinism. Man as painted by positivism was not a picture of beauty, possibility, and unity. As noted by Eckhardt (1972), positivism entailed a philosophy of science which valued serving the status quo rather than truth, while in meeting the challenging problems of today's society, a humanistic philosophy of science is more appropriate. As cogently argued by Eckhardt, a humanistic philosophy of science may offer a truth criterion which may truly serve to enhance the human condition, namely, "That theory is true which promotes altruistic practices which benefit others as well as oneself" (Eckhardt, 1972, p. 7).

The growing realization that traditional psychology may have placed its bets on an inappropriate philosophy of science is a relatively recent phenomenon. Althoush there are undoubtedly many internal and external factors involved in increasing the number of psychologists who have become disenchanted with the positivistic, mechanistic, deterministic paradigm, there is one particular set of factors which I believe has been instrumental. The youth movement of the sixties helped to give rise to an alternative model of man. Humanistic psychology rose during the sixties, and it was no accident that deep social transformations were being reflected and impelled by the youth movement. Let us now consider this parallel of events and examine their possible interrelationship.

GENERATIONAL THEORY, SOCIAL CHANGE, AND HUMANISTIC PSYCHOLOGY

The rise of humanistic psychology may be viewed as having its basis in part in the infrastructure of society. That one must look to social factors in accounting for the recent growth of humanistic psychology as a movement becomes apparent in historical perspective. Humanistic psychology has drawn heavily from such intellectual developments as existentialism and phenomenology—ideas that have been in existence for decades in Europe, although until recently, these ideas had little impact on the American scene. That small minority of scholars who pioneered humanistic psychology in America—people such as Allport, Maslow and Rogers—had laid the basic foundations for much of their later work during the forties and fifties and to some extent even in the thirties. One might well wonder why the humanistic movement was so late in coming—why did it take so long to become a truly significant force to be reckoned with? The answer to this puzzle, it seems, must be sought in the dramatic social changes occurring in the late fifties, early sixties, and coming to a head around the mid-point of the latter decade.

In order to grasp the intimate relationship between these social changes and the rise of humanistic psychology it is necessary to consider Mannheim's (1952) theory on generations and social change. Mannheim's views on a positivistic behaviorism are well expressed in his early writings, as documented elsewhere (Buss, 1975, 1976). In rejecting positivism, Mannheim embraced humanism, placing great faith in individuality and self-actualization.

More important, and perhaps more to the point, in adopting a nonpositivistic model of generations and social change, Mannheim's theory explicitly endorsed the idea that generational conflict resides in youth's criticism of the existing social order. As noted by Braungart (1974) and Lambert (1972), Mannheim's theory of generational change is revolutionary in nature, noting that generational conflict may lead to newer and "better" social structures. This view sees generational conflict as a potentially constructive force in the evolution of society to the extent that a breakdown of the existent social structure may pave the way for higher level, more sophisticated structures accommodating recent sociohistorical events.

In contrast, the major alternative model of generational conflict, the Eisenstadt-Parsons functionalist model (Eisenstadt, 1963; Parsons, 1963), sees the problem of generations as residing within youth rather than society. As noted by Braungart (1974) and Goertzel (1972), the functional model interprets generational conflict in terms of a problem of integration, wherein different age groups are not fully integrated into the ongoing continuous (accepted) social process. The functional model of generational conflict bears a close affinity to the early positivistic views of Saint-Simon and Comte, with an implicit acceptance of the status quo and integration into society, rather than with a breaking down of social structures leading to higher level social transformation, as the ultimate goal in dealing with youth's rebellion.

Given the revolutionary nature and pervasiveness of the Youth Movement of the Sixties, both Braungart (1974) and Goertzel (1972) argue for the superiority of Mannheim's generational model for interpreting the resultant social transformations. Although Mannheim's model has not thus far served as a framework for carrying out extensive empirical studies, both Buss (1974a) and Braungart (1974) (especially the latter) have offered some suggestions for translating this theory into testable empirical researches. Because of the superiority of Mannheim's theory for dealing with molar qualitative social change, it is fitting that we employ this theoretical framework in analyzing the role of youth in bringing into being a new and revolutionary model of man which may serve as an alternative to the positivistic, behavioristic, deterministic paradigm.

In Mannheim's (1952) view there were several important properties to be considered in any society. Thus, in a society where there is both a continuous emergence of new participants and a disappearance of former participants in the cultural process, cultural creation and cultural accumulation are not carried out by the same individuals at the same time. Each new generation of cohorts makes "fresh contact" with the accumulated heritage handed down by older generations, thereby altering or transforming that heritage to some degree by selecting and emphasizing certain aspects. The latter process occurs since the new generation comes into contact with the cultural heritage without the years of commitment to the existent ideology, and in the process of assimilating the cultural material will alter the interpretation of the legacy of older generations. The idea of "fresh contact" of each new generation thus provides the vehicle for social and cultural *change,* where each generation may reevaluate the existent cultural heritage and selectively emphasize certain aspects. If there were not a continuous process of succeeding generations, the existent social pattern would be perpetuated largely unaltered. If the latter were the case, the social structure would not provide for either adaptive additions or deleterious deletions.

The members of each generation in a given culture experience historical events at the same age or point in development. Since they have a common experiental base in development they may participate as an integrated group. Although different generations may experience the same historical event at the same time, because of age and previous experiental differences, the historical event will have differential effects on different generations. Older generations will tend to assimilate and interpret reality in terms of previously well formed structures and categories of experience, while youth's interpretation of reality will be quite different.

Those values, beliefs, theories, etc., which continue to prove their worth to a society in new situations are transmitted to incoming generations, while those aspects of the culture which are not of value fade out of existence along with the outgoing generations. However, the transmission of the cultural heritage is not strictly a one-way process from older to younger generations, since intergenerational interaction provides the opportunity for the old to learn from the young as well. In this way, the accumulated cultural heritage is constantly being transformed and modified.

According to Mannheim, whether a particular generation will play the role of mediating social change by participating as an integrated group or "generation unit" depends upon the trigger action of specific historical events. Thus it is the unique historical events which serve as catalysts in creating a distinct generational style of "entelechy." For example, the recent technical advances in the field of birth control have created the possibility for a new morality which can be more readily assimilated by younger generations. In this situation we may speak of the realization of the potential for implementing change that is inherent in each generation. Thus the biological given that we have a continuous succession of incoming generations does not guarantee the implementation of change, but merely provides for the possibility of change. There are several cultural groups that have successive generations and yet have little social change because of the lack of acceleration in tempo of social and cultural transformations. Thus any generational group may set in motion forces of social change, but it will be the incoming younger generations which will be readily able to assimilate such change and thereby transform the cultural heritage. (For a discussion of the implications of Mannheim's theory of generations and social change within the context of the lack of incoming new generations into academia and the future development of psychology, see Buss, 1974b.)

Mannheim's ideas on generations and social change are bound to the larger concern with the relationship between thought and social structure. In considering the social changes occurring in North America during the sixties, new forms of thinking about man and his nature were coming into being which were carried by the newly emerging youth generations. Thus the alienated youth and the rise of a counterculture (e.g., Flacks, 1971; Reich, 1970) may be seen as due in part to specific sociohistorical events making fresh contact with the incoming new generation. What were the specific sociohistorical events which triggered the distinct generational style of the sixties? Undoubtedly many factors were involved in this process, including, in no small way, the increasingly apparent contradictions between the professed normative values of individualism, freedom, and democracy, which "theoretically" underlay American society, and the existential or actual human conditions of suppression and discrimination characterizing large groups of Americans.

The new youth generations at this time took some of the American values seriously (i.e., the above mentioned) and found society wanting in its implementation of such values. Furby (1971) has put forth an interesting explanation of such generational differences—the idea being that, although two generations may experience similar socialization

practices and values, differing economic conditions will produce generational differences in sociopolitical values and behavior. Thus, values
upon which industrialized society was based were rejected in favor of
their polar opposites (Langman, 1971)—a situation which was in no small
way brought about by the relative economic affluence of this generation
(Furby, 1971). The civil rights movements, the student protests of the
Vietnam War, the cry for university reform and relevance of education,
all characterized the more general concern for man and society—a
concern which emphasized the humanness of man and the rejection of
"man's inhumanity to man."

As documented by Starr (1974), this generation was a "peace and
love" generation. That much of American society was undergoing a
process of dehumanization during the fifties and before has been
commented upon and much popularized by such writers as Goodman
(1956, 1962); Packard (1959); and Whyte (1956). In looking back in
historical perspective, one cannot fail to see that the popularized
sociological writings of the fifties were sounding an ominous bell
heralding the social upheavals and transformations which were to take
place in the sixties. Thus the emerging youth generations of the sixties
reflected and helped to give rise to considerable social change and a new
vision of man.

As noted by Mannheim, the intellectual elites do not constitute a
distinct social group reflecting a distinct style of thinking. Rather, they
may attach themselves to any of a number of existent social groups which
may be carriers of distinct modes of thought. Mannheim believed that
the intelligentsia held potentially great power and responsibility in
helping to determine the direction society was to take. One may view
the recent development of humanistic psychology within the perspective
of certain intelligentsia aligning themselves with certain aspects of the
youth movements of the sixties. Thus those professional academicians
who furthered the course of humanistic psychology may be seen as
paralleling the youth movement—giving academic "certified" approval
to the quest for enhancing human freedom, dignity, and experience. In
other words, the student protest movement and resulting social action
policies provided the necessary social climate to stimulate, encourage,
and foster the acceptance of a new psychological model of man within
academia. Thus youth's protest of the dehumanization of man in
twentieth century American society was isomorphic with certain psychologists protesting the dehumanization entailed by a positivistic behaviorism.

In summary then, the social-political-historical events of the late
fifties and sixties helped to give rise to a new humanistic approach to

psychological inquiry. The fundamental ideas on which a humanistic psychology rested had been laid down previous to the sixties, but it was not until recently that the social climate was such as to foster critical analysis and rejection of status quo ideas concerning how man should be studied psychologically. Those academicians who fought their battles against ideological thinking within psychology rather than on the campuses, in the ghettos, and in the protest lines had a new generation of graduate students which were able to endorse the new conception of man quite readily since it was consistent with the more general concerns of the youth movements. And, of course, such students had not yet made the deep commitment to behaviorism.

CONCLUSION: TOWARD A SOCIOLOGY OF PSYCHOLOGICAL KNOWLEDGE

The above interpretation of sociohistorical factors playing a significant role in the shaping of a psychological science may be viewed within the broader context of what may appropriately be called the *sociology of psychological knowledge* (which may be viewed as a special instance of the sociology of knowledge). Elsewhere (Buss, 1975) the case has been made for examining the social basis for the rise and fall of different psychological theories, models, and paradigms. To the extent that psychologists (as well as others) become more self-conscious of the broader social context of their work, they may explicitly recognize the relativisitic nature of the problems studied as well as the interpretations offered. By being more aware of the necessarily value-laden nature of the scientific enterprise, social scientists may evaluate their products in part on extra-scientific grounds. In this way, values may be *explicitly* recognized and science may be carried out in the service of *worthy* values.

References

Altbach, P. G. & Laufer, R. S. *The New Pilgrims: Youth Protest in Transition* (New York: David McKay, 1972).

Beit-Hallahmi, B. "Salvation and Its Vicissitudes: Clinical Psychology and Political Values." *American Psychologist 29:* 124–129 (1974).

Boring, E. G. *A History of Experimental Psychology* (New York: Appleton-Century-Crofts, 1950).

Brandt, L. W. "The Physics of the Physicist and the Physics of the Psychologist." *International Journal of Psychology, 8:* 61–72 (1973).

Braungart, R. G. "The Sociology of Generations and Student Politics: A Comparison of the Functionalist and Generational Unit Models." *Journal of Social Issues 30* (2): 31–54 (1974).

Buss, A. R. "Generational Analysis: Description, Explanation, and Theory." *Journal of Social Issues 30* (2): 55–71 (1974a).

Buss, A. R. "Psychology's Future Development as Predicted from Generation Theory." *Human Development 17:* 453–459 (1974b).

Buss, A. R. "The Emerging Field of the Sociology of Psychological Knowledge." *American Psychologist 30:* 988–1002 (1975).

Buss, A. R. "Karl Mannheim's Legacy to Humanistic Psychology." *Journal of Humanistic Psychology 16:* 79–81 (1976).

Eckhardt, W. "Practice, Theory, and Value." *Journal of Contemporary Revolutions 4:* 100–109 (1972).

Eisenstadt, S. N. "Archetypal Patterns of Youth." In Erikson, *Youth: Change and Challenge* (New York: Basic Books, 1963).

Flacks, R. *Youth and Social Change* (Chicago: Rand McNally, 1971).

Furby, L. "Political Socialization: The Need for a Cross-cultural Approach." *International Journal of Psychology 6:* 299–303 (1971).

Goertzel, T. "Generational Conflict and Social Change." *Youth and Society 3:* 327–352 (1972).

Goodman, P. *Growing Up Absurd* (New York: Vintage, 1956).

Goodman, P. *Compulsory Mis-education and the Community of Scholars* (New York: Vintage, 1962).

Kuhn, T. S. *The Structure of Scientific Revolutions* (Chicago: University of Chicago Press, 1962).

Lambert, T. A. "Generations and Change: Toward a Theory of Generations as a Force in Historical Process." *Youth and Society 4:* 21–45 (1972).

Langman, L. "Dionysius-Child of Tomorrow: Notes on Postindustrial Youth." *Youth and Society 3:* 80–99 (1971).

Lasswell, H. D. "Must Science Serve Political Power?" *American Psychologist 25:* 117–123 (1970).

Looft, W. R. "The Psychology of More." *American Psychologist 26:* 561–565 (1971).

Mannheim, K. "The Problem of Generations." In Mannheim, *Essays on the Sociology of Knowledge* (London: Routledge & Kegan Paul, 1952).

Packard, V. *The Status Seekers* (New York: David McKay, 1959).

Parsons, T. "Youth in the Context of American Society." In Erikson, *Youth: Change and Challenge* (New York: Basic Books, 1963).

Reich, C. A. *The Greening of America* (New York: Random House, 1970).

Starr, J. M. "The Peace and Love Generation: Changing Attitudes toward Sex and Violence among College Youth." *Journal of Social Issues 30* (2): 73–106 (1974).

Turner, M. P. *Philosophy and the Science of Behavior* (New York: Irvington Publishers, 1967).

Tyler, F. B. "Shaping of the Science." *American Psychologist 25:* 219–226 (1970).

Whyte, W. H. *The Organization Man* (New York: Simon and Schuster, 1956).

Wolman, B. B. "Does Psychology Need Its Own Philosophy of Science?" *American Psychologist 26:* 877–886 (1971).

Zeitlin, I. M. *Ideology and the Development of Sociological Theory* (Englewood Cliffs, N. J.: Prentice-Hall, 1968).

Chapter 8

Humanistic Psychology and the Liberal Tradition: Maslow's Theory

Humanistic psychology can best be understood within its cultural context. It is within this context that I advance the claim that humanistic psychology in general, and Maslow's theory of self-actualization in particular, have their genesis in liberalism. My purpose here is to try and reveal both the nature and consequences of the link between humanistic psychology and the liberal tradition, using Maslow's theory as a concrete case for analysis. This analysis is part of a larger goal: to examine the social and historical basis of psychological theory and ideas (e.g., Buss, 1975, 1976a, 1976b, 1977, 1978).

THE BIRTH OF HUMANISTIC PSYCHOLOGY

Over a period of some thirty years, Robert Nisbet (1953, 1966, 1968) has been arguing that the historical roots of classical sociological theory lie in the conservative response to modernity. Thus, the writings of Marx, Weber, Durkheim, Tönnies, and others may be seen as a *quest for community* in an age of increasing fragmentation, isolation, alienation, and bureaucracy. The latter are all due to forces of modernity such as the division of labor and the rationalization or routinization of institutional services. During the nineteenth century, when traditional

Reprinted with permission from the *Journal of Humanistic Psychology* (in press, 1979); original title, "Humanistic Psychology as Liberal Ideology: The Socio-Historical Roots of Maslow's Theory of Self-Actualization."

society was crumbling under the heavy weight of rapid scientific, technological, and sociopolitical change, sociological theorists attempted to preserve the idea of community. The rising tide of individualism (part of the growing liberal consciousness) seemed to show no sign of ebbing. Thus, we can modify Nisbet's thesis slightly: classic sociological theory can be seen as a conservative reaction to a growing liberalism that emphasized the autonomous individual.

Recently, Westkott has argued that modern (as opposed to classic) sociology is also conservative in nature (1977). However, in contrast to Nisbet's emphasis on conservative *theory*, Westkott (and before him, Birnbaum, 1971, pp. 81–93) has argued that modern sociology draws its conserving tendencies from *method*. Its methodology, inherited from Comte, emphasizes the present and the process of collecting facts; this produces "a 'situational conservatism' that justifies the factual reality it records" (p. 70). Positivism as a method "is the denial of philosophy, theory, politics, and imagination" (p. 70). It creates a conservative disposition that reproduces, rather than criticizes, social reality.

Comte's methodology has also influenced the other social sciences. When the social sciences became the behavioral sciences, positivistic methodology became the common denominator that united mainstream sociology, psychology, political science, and anthropology. It did not matter that most behavioral scientists were themselves self-professed liberals. Their individual politics are separable from the political consequences of their collective professional practice. Westkott's criticism applies to all the behavioral sciences. In Hampden-Turner's words:

Their [behavioral scientists'] conservatism is latent in the tools they employ. It comes about less by valuing conservatively than by the "value-free" selection of the less than human. . . . He who is silent assents, and to describe the status quo with detailed and passionless precision is usually to dignify it. (1971, pp. 17–18)

Although humanistic psychology has been branded by Maslow as the alternative to behaviorism and psychoanalysis—as "third force" psychology—it can more accurately be considered as "second force" psychology, *as the liberal reaction to conservatism* (albeit conservatism in two different guises). Anderson (1974) has recently noted that the political consequences of *both* behaviorism and psychoanalysis are conservative in nature. Given our previous distinction between conservative method and conservative theory, we can be somewhat more analytical than Anderson regarding the *sources* of the common conservative effect of both behaviorism and psychoanalysis. Whereas the conservative element in behaviorism stems from its positivistic *methodology,* in psychoanalysis it is more rooted in *theory.* Thus, Freud's deterministic, fatalistic, and pessimistic view of humanity offered little other than trying to get along as best one could in a basically static, evil society. For Freud, the nature of society was derived from the nature of the individual—from a biologically based, ahistorical view of humanity. Since human nature was basically irrational, destructive, and unchanging in his theory, there were no grounds for expecting improvement in the human condition, no plans for implementing social change. Humanistic psychologists reacted to a negative view of humanity that carried with it a latent conservatism (for a discussion of Freud's conservative theory, see Roazen, 1967). They certainly did not find in Freudian negativism any support for the idea of radical and revolutionary change that some others have seen (e.g., Brown, 1959; Jacoby, 1975; Marcuse, 1955; Reich, 1970; Robinson, 1969).

In summary, then, liberal humanistic psychologists rejected the conservative implications that both behaviorism and psychoanalysis seemed to entail. A mechanistic, deterministic conception of the individual left no possibility for an active, self-determining agent who could transform and change his/her situation. Behaviorism left no room for contemplation, speculation, or reflection about one's experience. Classical psychoanalysis offered little in this area as well, since one's experience and theorizing could never break through the prison of a deterministic past and a predetermined future. To the liberal mind, freedom, liberty, and personal development or progress were ideals inconsistent with the conservative methodology of behaviorism and the conservative theory of psychoanalysis. It was on the basis of such liberal values that humanistic psychologists launched their critique of the two "traditional" psychologies. Humanistic psychology thus began as a radical and revolutionary liberal movement—much like the liberalism associated with the Enlightenment, whose genesis also lay in criticizing the established order from the viewpoint of freedom, liberty, and individual progress.

In criticizing the conservative implications of both behaviorism and psychoanalysis, humanistic psychologists were really fighting a battle on two fronts: they were attempting to deal with the very real problem of an alienated, determined, controlled, and objectified human existence, and they were opposing the conservative ideology which had had the net effect of reproducing that reality. With respect to alienation, humanistic psychologists were reacting to the truth content of both behaviorism and psychoanalysis. That is to say, the origins of both behaviorism and psychoanalysis can be seen as tied to a specific sociohistorical condition, and as such, they offer certain insights into that condition. A deterministic, mechanistic, and pessimistic conception of the individual was tied to a social reality indeed consistent with such an image. However, the error of both behaviorism and psychoanalysis was to accept current reality as absolute reality. Behaviorism in method, and psychoanalysis in theory, universalize, and thus conserve and preserve, a human condition that should be transformed. Their built-in conserving tendencies tend to perpetuate the social reality that spawned them. Thus, they are both ultimately ideological in the Marxian sense (e.g., see Lichtman, 1975) of that term. That is to say, both behaviorism and psychoanalysis "reflect" social reality (the deterministic, alienated, mechanistic existence associated with advanced industrial capitalistic society), and this is their truth content. Yet, *at the same time*, both also involve a distortion, or an "inversion" of that social reality, by which is meant that both absolutize what is really a historically unique situation. This is their "falseness" dimension. For Marx, an ideology both "reflected" and "inverted" social reality, and thus contained both truth and falseness.

Although humanistic psychology as a liberal theory offers quite a different view of humanity than do the conservative theories of both behaviorism and psychoanalysis, it does not escape their ideological fate. Although it started out with a revolutionary bang, humanistic psychology has ended up with a coopted whimper. There can be little doubt that, historically speaking, third force psychology has been a progressive movement. Its critical foundations, however, have gradually been eroded as it has become institutionalized within the APA as the "official" oppositional wing. What was once an "out" group is now very much an "in" group. The rhetoric of individual development and self-actualization has been taken over by government, industrial, and organizational psychologists (e.g., Harman, 1974), and has been turned into an ideology that maintains the status quo. What was once a theory of revolutionary liberal psychologists is now part of the received doctrine of the liberal establishment—what might be called "conservative liberalism."

The excessive individualism contained in the doctrine of self-actualization serves to mask the larger social questions surrounding society's structures and institutions. A theory that predisposes one to focus more upon individual freedom and development than the larger social reality works in favor of maintaining that social reality. Several people have already noted the conformist implications of humanistic psychology (Adams, 1977; Beit-Hallahmi, 1977; Glass, 1971; Nord, 1977), but thus far there has not been an adequate sociohistorical interpretation of this dimension. What is required to situate the theory of humanistic psychology within a larger social and political matrix and, more specifically, to reveal the liberal foundations of the theory. The latter permits a deeper, more meaningful critique in the sense of pointing out that it is necessary to transform the social props that support liberal humanistic psychology in order to transcend its individualistic bias. In other words, it is through praxis that more valid theory will develop (and, being good dialecticians, our theory should also inform our praxis). Let me now try and make these rather abstract ideas more concrete by focusing on Maslow's theory of self-actualization.

THE LIBERAL BASIS OF MASLOW'S THEORY OF SELF-ACTUALIZATION

Having alluded to the link between humanistic psychology and liberalism, I will become a little more specific about that relationship by looking at the structure of Maslow's theory. Conceptually, there can be little doubt that Maslow's psychological theory is founded upon, and implies, the tenets of liberalism. Such themes in his writings as growth, becoming, self-actualization, individual freedom, and tolerance are all the psychological embodiment of the liberal frame of mind, which emphasizes optimism, pluralism, individual freedom, piecemeal progress, and a gradual movement toward perfection. Thus, although Maslow rejected positivism as a methodology, he adopted a positive, or optimistic, rather than a negative, or critical, approach (Maslow, 1954, pp. 353–362). In this way he shared the liberal disposition to concentrate on the "good" rather than on the "bad," and to attempt piecemeal social change through the education of individuals, rather than by transforming the deeper structures of society.

Maslow had a vision of the ideal liberal society in which freedom and individual development reigned supreme—a psychological utopia he called "Eupsychia." Thus, in common with other liberal thinkers, Maslow shared the dual commitment to finding out the "truth"—describing reality as it "really" is—and hinting at a social reality we "ought" to nurture into being. And the two tasks were often unconsciously fused. Maslow never did adequately distinguish between, and resolve to *some* degree of satisfaction, the "is" and the "ought." He attempted to pass his own theory off as one based on purely descriptive statements, rather than one containing a hard normative core (Smith, 1969, p. 169). Thus, his theory lacks an explicit and self-conscious appreciation of its own value-laden nature, and more specifically, its affirmation of liberal values. The latter was the case in spite of the fact that Maslow gave considerable attention to the study of values.

In regard to Maslow's own values, his original sample of self-

actualizers—his own personal selection of individuals he considered to
be self-actualized—appears to epitomize liberal values. According to
Maslow, these people were democratic, autonomous, individualistic,
and—true to the liberal penchant for piecemeal progress—preferred to
work from within the system on matters relating to social injustice. Like
nineteenth-century liberals such as Herbert Spencer, Maslow grounded
his notion of individual progress on the universal laws of biology.
Maslow's absolute, ahistorical view of human nature, as anchored in his
concept of "instinctoid," was the foundation for his theory of self-
actualization. His conception of human nature as primary, and the
environment as secondary, was much like that of an earlier champion of
liberal ideals—Rousseau. Rousseau's "natural man" would almost seem
to have inspired Maslow's "concept of the psychiatrically healthy man, or
the eupsychic man, who is also in effect the natural man" (Maslow, 1954,
p. 340). Thus, for Maslow, "Man demonstrates *in his own nature* a
pressure toward . . . more perfect actualization. . . . The environment
does not give his potentialities" (Maslow, 1968, p. 160, original
emphasis).

   Whereas Freud's conception of an unchanging human nature was
one that emphasized destruction, negation, and despair, Maslow's liberal
essentialism was one of construction, affirmation, and hope. The
important point here is that the *structure* of both Freud's and Maslow's
views of humanity is *identical* (ahistorical, essential, unchanging, biological), although the *content* differs. Although he is not specifically
discussing humanistic psychology, Lichtman's observations on various
reactions to psychoanalysis are indeed appropriate:

The tendency is to negate the Freudian *characterization* of human nature . . .
[and] assert the view that the new set of attributes is *given fact* about human
beings. Men and women are transformed into a *new* entity, but an *entity*
nonetheless. . . . What distinguishes human life, however, what constitutes its
dignity and unique value, is our capacity to create ourselves in history . . . the
view of a fixed human nature is one of the basic mystifications to be opposed.
(Lichtman, 1977, p. 81, original emphasis)

Thus, the theories of both Maslow and Freud are ideological to the
extent that they view human nature as an absolute.
   Part of Maslow's view of human nature included a consideration of
values and ethics. Maslow also attempted to ground his own values and
ethics in biology, and then passed them off as universal. As noted by
Smith (1973), this move is problematic for a truly humanistic approach—

that is, an approach that rests upon choice, dialogue, and criticism within the context of a changing sociohistorical reality.

Along with his emphasis upon an essential rather than a historical or transformable human nature, Maslow also stressed inner rather than outer freedom:

Healthy individuals are not externally visible. . . . It is an *inner* freedom that they have . . . they may be considered to be psychologically autonomous, i.e., relatively independent of culture. External freedom seems to be less important than inner freedom. (Maslow, 1954, p. 351)

Here Maslow is following J. S. Mill's emphasis on freedom or liberty in the internal rather than in the external sphere. Mill's entire essay of 1859, *On Liberty*, is an exploration of the limits of society's constraint over the individual. The major theme Mill defends is one in which there is "absolute nonintervention in the private sphere of human affairs" (Wolff, 1968, p. 7). It is a position that Wolff has dubbed "Mill's Doctrine of the Liberty of Inner Life," and would seem to find its *psychological* expression in Maslow's theory of inner freedom and self-actualization. Finally, in regard to the political content of Maslow's theory, we can note that in reading various political analyses of liberalism, it is very easy indeed to find passages that could have been written by Maslow. Thus, such classic liberal works as Mill's *On Liberty*, (1859) and Hobhouse's *Liberalism*, (1911) contain many references to the idea of individual development and self-actualization.

Important as these observations are concerning the liberal foundations of Maslow's theory, we can go beyond a "mere" conceptual link between his concepts and the liberal tradition; we can examine the deeper sociohistorical roots that nourished the specific form of liberalism which permeates his psychological categories. My strategy here is to single out the major underlying contradiction within Maslow's theory— *the tension between his democratic and elitist tendencies*—and place this contradiction within its sociohistorical context.

THE SOCIOHISTORICAL DIMENSION IN MASLOW'S THEORY

The major implicit contradiction within Maslow's theory has recently been made explicit by Aron (1977). According to Aron, Maslow held two contradictory views of self. One view involved a *democratic* conception of self. It emphasized equality of rights, individual sovereignty, pluralism, and a toleration of others. This side of Maslow placed a premium on individual choice and development, and was based on a relativistic notion of values. "Maslow's other child" involved what Aron has called an aristocratic or *elitist* view of the self. This elitist view derived from Maslow's judgment that, in reality, some values *are* better than others; there are better ways of living than others, better people than others. According to this side of Maslow, there are two distinct kinds, or what we might call classes, of people: (1) those who are self-actualizing, worthy of emulation, psychologically healthy, and in control of their lives (one percent of the general population, according to Maslow); and (2) those who are nonactualizing, nonworthy of being emulated, psychologically unhealthy, and impotent vis-à-vis successfully charting themselves around life's obstacles. Maslow revered the former and disparaged the latter.

Although Aron has detected and revealed this contradiction within Maslow's thought, she has not explained its existence. Thus, it is not enough to psychologize such a contradiction and state that "Maslow committed an error in reasoning that cannot be rectified" (Aron, 1977, p. 14). It makes no sense to ask "where in this wild dialectic is the *real* Maslow?" (p. 15, original emphasis), since it is not necessary to choose between Maslow the democrat and Maslow the aristocrat. The "real" Maslow was both. The contradiction in his theory is not a conceptual one. There is no error in logic. Rather, the contradition is a *real* contradiction. It is an historical contradiction rooted in a concrete social reality. *Maslow's contradiction is part of a larger contradiction—the contradiction between democratic theory and democratic practice within modern liberal society*. A more adequate explanation of Maslow's psychological concepts (and their contradictory nature) must involve unearthing their social content—peeling away their surface layers and laying bare their historical origins.

Maslow's first systematic presentation of his views, *Motivation and Personality*, was published in 1954. This book, which contains revisions of several essays dating from 1941, was thus written over a period which witnessed some significant political events revolving around the undermining of classical democratic theory. Several mass movements, all of which took a totalitarian turn (Nazism, Fascism, and McCarthyism), shook the very foundations of classic liberal democratic theory, which had considered the masses as the protectors of freedom and liberty. The growing postwar prolitarian support for communist parties in such Western countries as France and Italy posed somewhat of a threat to classical liberal democratic theory. Rather than seeing the franchise and the further delegation of power to the masses as guaranteeing the preservation of democracy, there developed a growing realization that perhaps the masses could not be trusted to exercise such increased responsibility in a way consistent with preserving liberal values. During the early 1950s the common person's lack of political sophistication was being increasingly documented by social scientists. Such findings helped to fuel a growing disillusionment with classic liberal democratic theory and the acceptance of elitist theories of democracy (see Bachrach, 1967, for a useful discussion of this point).

The tension between the theory and practice of classic democracy during this period could no longer be ignored. The historical setting that nurtured the development of democracy—that is, the small rural village in which each individual was assured of a hearing—was no longer the prototype for the modern democratically run state. In an age of the nation-state there was little opportunity for direct participation of the masses. Democratic government increasingly involved fewer and fewer decision-makers. Those who continued to espouse classic democratic theory were by now uttering rhetoric. The reality could no longer be ignored: democracy was increasingly becoming the tool of a very small but powerful elite. What Bachrach (1967) has called *democratic elitism* had replaced classic democratic theory. As outlined by Bachrach, the flames of democratic elitism were fanned by the mass movements of the 1930s and 1940s, and this liberal doctrine became a force to be reckoned with during the aftermath of World War II. Whereas earlier liberals had believed that values such as liberty, freedom, individual development, tolerance, and pluralism were to be defended and preserved through increasing the franchise and individual rights, postwar liberals began to take the opposite view: Liberalism was endangered by further democratization and needed a "power elite" to safeguard its existence.

We are now in a position to understand the social basis of Maslow's theory of self-actualization, and the historical roots of the contradiction between the democratic and elitist views of self. Maslow's elite—the one percent of the general population who define and thus control what is meant by self-actualization—are the psychological embodiment of the social elite who are society's decision-makers. *The structure of Maslow's psychological theory can be seen as incorporating the structure of his society. Maslow's hierarchical or "class" theory of self-actualization consists of social categories projected onto the individual.* His is a liberal psychological theory that contains the real sociohistorical contradiction between democracy and elitism—the contradiction that had evolved within the modern liberal democratic state. The tension in Maslow's theory of self-actualization between democracy and elitism—between the nonactualized masses and the actualized few—is part of the tension liberal theorists were experiencing and trying to resolve in the 1940s and 1950s. Whereas the latter attempted a conceptual solution involving a defense of democratic elitism, Maslow, as Aron (1977) has made clear, was never sufficiently conscious of the contradictory strains in his theory to attempt such a solution.

Thus, contrary to Hampden-Turner's argument that Maslow sought to synthesize "apparent" contradictions and transcend false dualisms, I believe that the democratic-elitist tension remains intact and below consciousness in his work. It is driven underground where it can serve an ideological function. Even if Maslow had been conscious of the contradiction in his theory, an attempt to perform conceptual surgery by synthesizing the polarity would not have been the way out. False syntheses are no better than false dualisms. We should guard against applying dialectical thinking in a mechanical or undialectical manner. We need a truly critical approach. We need to turn dialectics upon itself and adopt a perspective that Adorno (1973) has called "negative dialectics" in order to detect the *actual* contradictory and fragmentary social reality underlying our theory. In other words, theory alone will not suffice to save Maslow's work from its contradictions. Since the contradiction of which we are speaking is not conceptual but a real one anchored in a concrete sociohistorical reality, its resolution requires transforming that social reality. Thus, theory guiding praxis, and praxis in turn guiding theory are necessary to resolve the contradictory democratic and elitist dimensions in Maslow's theory. The solution to Maslow's contradiction is part of a larger social solution—undermining the structural basis of democratic elitism and establishing a form of democracy with a broader base.

Reestablishing the very important core of classic liberal democratic theory—that is, a broadly based type of political participation—is absolutely necessary in order to achieve the kinds of goals Maslow's theory of self-actualization is purportedly trying to achieve. Classic democratic theory "is based on the supposition that a man's dignity, and indeed his growth and development . . . is dependent upon an opportunity to participate actively in decisions that significantly affect him" (Bachrach, 1967, p. 98). Having the freedom to be an effective part of those collective decisions that affect one's life must be a prerequisite reality, rather than a myth, if Maslow's goal of widespread self-actualization is to be a realistic one. Democratic elitism, which sustains Maslow's self-actualized elite, must give way to mass self-actualization. This, in turn, requires mass democracy. It is in this way that the structure of Maslow's psychological theory can inform our social praxis.

Political action and psychological theory are thus connected, dialectically.

Of course, a plea for a return to the practice of classic liberal democratic theory is unrealistic in the age of the "global community." Increasing centralization of the decision-making process has gone beyond the "mere" establishment of national governing bodies to the establishment of those with international powers. We must take account of the reality of C. Wright Mills' "power elite" in an age of increasing complexity, sepcialization, and bureaucracy (1956). What, then, is a realistic, yet more democratic alternative to democratic elitism in the age of mass society? Bachrach's proposal for transcending democratic elitism would seem to provide at least a valuable hint for finding a solution to the social contradiction that Maslow's psychological theory contains. According to Bachrach's "self-developmental theory of democracy," it is necessary to go beyond a nineteenth-century notion of political decision-making: "Large areas within existing so-called private centers of power are political and therefore potentially open to a wide and democratic sharing in decision-making" (Bachrach, 1967, 102). Thus, greater effort should be made so that the common person can actively participate in those decisions that affect him/her in the factory and in the community—decisions he/she considers important and vital, rather than tangential and irrelevant to day-to-day living.

CONCLUSION

In giving Maslow's theory of self-actualization a critical and dialectical reading, we are able to understand its liberal ideological foundations and go beyond them. Ideologically speaking, the validity of Maslow's theory derives from the contradictory social reality it "reflects" and supports—democratic elitism, a two-class theory of individual freedom and development. However, Maslow's theory is at the same time an "inversion" of that social reality to the extent that its psychological categories universalize a historically specific condition—namely, democratic elitism. Maslow's biologically rooted theory of self-actualization freezes human nature circa 1950, and makes an absolute of two historically evolved classes of individuals. As such, it contains a hidden plea for social transformation once we appreciate that human nature is itself historical, and that humanity can create and re-create its own nature through its making of history.

References

Adams, H. "Toward a Dialectical Approach to Counseling." *Journal of Humanistic Psychology 17:* 57–67 (1977).

Adorno, T. W. *Negative Dialectics* (New York: Seabury, 1973).

Anderson, W. "Politics and the New Humanism." *Journal of Humanistic Psychology 14:* 5–26 (1974).

Aron, A. "Maslow's Other Child." *Journal of Humanistic Psychology 17:* 9–24 (1977).

Bachrach, P. *The Theory of Democratic Elitism: A Critique.* (Boston: Little, Brown, 1967).

Beit-Hallahmi, B. "Humanistic Psychology: Progressive or Reactionary?" *Self and Society 5:* 97–103 (1977).

Birnbaum, N. *Toward a Critical Sociology* (New York: Oxford University Press, 1971).

Brown, N. O. *Life against Death: The Psychoanalytic Meaning of History* (Middletown, Conn.: Wesleyan University Press, 1959).

Buss, A. R. "The Emerging Field of the Sociology of Psychological Knowledge." *American Psychologist 30:* 988–1002 (1975).

Buss, A. R. "Development of Dialectics and Development of Humanistic Psychology." *Human Development 19:* 248–260 (1976a).

Buss, A. R. "Galton and the Birth of Differential Psychology and Eugenics: Social, Political, and Economic Forces." *Journal of the History of the Behavioral Sciences 12:* 47–58 (1976).

Buss, A. R. "Piaget, Marx, and Buck-Morss on Cognitive Development: A Critique and Reinterpretation." *Human Development 20:* 118–128 (1977).

Buss, A. R. "Critical Notice of Izenberg's Psychohistory and Intellectual History." *History and Theory 17:* 94–98 (1978).

Glass, J. F. "The Humanistic Challenge to Sociology." *Journal of Humanistic Psychology 11:* 170–183 (1971).

Hampden-Turner, C. *Radical Man.* (Garden City, N.Y.: Anchor Books, 1971).

Hampden-Turner, C. "Comment on 'Maslow's Other Child.'" *Journal of Humanistic Psychology 12:* 25–31 (1977).

Harman, W. W. "Humanistic Capitalism: Another Alternative." *Journal of Humanistic Psychology 14:* 5–32 (1974).

Hobhouse, L. T. *Liberalism* (New York: Oxford University Press, 1964, originally published in 1911).

Jacoby, R. *Social Amnesia: A Critique of Contemporary Psychology from Adler to Laing*. (Boston: Beacon Press, 1975).

Jay, M. *The Dialectical Imagination: A History of the Frankfurt School and the Institute of Social Research 1923–50*. (London: Heinemann, 1973).

Kaufman, A. S. *The Radical Liberal* (New York: Atherton Press, 1968).

Lichtman, R. "Marx's Theory of Ideology." *Socialist Revolution 5:* 45–76 (1975).

Lichtman, R. "Marx and Freud, Part 2: Antagonistic Themes." *Socialist Revolution 7:* 59–84 (1977).

Marcuse, H. *Eros and Civilization: A Philosophical Inquiry into Freud* (Boston: Beacon Press, 1955).

Maslow, A. H. *Motivation and Personality* (New York: Harper, 1954).

Mill, J. S. *On Liberty* (New York: Norton, 1975, originally published in 1859).

Mills, C. W. *The Power Elite* (New York: Oxford University Press, 1956).

Nisbet, R. A. *The Quest for Community* (New York: Oxford University Press, 1966).

Nisbet, R. A. *The Socialogical Tradition* (New York: Basic Books, 1966).

Nisbet, R. A. *Tradition and Revolt: Historical and Sociological Essays* (New York: Random House, 1968).

Nord, W. "A Marxist Critique of Humanistic Psychology." *Journal of Humanistic Psychology 17:* 75–83 (1977).

Reich, W. *The Mass Psychology of Fascism* (New York: Farrar, Straus and Giroux, 1970, originally published in 1933).

Roazen, P. *Freud: Political and Social Thought* (New York: Knopf, 1968).

Robinson, P. A. *The Freudian Left* (New York: Harper and Row, 1969).

Smith, M. B. *Social Psychology and Human Values* (Chicago: Aldine-Atherton, 1969).

Smith, M. B. "On Self-actualization: A Transambivalent Examination of a Focal Theme in Maslow's Psychology." *Journal of Humanistic Psychology 13:* 17–33 (1973).

Volkomer, W. E. (edl). *The Liberal Tradition in American Thought*. (New York: Putnam's, 1969).

Westkott, M. "Conservative Method." *Philosophy of the Social Sciences 7:* 67–76 (1977).

Wolff, R. P. *The Poverty of Liberalism* (Boston: Beacon Press, 1968).

Chapter 9

Theories of Cognitive Development: Piaget, Marx and Buck-Morss

In an extremely penetrating and provocative article, Buck-Morss (1975) has recently attempted to interpret cross-cultural differences in performance on Piagetian reasoning tests as being associated with underlying differences along certain socio-economic variables. More specifically, she has adopted a Marxian framework, which leans heavily upon the forces and relations of production as the substructure underlying superstructure or consciousness, in accounting for cultural differences in the existence, level and/or time necessary to achieve abstract formal reasoning. While I am very sympathetic with the approach taken by Buck-Morss, and further, agree with much of her analysis, it is also true that I believe that her interpretation of extant cross-cultural differences in abstract formal reasoning can be placed within a more general perspective. The latter tack, it will be argued, has the added advantage of resolving some of the tensions and non-real contradictions which are a consequence of her adopted Marxian framework.

The purpose of the present brief chapter is to take a "critical" look at Buck-Morss' thesis on socio-economic bias in Piaget's theory, and, hopefully, partake in what will become an ongoing dialogue in the ambitious attempt to better understand the social context of psychological theory (Buss, 1975). Thus, consistent with the intellectual heritage within which Buck-Morss is operating, I wish to make a modest attempt

Reprinted with permission from Human Development 20: 118–128 (Karger, Basel, 1977); original title, "Piaget, Marx, and Buck-Morss on Cognitive Development: A Critique and Reinterpretation."

to use the dialectic as a method in order to try and advance some of her ideas on Piaget's theory of cognitive development and its relationship to the real dialectic between the individual and society, thought and action, theory and praxis. As an introduction to Buck-Morss' position, although also of value in its own right, a brief comparison is undertaken below of Piaget's and Marx's theories of cognition (a "mini-structural analysis"). Then, after noting some inconsistencies and/or non-real contradictions inherent in Buck-Morss' Marxian interpretation of cross-cultural differences in abstract formal thought, some of the more recent ideas of those social theoreticians in the "critical" tradition are considered in an attempt to transcend the limitations of Buck-Morss' position.

THE CONTEXT

Readers of this chapter are well aware of Piaget's theory of cognitive development. What they may not be so well aware of is that Marx also had a theory of cognition—a theory which is only recently beginning to receive attention (Kolakowski, 1968). It is in the *Philosophical and Economic Manuscripts* of 1844 that Marx, while not outlining a detailed theory of cognitive development, does provide enough material to piece together the basics of such a theory. Marx considered cognition from a developmental perspective, but in this case the term "development" is to be understood as *historical* development rather than, as in Piaget's case, *ontogenetic* development.[1] For Marx, "The cultivation of the five senses is the work of all previous history," where "it is not only the five senses, but also the so-called spiritual senses, the practical senses (desiring, loving, etc.), in brief, human sensibility and the human character of the senses, which can only come into being through the existence of *its* object, through humanized nature" (Marx, 1964, p. 161). In Marx's view, nature was not to be understood in terms of immanent categories which are trans-historical. It is social people with human needs who appropriate and understand nature in terms of cognitive categories related to those needs. In the process of objectivizing nature, new needs are created and thus new cognitive categories come into being. Cognition is therefore historical in that the world and nature are known through cognitive categories which are the product of a changing human nature (new needs) interacting with a changing social reality.

Marx's largely implicit theory of cognition which runs through the Paris manuscripts (see especially the third manuscript) may be viewed within the context of an enduring problem of Western philosophy—the relationship between theory and practice. While a detailed treatment of the relationship between theory and practice is beyond the scope of the present chapter (e.g., see Lobkowicz, 1967, for a history of the ideas relating to this relationship from Aristotle to Marx), some passing comments and distinctions are necessary in order to clarify Buck-Morss' contention that, for Piaget, "the culmination of learning is when the child can 'do' everything in his head, that is, when he can divorce theory from practice." (1975, p. 41).

As pointed out by Bernstein, there has been much confusion over the issue of the relationship between theory and practice due to the "ambiguity of what we might label the 'high' and 'low' senses of 'practical'" (1971, p. X). Marx carried on in the Aristotelian tradition; that is, practice, or *praxis*, denoted and connoted distinctly human activities typically within a political or ethical context (e.g., labor, production, relentless criticism, revolutionary activity, etc.) rather than simply low-level action in the real world. Out of human praxis arises critical theory, where critical theory, in turn, is to guide better practice. In this way, Marx attempted to unite theory and practice, thought and action, values and facts, "ought" and "is," prescription and description. According to Marx, then, cognition is rooted in praxis, where changing needs and praxis yield changing cognitive categories and changing theory. Truth is thereby historical rather than absolute.

Piaget's theory of cognitive development may be viewed as a very different outcome in the attempt to deal with some similar problems and issues as concerned Marx. Both Piaget and Marx shared an uneasy attitude towards philosophy, although each proposed a somewhat different solution for transcending philosophy. For Marx, philosophy must be realized through praxis in order to abolish it. In his last thesis on Feuerbach written in 1845, Marx reveals his disenchantment with pure speculation: "The philosophers have *interpreted* the world in various ways; the point, however, is to *change* it" (Marx, 1941, p. 84). In an autobiographical account of his intellectual development, Piaget has outlined the reasons which led him away from speculative philosophy towards an attempt "to make epistemology into a science" (1971a, p. 55). The insight which Piaget shared with Marx, namely, "the close relation that exists between philosophical thought and the underlying social factors" (Piaget, 1971a, p. 15), effected in Piaget (in contrast to Marx) an attempt to break out of relativism by an ahistorical scientific study of the development of epistemic operations. In this way, theory and praxis were torn asunder in that there was created an unbridgeable gap between fact and value, description and prescription, the "is" and "ought," by adopting a universalist, natural science structuralist model of cognitive development (for an account of the intellectual tradition into which Piaget's theory falls—French Structuralism—see Piaget, 1971b). Since for Piaget metaphysics, speculative thought, or a kinder term, "critical reason," were all devalued and even banished as legitimate means for arriving at truth, one can view his theory as an example *par excellence* of what Horkheimer was to call the "eclipse of reason" (see below).

At another level, however, Piaget *did* attempt to reconcile theory and practice, where *both* of these two terms should now be understood in their "low" sense, that is, respectively, abstract formal thought or mental operations (as opposed to critical-evaluative-content-type thought), and physical action, manipulation, or control of the real world (as opposed to distinctly human projects concerning the better life). For Piaget, mental operations were seen as an outgrowth of action in the real world, where abstract thought was viewed as covert action. Thus, both Piaget and Marx placed a priority on practice in that, out of practice, developed (ontogenetically and historically, respectively) cognition, although the meanings of these terms were certainly not the same for them.

Whereas Marx was concerned with the historical development of the content of cognition, Piaget has been addressing the ontogenetic development of the form of cognition. Each, in his own unique way, has been critical of positivism and empiricism, and both have attempted to go beyond mere appearances and the given facts in order to penetrate to the underlying structural reality of cognitive content and form, respectively. Each has stressed an active, constructing organism interacting in a dialectical way with the environment; and thus both incorporated certain aspects of German idealism into their cognitive theories. While the logic of Marx's theory of cognition is, in principle, able to explain the historical development of different categories and types of knowledge, Piaget's theory is confined to accounting for the development of Western scientific thinking within each individual. Thus, Piaget's characterization of his endeavor as "genetic epistemology" as a misnomer (but could be used to characterize Marx, if by "genetic" one meant "historical") insofar as he is really focused upon what may be termed "genetic philosophy of science." Piaget has slipped into that positivistic conceptual error of equating epistemology and philosophy of science. As pointed out by Habermas, epistemology contains the study of science (i.e., the philosophy of science) as one category of knowledge. When one falls into the position of equating epistemology with the philosophy of science, the result is a scientism which "means science's belief in itself: that is, the conviction that we can no longer understand science as *one* form of possible knowledge, but rather must identify knowledge with science" (1971, p. 4). In *this* respect, Piaget is very much a positivist, since he believes that there is only one absolute truth which is only knowable through the scientific method. Philosophy, or what might be called metaphysics or critical thought, is a "wisdom" which "man as a rational being finds essential for coordinating his different activities, but is not knowledge properly so called" (Piaget, 1971a; p. xiii). For Piaget, "wisdom" means "the taking up of a vital position" and implies "there can be several wisdoms, while there exists only one truth" (1971a, p.210).

Thus far, I have been preparing the way for a brief outline of Buck-Morss' interpretation of cross-cultural differences in Piagetian reasoning as associated with certain socio-economic variables. As implied by the above discussion, and as cogently argued by Buck-Morss, Piagetian type formal reasoning may be viewed as a specific historically conditioned form of cognition (i.e., cognitive content) which can be explained in terms of the theory of historical materialism or some modification thereof. Briefly stated, Buck-Morss draws upon Marx's theory of commodity structure in Western industrial capitalism (i.e., abstraction of: form from content, objects from the processes of their production and reproduction, phenomena from history so they appear as universals) in accounting for abstract formalism as a pervasive mode of thought (1967). Supported by Lukacs' (1971) claim that there is a structural correspondence between cognition and social reality and that, therefore, abstract formal thought "reflects"[2] the abstraction inherent in the commodity structure of industrial capitalism (i.e., the "exchange principle," "reification," "alienation," "fetishism"), Buck-Morss argues that it is cross-cultural differences in the presence and degree of development of Western industrial capitalism which accounts for cross-cultural differences in performance in Piagetian abstract formal reasoning. In addition to the objective variable of the presence and level of a capitalistic political economy, Buck-Morss introduces the subjective variable of the existence and level of consious participation in bringing about social change in order to account for within-cultural differences in abstract reasoning between, say, different socio-economic groups. The argument here is that lower socio-economic strata within, say, highly industrialized capitalist societies encounter a concrete reality over which they can exert little control and where there is little to reinforce the mental operations of manipulation, transformation, and abstract formal reasoning in general.

THE NON-REAL CONTRADICTION

There can be little doubt that Buck-Morss' attempt to give a
Marxian historical interpretation of Piagetian abstract formal thought
deserves serious attention. While the thesis is "radical" (in the everyday
sense of this term, as well as etymologically, that is, going to the root or
origin), it's spirit is not without historical precedence. Thus, in 1912,
Durkheim argued that Aristotelian categories of thought such as time,
space, class, number, cause, force, etc. (all epistemic categories with
which Piaget's theory of abstract reasoning has been concerned) were not
immanent in the Kantian sense, but, rather, were socially constructed
and historically derived and, therefore, not necessarily invariant across
cultures (1964). However, Durkheim went beyond Marx's attempt to
explain consciousness exclusively in terms of socio-economic relationships in that he included other kinds of social relations in his sociological
theory of knowledge. Durkheim's attempt to broaden the base of the
Marxian tradition is a trait he shared with recent neo-Marxist social
theorists—a point to which I will subsequently return in some detail.

In carefully examining the arguments advanced by Buck-Morss, one
can detect a non-real contradiction which is the source of some tension—
tension which cries out for resolution—hence, this chapter. Simply put,
"the problem" is that for Buck-Morss the high point of abstract formal
thought is directly tied to the underlying structure of Western industrial
capitalism, yet it is apparent that societies with communist political
economies share the *same* pervasive organizing principle of abstract
formal thought. In other words, if it is the commodity structure of
Western industrial capitalism which is the basis for abstract formal
thought as a "world view," how can one account for this same "world
view" in non-capitalistic industrial societies? Buck-Morss treks over
rough terrain on this issue and, in my judgement, unavoidably falters
along the way. It is clear that she has some awareness of the problem
insofar as she feels compelled to acknowledge a point which in the end
undermines her thesis, namely, that "The formal, abstract nature of
thought and social reality seems to be equally characteristic of industrialization in communist countries as the neo-Marxists who 'rediscovered'
Lukacs in the 1960s have argued" (Buck-Morss, 1975, p. 39). And
whereas, previous to the statement just quoted, there is a high frequency
of the term "capitalism" in association with abstract formal reasoning,
subsequent to this statement Buck-Morss tends to substitute the term

"industrialization," almost, one might think, in a mid-stream attempt to resolve the contradiction just hovering below consciousness. But this tack will not do, since her whole argument and explanatory interpretation rest upon the structure of commodities in Western industrial capitalism rather than the more general structure of industrialization.

THE RESOLUTION

Buck-Morss' interpretation of cultural differences in abstract formal reasoning as being rooted in differences in the development of Western industrial capitalism can be considered accurate and true only in a historical sense, that is, if it were first presented 30 or more years ago at a time before the industrial communist experience. It can also be considered to be problematic for the contemporary situation and hence "dated" to the extent that Western industrial capitalism reached its zenith during the 19th century. To the extent Buck-Morss is using the term "industrial capitalism" in its specific historical sense, changes and qualifications would be required in her thesis as we move through to finance capitalism (the first third of the 20th century) and, especially, on to present day welfare or state capitalism. Is the commodity structure of Western industrial capitalism the same as in welfare capitalism? Only if the answer to this question is in the affirmative, and only if it can be sufficiently justified, is it possible to even consider retrieving for today what would seem to be Buck-Morss' outmoded interpretation of the socio-economic bias in Piagetian abstract reasoning.

In light of the above historical considerations and the soon-to-be discussed recent theoretical advances made by certain neo-Marxists, the truth value of Buck-Morss' interpretation of cross-cultural differences in Piagetian abstract formal reasoning must today be judged to be more negative than positive. It is in the writings of Hegelian-Marxists (though of a more recent vintage than Lukacs' 1923 *History and Class Consciousness*) where one can find the theoretical basis for transcending the non-real contradiction inherent in Buck-Morss' thesis, and, thereby in the process, reaffirm her effort as a positive contribution in an ongoing dialectic. The neo-Marxist social theoreticians who I believe can provide the means for rescuing an historical interpretation of abstract formal reasoning from history and give it *contemporary* validity are those individuals who comprised the inner core of the Frankfurt Institute for Social Research (more commonly known as the "Frankfurt School") during the 1930s and early 1940s (i.e., Adorno, Horkheimer, and Marcuse) as well as certain more contemporary social theorists in the "critical" tradition (e.g., Habermas, Jacoby, Jay, Leiss, and Wellmer). It was during the 1940s that they key people of the Institute began to formulate a view which involved a shift from the Marxist notion of class antagonisms as the motor of history to an emphasis upon humanity's relationship to nature and, more specifically, the mastery of nature. Leiss (1972a, 1972b, 1975) has provided an excellent analysis of the "dominance of nature" theme of the Frankfurt school, while Jacoby (1970), Jay (1973), and Wellmer (1971) have provided useful but shorter interpretive summaries. In Jay's assessment of this "critical" point in the development of "critical" theory: "The focus was now on the larger conflict between man and nature both without and within, a conflict whose origins went back to before capitalism and whose continuation, indeed intensification, appear likely after capitalism would end. . . . The capitalist mode of exploitation was now seen in a larger context as the specific, historical form of domination of the bourgeois era of Western history" (1973, p. 256).

This theme of the struggle for the dominance of nature (and by implication, people dominating people insofar as people are part of nature) was taken up in the 1940s by Horkheimer (1974), Horkeimer and Adorno (1972), and later in the 1960s and 1970s by Marcuse (1964, 1972), and has important consequences for any argument that attempts to link abstract formal thought to the commodity structure of Western industrial capitalism.

In Horkheimer's view, "the social need of controlling nature has always conditioned the structure and forms of man's thinking and thus given primacy to subjective reason" (1974, p. 75). By subjective reason, Horkheimer meant abstract formal thought or instrumental reason, that is, formal logic and mathematical techniques which can operate on, and manipulate the objects of, thought, regardless of their specific content. Implicit in Horkheimer's view is the notion that the degree of abstract formal thought or instrumental reason present in any society is directly correlated with the level of sophistication a society has arrived at in mastering nature, that is, its scientific and technological know-how. Paradoxically, the more successful a society is in mastering nature, the greater the danger that abstract or instrumental reason will become dominant and serve as a "world view" at the expense of objective or critical reason. To the extent the latter is the case, what has the potential of creating the conditions for human liberation and emancipation, that is, subjective reason in the service of mastering nature, becomes an irrational force such that humanity becomes objectified, manipulated, controlled, and dominated by an instrumental rationality.

The main point to be emphasized in the present context, then, is the crucial shift in the Frankfurt School's interpretation of superstructure or consciousness as based upon not the Marxian substructure of economic relations and forces, but, rather, the more general deep structure of the dominance of nature.[3] The need to master or dominate nature has historically been the mainspring for the development of an instrumental rationality or abstract formal thought. Instrumental rationality in the service of mastering nature became crystallized as a pervasive mode of thought during the Enlightenment, and has reached its ultimate development in present day Western science and technology. In Habermas' words: "Technological development thus follows a logic that corresponds to the structure of purposive-rational action . . . [where] the components of the behavioral system of purposive-rational action, which is primarily rooted in the human organism . . . [are projected] one after another onto the place of technical instruments" (1970, p. 87).

In other words, for Habermas the development of abstract formal thought, instrumental reason, or subjective reason, involves the realization of the telos of an action system[4] intrinsic to the human predicament—the need to gain control over one's environment. The pinnacle of the rationalization of the mastery of nature (i.e., abstract formal reasoning) is considered to be the technological or instrumental rationality prevalent today in *both* capitalist and communist societies—a type of rationality which must be accompanied by critical reason in order to avoid becoming irrational.[5] Thus, Habermas (like Marcuse) has continued the tradition established by Adorno and Horkheimer in the 1940s, that is, criticizing the Enlightenment legacy—the dominance of instrumental or technological reason. Habermas, however, in contrast to Adorno, Horkheimer, and Marcuse, gives this theme a new twist by grounding the historical content of cognition (including form as a special case) upon the ahistorical human behavioral system, "purposive-rational action."

The relevance of the new emphasis in critical theory upon the mastery of nature and the criticism of the modern historically evolved cognitive product (i.e., instrumental or technological reason) should now be apparent vis-à-vis Buck Morss' interpretation of cross-cultural differences in Piagetian-type reasoning tasks. The structure of commodities in Western industrial capitalism can now be seen as a special case of, or a historical expression of, the structure of appropriating and objectivizing nature, that is, mastering nature. By linking the development of abstract formal thought to the development of the forces for the control and dominance of nature (i.e., science and technology), the previously noted problems and contradictions inherent in Buck-Morss' interpretation are transcended. Thus, the prevalence of abstract formal thought in advanced communist countries is no longer an embarrassment to a "mastery of nature" explanation as it was to a "structure of commodities in Western industrial capitalism" type of explanation. In addition, the problem of the historical casing of Buck-Morss' interpretation, that is, its lack of contemporary truth value (but having "historical" or "dated" truth), is resolved by the more general interpretation of cross-cultural differences in abstract formal thought as being associated with differences in the level of the mastery of nature. In the present view, then, post-industrial capitalistic societies may be coming to be less capitalistic, yet are more advanced in mastering nature and, therefore, more advanced in abstract formal reasoning.

Another advantage of the "mastery of nature" explanation is that it is able to incorporate Buck-Morss' two separate explanatory factors within a single theoretical framework. Thus, as previously mentioned, Buck-Morss outlines the socio-economic objective factor of industrial capitalism and the subjective factor of the degree of participation in social change in, respectively, accounting for between- and within-cultural differences in abstract formal thought.[6] However, just as the objective socio-economic factor of industrial capitalism can be seen as a special case of the more general "mastery of nature" explanation, the same holds for the subjective factor of degree of participation in bringing about social change. The latter involves changing one's physical and psychological environment, that is, the control, manipulation, dominance, or mastery of nature. Thus, group (e.g., class) differences in abstract formal thought can be linked to both an objective and subjective aspect of the degree of mastery of nature.

In conclusion, it should be noted that Buck-Morss has provided a scholarly analysis of socio-economic bias in Piaget's theory, although I believe that it is necessary to cast a broader nomological net in order to effect a more adequate explanation of the "facts."

Notes

1. It should be noted that, while Piaget on occasion uses the term 'historical' to characterize his theory of cognitive development, by this term he means to refer to the *individual's* history rather than to social (i.e., cross-generational) history.

2. Perhaps this is a poor choice of terms, since Lukacs (1971) actually argued against the "copy" theory of cognition as developed by "vulgar" Marxist-Leninists

and placed more weight on an active subject, thereby reaffirming the Hegelian dimension in Marx.

3. It should be noted that members of the Frankfurt School (especially Marcuse) did recognize the need for a social psychology in explaining the link between substructure and superstructure, and spent considerable effort on this problem. Also, by this time it was recognized that the "vulgar" Marxists' notion of substructure conditioning or determining superstructure in a simple direct manner was problematic insofar as in welfare or state capitalism the state (i.e., superstructure) intervened in the operation of the economic base (i.e., substructure).

4. Habermas, like Piaget, makes action the more fundamental component in the dialectic between thought and action, although, like others of the Frankfurt School, action is taken in its "high" sense.

5. The whole issue of the rational versus irrational use of technology or the control of nature, that is, whether abstract formal reason is or is not accompanied by critical reason, respectively, is tangential to the argument of this article and is, therefore, bracketed. It can be noted in passing, however, that in Horkheimer's (1974, p. 174) view the solution to the tension between abstract and critical reason was to "foster a mutual critique and thus, if possible, to prepare in the intellectual realm the reconciliation of the two in reality." See also Marcuse (1964) for an analysis of the dialectic between abstract and critical reason.

6. It should be noted in passing that the subjective factor will also be part of any explanation of between- or cross-cultural differences.

References

Bernstein, R. J. *Praxis and Action* (Philadelphia: University of Pennsylvania Press, 1971).

Buss, A. R. "The emerging field of the Sociology of Psychological Knowledge." *American Psychologist 30:* 988–1002 (1975).

Buck-Morss, S. "Socio-economic Bias in Piaget's Theory and Its Implications for Cross-cultural Studies." *Human Development 18:* 35–49 (1975).

Durkheim, E. *The Elementary Forms of Religious Life* (London: Allen & Unwin, 1964).

Habermas, J. *Toward a Rational Society* (Boston: Beacon Press, 1970).

Habermas, J. *Knowledge and Human Interests* (Boston: Beacon Press, 1971).

Horkheimer, M. *Eclipse of Reason* (New York: Seabury Press, 1974).

Horkheimer, M. & Adorno, T. W. *Dialectic of Enlightenment* (New York: Herder and Herder, 1972).

Jacoby, R. "Reversals and Lost Meanings." In Breines, *Critical Interpretations* (New York: Herder and Herder, 1970).

Jay, M. *The Dialectical Imagination. A History of the Frankfurt School and Institute of Social Research* (London: Heinemann Educational Books, 1973).

Kolakowski, L. *Toward a Marxist Humanism* (New York: Grove Press, 1968).

Leiss, W. *The Dominance of Nature* (New York: George Braziller, 1972a).

Leiss, W. "Technological Rationality: Marcuse and His Critics." *Philosophy of the Social Sciences* 2: 31–42 (1972b).

Leiss, W. "The Problem of Man and Nature in the Work of the Frankfurt School." *Philosophy of Social Science* 5: 163–172 (1975).

Lobkowicz, N. *Theory and Practice. History of a Concept from Aristotle to Marx* (Notre Dame: University of Notre Dame Press, 1967).

Lukacs, G. *History and Class Consciousness* (Cambridge: MIT Press, 1971).

Marcuse, H. *One-dimensional Man* (Boston: Beacon Press, 1964).

Marcuse H. *Counterrevolution and Revolt* (Boston: Beacon Press, 1972).

Marx, K. "Thesis on Feuerbach." In Engels, *Ludwig Feuerbach* (New York: International Publishers, 1941).

Marx, K. "Economic and Philosophical Manuscripts." In *Karl Marx: Early Writings,* Bottomore, ed. (New York: McGraw Hill, 1964).

Marx, K. *Capital: A Critique of Political Economy,* vol. 1 (New York: International Publishers, 1967).

Piaget, J. *Insights and Illusions of Philosophy* (New York: New American Library, 1971a).

Piaget, J. *Structuralism* (London: Routledge & Kegan Paul, 1971b).

Wellmer, A. *Critical Theory of Society* (New York: Herder & Herder, 1971).

Chapter 10

Conceptual Issues in Life-Span Developmental Methodology

Over the past decade or so several studies using bifactorial analysis of variance (ANOVA) designs for the description and/or explanation of developmental phenomena have been reported in the literature. As formulated by Schaie, Baltes, and others, these bifactorial ANOVA designs consist of taking any two of age, cohort, or time of measurement as the independent variables. The logic of these designs is carefully considered below in terms of their adequacy in answering descriptive and/or explanatory developmental questions. It is argued that the employment of ANOVA in the manner recommended by Schaie, Baltes, and others has led us down a blind alley with respect to addressing developmental phenomena.

SCHAIE'S GENERAL DEVELOPMENTAL MODEL

Researchers concerned with gathering life-span developmental data have been confronted with difficult problems both in gathering such data and in deciding the permissible kinds of analyses and attendant interpretations these data afford. As is well known by now, cross-sectional data, which are obtained at one point in time for various age groups, are not open to an unambiguous interpretation, since the various age groups differ in terms of both age and cohort (year of birth). Gathering longitudinal data, which typically involves repeated measures of a given cohort through time, is thought to be a better strategy insofar as age and cohort are not confounded, and one is describing age-related changes rather than age (confounded with cohort) differences. Although a simple longitudinal design may be descriptive of age-related changes, such a description refers only to the specific cohort sampled. To the extent that there may be cohort differences in age-related changes, one cannot generalize beyond the cohort sampled in a simple longitudinal design. Concerns such as these with respect to the two traditional data-gathering designs have led to an active attempt to elaborate more useful life-span methodological designs. Schaie's 1965 general developmental model was an important attempt to wrestle free from the limitations of the simple cross-sectional and longitudinal designs. His contribution has led to much debate on developmental methodology, and brief summary of this debate will pave the way for a reappraisal of the central issues and their implications for methodology in developmental data analysis.

Essentially Schaie's model consists of three separate bifactorial designs, the *cross-sequential* (cohort × time of measurement), the *time-sequential* (age × time of measurement), and the *cohort-sequential* (age × cohort). The three were formulated by Schaie on the basis that there are three conceptually distinct time indicants for indexing a particular developmental datum—a person's year of birth, his/her age, and that point in historical time at which the measure is taken. The reason that one cannot carry out a three-way ANOVA is that any two of age, cohort, or time of measurement completely determine the third variable (e.g., a measure of a 10-year-old born in 1960 *must* be taken in the year 1970). This logical property precludes varying simultaneously, and independently, the three variables age, cohort, and time of measurement in a single trifactorial design—a necessary requirement for the independence assumption of ANOVA. Taking any two of these three variables at a time satisfies the general requirement of the independence of the independence variables, but does not aovid the problem of the third variable being confounded with the dependent variable. As Schaie recognized, it is necessary to assume that the third variable in any one of his three bifactorials is in fact unrelated to the dependent variable in order to unambiguously interpret the results.

In addition to its descriptive aspect, Schaie proposed employing his general developmental model for explanatory purposes. Thus the three variables age, cohort, and time of measurement were given functional interpretations, where age was thought to reflect a maturational effect, time of measurement an environmental effect, and cohort an environmental and/or genetic effect. Schaie's original article stimulated some debate as the adequacy of his proposal regarding the simultaneous use of his three bifactorial ANOVA designs, as well as his functional interpretation of the variables age, time of measurement, and cohort. Thus Baltes

(1968) at this time correctly argued that, if one wished to tease apart effects due to maturational, environmental, and genetic factors, much more elaborate and different kinds of designs were required. Baltes argued for one particular bifactorial ANOVA design—the age × cohort— as opposed to the simultaneous application of all three of Schaie's bifactorial ANOVA designs to the same data. Cattell (1970) also proposed a design similar to Baltes' age × cohort, or Schaie's cohort-sequential design, as the preferred developmental design. In more recent writings (1970, 1973), Schaie has modified some of the equations in his original model in light of Baltes's criticisms, but has stood firm on the essential aspects—that is, the concerted application of his three bifactorial ANOVA designs is necessary for explaining the variance associated with maturation, environmental impact, and genetic factors.

    In a critical review of the developmental models of Baltes, Cattell, and Schaie, I presented additional arguments in support of Baltes's original criticisms of Schaie's general developmental model concerning the value of all three bifactorials, as well as the functional interpretation of age, time of measurement, and cohort (Buss, 1973b). These arguments will not be repeated here, but in essence they were felt that the age × cohort ANOVA design was to be preferred for addressing developmental questions, since each of the other bifactorials must assume that either age or cohort is not related to the dependent measure—assumptions not defensible in any developmental study. It was also argued that time of measurement did not confound the age × cohort ANOVA design. At the time, Baltes in a personal communication pointed out that his true position in regard to Schaie's model was not adequately represented in his 1968 article. Baltes stressed that he did not object to using any one of Schaie's three bifactorial ANOVA designs, but he did object to their *simultaneous* application to the same set of data because of the confounding of the three variables. However, Baltes did maintain that for substantive reasons he still preferred the age × cohort design.

    Further refinements and arguments as to the value of the age × cohort model were subsequently presented in which it was felt that a distinction between data-gathering strategies and data-analysis designs was useful (Buss, 1974b). Thus, in terms of data-gathering strategies, any of Schaie's three matrices will potentially yield the same data, although it would be most efficient to collect cross-sectional sequential data in the manner suggested by Baltes (1968) and as indicated in Figure 2. Having gathered data, say, on several cohorts over time, one may fit such data into any one of Schaie's three bifactorial designs by appropriate arrangement of the cells and carry out an ANOVA. In Figure 2 the data are organized into an age × cohort data matrix, where the cells are indexed by the third variable—time of measurement. The latter may easily be made an independent variable with these data by rearranging the cells and indexing them with either age or cohort. Also indicated in Figure 2 are two data analyses—the longitudinal sequential and time-lag sequential—which are really just segments of the more inclusive analysis of the age × cohort bifactorial design.

Further argument as to the superiority of the age × cohort model as a data analysis design followed my article (e.g., see a reply by Labouvie, 1975, and a counterreply by Buss, 1975b, as well as Schaie and Baltes, 1975). The most recent reply deserves consideration at this point. Schaie and Baltes attempted to clarify their respective positions, and the growing controversy, by issuing a joint statement emphasizing their agreements rather than disagreements. The impetus for this "position paper" stemmed partly from their previous writings, which, inadvertently they feel, led others to believe they had major disagreements (e.g., see Buss, 1973b, and Wohlwill's 1973 discussion of what he called the "Baltes-Schaie debate"). Their chapter stresses their most recent stand on the issue and therefore deserves careful consideration—especially since it is aimed toward correcting misinterpretations. In their article, Schaie and Baltes distinguish between the description and explanation of developmental change vis-à-vis Schaie's three bifactorial ANOVA designs. They argue that, with respect to developmental questions, the age × cohort design is to be preferred to the extent that one is interested in describing intra-individual change (i.e., aging) as well as interindividual differences (cohort differences) in intra-individual change. This recommendation would indeed seem to be a valid procedure and, in general, consistent with my previous writings. However, at this stage in my thinking, I am coming to question even the value of the age × cohort bifactorial model, as conceived by Schaie and Baltes, as a useful way to describe developmental change. In order to develop this point adequately, it is necessary to make an even finer distinction with respect to the description of developmental change within the context of an age × cohort data matrix.

THE DESCRIPTION OF DEVELOPMENTAL PHENOMENA

As viewed by Schaie and Baltes, the description of developmental change in an age × cohort data matrix is synonymous with carrying out an ANOVA and partitioning the variance into age, cohort, and interactional components. However, the description of developmental change within an age × cohort matrix does not necessarily entail carrying out an

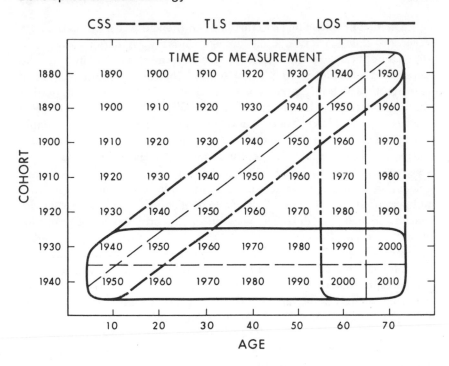

Figure 2. A modification of Baltes' Age × Cohort bifactorial developmental model where each cell is indexed by time of measurement. The cross-sectional sequential (CSS) is best thought of as a data gathering strategy while the longitudinal sequential (LOS) and time-lag sequential (TLS) may be best considered as data analysis designs. The actual dates are illustrative only and are not meant to reflect recommended ranges of time intervals.

ANOVA—or any other kind of data analysis. Consider first the description of developmental change as afforded by an age × cohort ANOVA. The assumption here is that the third variable, time of measurement, is in fact not related to the dependent variable, since time of measurement is not uniform across rows or columns. To the extent that time of measurement is related to the dependent variable, the variance components associated with age, cohort, and interaction will be contaminated and therefore erroneous. The importance of this error should be stressed, since the variance components associated with age, cohort, and their interaction will not be good approximations or estimates of their "true" value if time of measurement is related to the dependent variable; they will simply be wrong.

On further reflection as to the value of the age × cohort matrix *with respect to doing ANOVA*, I am forced to modify my earier view, since the assumption required (time of measurement not related to the dependent variable) is simply not tenable in the substantive areas of research to which this model has been applied. This is not to deny that the age × cohort data matrix is potentially valuable for descriptive purposes (see below). Time of measurement, of course, is a variable associated with numerous factors such as changes in educational quality, nutrition, better health care, cultural mores, social values, life styles, sociohistorical and political events, etc. Such factors undoubtedly are related in complex ways to changes and differences in abilities and temperament—the two main psychological domains studied using the Schaie and Baltes models. The way out of this problem is not to opt for an age × time of measurement ANOVA design, since the confounded variable is now cohort—and cohort is also related to some of the *same* variables mentioned above, which are related to time of measurement. Support for the latter point comes from Goulet, Hay, and Barclay (1974), who convincingly argue, among other things, that time-of-measurement-related variables and cohort-related variables are clearly not independent. In light of the nonindependence of time-of-measurement and cohort-related variables, the cohort × time of measurement ANOVA design presents *insurmountable* difficulties of interpretation. In addition, the cohort × time of measurement ANOVA design would need to assume no relationship between the dependent variable and age—hardly a wise tactical move to get at descriptive developmental phenomena. Is there any way out of this morass of indefensible ANOVA designs? Before offering what I think are some useful models that provide at least a partial solution to this perplexing dilemma, let me consider further the real futility of getting at the description of developmental change by using ANOVA designs, followed by a consideration of the Schaie-Baltes position regarding such designs in the explanation of developmental change.

Schaie and Baltes reaffirm previous recommendations that developmental psychology should focus on intra-individual change and interindividual differences in intraindividual change (e.g., Baltes & Nesselroade, 1973; Buss, 1973a, 1974a; Wohlwill, 1970, 1973). Actually, as pointed out elsewhere (Buss, 1974a), no less than eleven kinds of data-gathering strategies and designs may be of interest to developmental psychologists, where such strategies are generated by considering some of the various permutations of intra-individual change, interindividual differences, and intra-individual differences taken singly, two at a time, and all three together. If we accept for the moment, however, that the study of intra-individual change and interindividual differences in intra-individual change is an important paradigm for exploration of development, we should note that thus far few researchers (Meyers, 1974, is one) have taken up such a study empirically—contrary to what Schaie and Baltes imply. Are the models proposed by Schaie and Baltes equipped to deal with this issue?

The age × cohort data matrix is *potentially* a workhorse for the description of interindividual differences in intra-individual change *if* one approaches the problem from a single-organism strategy (e.g., see Hoyer's 1974 discussion, as well as Wohlwill, 1970, 1973). However, if one adopts the strategy of operating upon this matrix in the fashion in which Schaie and Baltes have in all their reported empirical research, such description is elusive. ANOVA, which groups the data according to age and cohort, forfeits any possibility of the description of interindividual differences in intra-individual change simply because the individual is lost. The logic of such a design can provide no basis whatsoever for making inferences about intra-individual change, and therefore interindividual differences in intra-individual change. An ANOVA, of any of Schaie's three bifactorials falls into that group which have been called "mixed designs" (Lindquist, 1953) or "split-plot designs" (Kirk, 1968). Such designs allow for repeated measures of individuals across treatments (or matched subjects across treatments), but the inferences permitted are with respect to *groups* of individuals. Thus applying ANOVA to an age × cohort data matrix permits only measurement of intra*group* change and inter*group* differences in intra *group* change. The latter holds, however, only if we assume that it is meaningful to carry out an ANOVA on an age × cohort data matrix—an assumption that is not tenable, as I have argued above and will further elaborate below.

Of course, Schaie and Baltes would admit to the possibility of analyzing an age × cohort data matrix in ways other than a split-plot ANOVA, and they never explicitly state that an ANOVA of an age × cohort data matrix does provide a useful description of interindividual differences in intra-individual change, although the context of their discussion strongly suggests the link. Elsewhere, however, Nesselroade and Baltes state that, with respect to their reported ANOVA on a time of measurement × cohort matrix dealing with personality measures, "The evidence obtained will be used to estimate developmental gradients allowing for both *individual* (ontogenetic) and historical (generational) change components and their interaction" (1974, p. 10, emphasis added). Clearly this is a promise they cannot deliver on the basis of their analyses. Even assuming that the authors meant to say "age" rather than "individual" (as one might hypothesize, since the word "ontogenetic" follows "individual"), this is also a contradiction insofar as what they say they are going to do, and what in fact they logically can do, are entirely different. A time of measurement × cohort ANOVA logically entails the assumption of no age (ontogenetic) effects with respect to the dependent variable (see below). Even if we grant Schaie and Baltes the benefit of the doubt, however, their emphasis on the importance of the description of interindividual differences in intra-individual change remains unrealized in the descriptive analyses which they have so far reported.

More important, perhaps, is the Schaie-Baltes position with regard to the choice of which of the three bifactorials to use for descriptive purposes. Thus, they state: "Baltes, however, agrees with Schaie (1973) that application of age-time and time-cohort matrices may be useful also for descriptive purposes. On the one hand, these matrices are approximations to a direct assessment of developmental change via age-cohort matrices, the preferred mode" (Schaie and Baltes, 1975, p. 5). Since all three bifactorials may operate on the exact same data, why is it necessary to give up the "age-cohort matrices, the preferred mode"? Why use an "approximation" if one may just as easily use the ideal design? Unfortunately, Schaie and Baltes provide no rationale for this position, probably because there is none to offer. They do state, however, that age × time of measurement and time of measurement × cohort designs are useful for considering sociocultural change rather than individual development. This is potentially defensible (see below), but to the extent that one operates upon such data matrices using ANOVA, as Baltes and Schaie have, it is necessary to make the untenable assumption that the third variable is unrelated to the dependent variable. This last point is not a minor one. Consider, for example, the recent monograph by Nesselroade and Baltes (1974) entitled "Adolescent personality Development and Historical Change: 1970–1972," which is an extension of data reported earlier (Baltes and Nesselroade, 1972). In this study the authors opt for a time of measurement × cohort ANOVA design. Such a design *must* assume that age is unrelated to the dependent variable—and there is simply no way this assumption can be avoided. Hence, such research cannot make inferences in regard to age-related change; and to call it a study of adolescent personality "development" is a misnomer and misleading. These same criticisms apply to "Ontogenetic and Generational Components of Structural and Quantitative Change in Adult Behavior" by Nesselroade, Schaie, and Baltes (1972), in which a time of measurement × cohort bifactorial ANOVA was carried out. They also apply to "Generational versus Ontogenetic Components of Change in Adult Cognitive Behavior: A Fourteen-Year Cross-Sequential Study," by

Schaie and Labouvie-Vief (1974), again using a time of measurement ×
cohort bifactorial ANOVA design, as well as to the early study by Schaie
and Strother (1968a) employing the same bifactorial ANOVA design, yet
again talking about "developmental" phenomena.

Nesselroade and Baltes acknowledge that age is indeed confounded in
their design, yet throughout their report they talk about effects
associated with age changes and cohort differences—effects presumably
based upon their data analyses. However, they simply cannot talk about
effects (age) that their model must assume to be zero. Why did they opt
for such a design in light of the developmental questions they sought to
address? They state that:

The underlying belief is that sequential strategies are basically descriptive in
nature unless they are tied to additional (superimposed) experimental conditions.
The choice of data analysis, therefore, is primarily guided by principles of
parsimony. Which form of analysis is to be used, we maintain, is dictated by
constraints inherent in the data matrix. In some cases the choice may be one that
involves an age by cohort . . . in others an age by time arrangement . . . in still
others, a cohort by time setup. (1974, p. 7)

Unfortunately, no adequate rationale is proposed in this statement,
or elsewhere in the text, to justify looking at developmental questions by
assuming a priori that there are no age-related effects. What are the
"principles of parsimony" and the "constraints inherent in the data
matrix"?

THE CONCERTED APPLICATION OF BIFACTORIAL ANOVA DESIGNS

Thus far I have been arguing that applying ANOVA to any of
Schaie's three data matrices leads to faulty descriptive inferences, given
that in each instance the third variable is always confounded in the
design. Whenever one of the three bifactorials is analyzed, there has
been, and can be, no justification for assuming the third variable is
unrelated to the dependent variable. Although it would seem that a
single ANOVA employing any one of Schaie's data analysis designs is
inadvisable, error compounded upon error is the result of applying two
or more of these data analyses to the same data. Baltes (personal
communication, 1973) disagreed with Schaie's strategy of the simultaneous application of more than one bifactorial ANOVA to the same
data, but more recently he seems to be not as opposed to such a
procedure. Apparently the justification for this strategy is to get at an
explanation of observed effects. Thus, Schaie and Baltes state:

Schaie's position is—and Baltes does not disagree with the general rationale but is only dissatisfied with the obtained level of usefulness—that concerted application of his three sequential models of data analysis shed light on the substantive meaning (genetic, environmental, etc.) of the age, cohort, and time effects involved. (1975, p. 7)

Bracketing the explanatory issue for the moment, let us examine the underlying logic of applying two or more bifactorial ANOVA designs to the same data. Using an age × cohort bifactorial, Baltes and Reinert (1969) reported significant effects associated with age, cohort, and interaction, where the dependent variables were ability measures. Such an ANOVA design confounds time of measurement with the dependent variables, especially since no justification is (nor could it be) given for assuming that such confounding does not exist. These same data were then analyzed by Baltes, Baltes, and Reinert (1970) using an age × time of measurement ANOVA. Significant age, time of measurement, and interaction effects were reported. In this instance the authors must assume (but make no justification) that the cohort variable is unrelated to the dependent variable! But it was previously found that, for the same data, there were significant effects associated with cohort! In the first analysis it must be assumed that there are no time of measurement effects, yet the second analysis found such significant effects! Which analysis is to be accepted? In fact, of course, neither analysis is acceptable alone, and together the difficulties of carrying out ANOVA on such data cannot but make one despair. Applying a single ANOVA to data collected by, say, cross-sectional sequences is a grave sin, but applying more than one of Schaie's ANOVA designs to the same data is a graver sin. Error compounded upon error can only lead to greater descriptive confusion. Explanatory goals cannot proceed on the basis of noninterpretable descriptive analyses.

Schaie has been the major proponent of doing simultaneous bifactorial ANOVA on the same data, and in several publications (e.g., Schaie, Labouvie, and Buech, 1973; Schaie and Strother, 1968b) he has opted for applying both the cohort × time of measurement and age × time of measurement bifactorial ANOVA to the same data (what happened to the "preferred" design—the age × cohort?). *Mutatis mutandis*, the same criticisms outlined above concerning Baltes' application of two bifactorial ANOVA designs to the same data apply here. It is interesting to see the justification of this strategy given by Schaie. Thus, Schaie, Labouvie, and Buech state:

Under the assumption that cohort (birth year)-related differences represent a major variance contribution, the data may be organized into a *cross-sequential*

Cohort × Time of Measurement × Sex design. Alternately, assuming that genuine age-related differences are of significance, the data may be grouped according to age levels yielding a *time-sequential* Age × Time of Measurement × Sex design. (1974, p. 153)

What is interesting in these comments is that a particular bifactorial ANOVA is selected on the basis of assuming that there will be significant effects associated with *one* of the two independent variables in the design, rather than starting with the only logical assumption—that the third confounded variable in a particular bifactorial design is in fact *not* related to the dependent variable. The choice of a single bifactorial design must rest on an assumption that one of the three variables of age, cohort, and time of measurement is in fact *not* related to the dependent variable, rather than on which one *is* related (and dragging along a second independent variable). Selecting two bifactorial ANOVA designs, as Schaie and others have done, and then applying them to the same data, is to defy, in a gross manner, any semblance of consistency in research strategy. More important, such a choice violates several rules of logic in data analysis. All the problems of applying several bifactorial ANOVA designs to the same data have been criticized at the descriptive level. Surely a prudent researcher would not risk making explanatory inferences on the basis of such contaminated descriptive data. Of course, I am arguing here that the data are contaminated only to the extent that one applies ANOVA to get at the description of developmental phenomena. I am not arguing that the data are intrinsically contaminated; they are contaminated only insofar as they are analyzed using statistical models whose assumptions cannot be met, thus resulting in serious confounding.

THE EXPLANATION OF DEVELOPMENTAL PHENOMENA

In regard to the extra descriptive value of Schaie's three bifactorial ANOVA designs, Schaie's and Baltes's position is clear: Concerted application of all three bifactorial designs is thought to lead to the possibility of teasing apart genetic and environmental effects. Bracketing the previous argument that it would *never* make any sense to apply several of Schaie's bifactorial ANOVA designs to the same data, for descriptive or explanatory reasons, we should note that if we wish to tease out the genetic and environmental variance components of a dependent variable, there is no way to do this with any of Schaie's bifactorial ANOVA designs, applied either singly or in concert. Previous arguments on this point presented elsewhere (Buss, 1973b) will not be repeated. A couple of additional comments, however, would seem to be in order.

Unraveling the genetic, environmental, and interaction variance components that produce individual differences is currently an active area of research. Most important for my purposes here is to note that statistical models which attempt to estimate, say, the *heritability* of a trait (the proportion of individual differences variance associated with genetic factors) rest upon very complex designs (e.g., Cattell, Jinks and Fulker, 1970). Of fundamental concern is the partitioning of individual differences variance at one point in time. Although one may chart out changes in genetic, environmental, and interaction individual differences components over time (e.g., see Buss, 1973b; Cattell, 1970), it makes no conceptual sense to partition intra-individual change data into genetic, environmental, and interactional components. Stated another way, if one had longitudinal data on several different groups for, say, an ability measure, there is, to my knowledge, no meaningful way to talk about getting estimates of the genetic and environmental variance components for *change* data.

Separating genetic and environmental variance components makes sense only when we are talking about individual differences, not intra-individual changes (group or individual data). Schaie's and Baltes's belief in the value of applying concerted bifactorial ANOVA designs to cross-sectional sequential gathered data is seriously misguided, and rests upon an inadequate appreciation of the tricky concepts of genetic and environmental factors as these are related to sources of individual differences. Genetic and environmental factors simply cannot be quantified into variance components that account for intra-individual change. This is not to say, of course, that genetic and environmental factors are not operating during ontogeny. Rather, they cannot be separated into variance components in terms of causing intra-individual change. Thus Schaie's and Baltes's proposal that "the concerted application of these models leads to explanatory inferences about genetic and environmental agents of change" (1975, pp. 6–7) is simply not true.

In regard to my previous criticisms of the value of Schaie's three bifactorial ANOVA designs for explanatory purposes (Buss, 1973b), Schaie and Baltes note that:

The decision on whether to use the explanatory part of Schaie's General Developmental Model and his three sequential modes of data analysis and interpretation is more a matter of theory-model match and acceptability of assumptions than one of *internal logic* as was suggested by Buss (1973). In short,

there are many useful ways to explicate developmental change and the one
proposed by Schaie (1965) is one of them. (1975, p. 9, emphasis added)

As I have taken pains to show, matters of internal logic pertaining to
the assumptions of ANOVA for both the single and concerted application
of Schaie's three bifactorial designs for either descriptive or explanatory
goals *is* the issue. The several inadequacies of the Schaie-Baltes approach
to the description and/or explanation of developmental change cannot be
skirted by statements such as the following:

It is not only reasonable but, in line with a pluralistic approach to theory
building, desirable to expect that some researchers will judge the models and
their assumptions to be acceptable, while others will reject them for an
insufficient match with their explanatory hypotheses. (1975, pp. 8–9)

But the selection of a particular model for the description and/or
explanation of a phenomenon is not automatically acceptable, given the
desirability of a pluralistic approach to theory building. Each model must
be taken seriously, and therefore evaluated seriously, *within* the context
of the principles, assumptions, and logic of *its* particular metamodel or
family paradigm. Thus, the arguments I have advanced concerning the
serious shortcomings of the Schaie-Baltes approach have been constructed within the framework of their paradigm model. In other words,
the disagreements cannot be dismissed as stemming from different and
logically irreducible model differences (e.g., Kuhn, 1970; Overton and
Reese, 1973, Reese and Overton, 1970). I would certainly agree with
Schaie and Baltes that paradigmatic model differences are based upon
different underlying metaphysical assumptions, and thus such conflicts
are not resolvable—either by logical refutation or empirically.
    It is therefore somewhat surprising to find Baltes and Nesselroade
(1972) and Nesselroade and Baltes (1974) arguing, on the basis of their
data, against an organismic stage model of personality development,
even though they are aware that their bipolar trait approach has loaded
the dice, to say the least, against finding evidence for sequential stages.
Similarly, their argument against a mechanistic cumulative linear model
of personality development on the basis of their data is equally not
warranted—especially since their model is compatible with such a view!
One needn't have a nice linear function to hold a mechanistic view.
Personality traits are bipolar rather than unipolar, and there is no reason
to expect the kind of developmental (negatively accelerating) curves
(appearing linear over short timespans) found in the abilities domain.

THE INEFFICIENCY OF ANOVA FOR DEVELOPMENTAL DATA

Thus far I have criticized the Schaie-Baltes position as to the value of applying bifactorial ANOVA designs for purposes of the description and/or explanation of developmental phenomena on the grounds of internal inconsistencies and contradictions. Although aware of these internal problems, they have attempted to avoid them by alluding to unacceptable assumptions; by falling back on the idea that model selection is always accompanied by adversaries who will disagree with it; or, even worse, by not dealing directly with the contradictory implications their assumptions entail. One may argue against their strategy on still other grounds, and I will now attempt to point out yet additional problems of doing ANOVA on cross-sectional sequentially gathered data from more general considerations.

As mentioned previously, Schaie's three bifactorial ANOVA designs fall into that group known as "mixed designs" (Linquist, 1953) or "split-plot designs" (Kirk, 1968). Such designs do not have equal efficiency in estimating the main and interactional effects. The nonrepeatable block treatments (cohort in the age × cohort and time of measurement × cohort designs, and age in an age × time of measurement design) tend to be not as accurately estimated as the repeatable treatments and the interaction between the two independent variables (Kirk, 1968, pp. 282–283). The logic of the model necessitates increasing the accuracy of the estimates of the effects of the latter two components at the expense of accuracy in the former. Thus, such a design should be used only when the experimenter is not as interested in the nonrepeatable block treatment effects as he is in the repeatable treatment and the interaction effects. Is this consistent with the objectives of the research strategies of Schaie and Baltes? I think not, to the extent that they have not taken this property of the split-plot design into consideration in selecting a particular bifactorial design. Of course, the simultaneous application of two or more bifactorial ANOVA designs would introduce a more complex decision-making (rational?) rationale. The above-mentioned property of the split-plot design is probably superseded to the extent that, as argued previously, it makes no sense to apply ANOVA techniques to such data given the contradictory restrictive assumptions one must make.

Further, ANOVA is a very inefficient statistical model when the independent variables are of a continuous nature. Grouping subjects together by arbitrarily demarcating a continuous variable (as is done for age and cohort) results in a serious loss of useful information. As noted by Kerlinger and Pedhazur in discussing the merits of ANOVA versus multiple-regression techniques when organismic variables are the independent variables:

When one dichotomizes a variable that can take on a range of values, one loses considerable variance. This can mean lowered correlations with other variables and even nonsignificant results when addicted to an elegant and powerful method like analysis of variance (or factor analysis or multiple regression analysis) and force the analysis of research data on the procrustean bed of the method. (1973, p. 8)

It would seem that for Schaie, Baltes, and their collaborators, ANOVA has been largely accepted a priori as *the* model for descriptive developmental research.

CAN ANCOVA PROVIDE DESCRIPTIONS OF DEVELOPMENTAL PHENOMENA?

Before outlining the kind of regression analysis that might yield relatively adequate description of developmental phenomena, we should consider a type of ANOVA design that makes use of both analysis of variance and regression analysis and would seem to be able to handle the problem of the confounded third variable in any one of Schaie's bifactorials. Thus, since we cannot in fact assume that the third variable in any of Schaie's designs has zero effects associated with the dependent variable, is there a way to control such confounding using ANOVA? Analysis of covariance (ANCOVA) is a design specifically equipped to control, through statistical procedures, the effects of a concomitant variable or "covariate" on the dependent variable, where the effects of the covariate cannot be experimentally controlled through randomization. Such being the case, it would seem to be a design ideally suited for analyzing the data, say, in an age $\times$ cohort matrix.

In ANCOVA, the effects of the covariate associated with the dependent variable are assessed using regression analyses and are then removed from the total sum of squares. Thus, in considering the case of a regression (linear or otherwise) of the dependent variable on the covariate time of measurement, one would be interested in the variance *no* predictable by time of measurement—that is, the sum of the squared deviations of the dependent measures and their predicted scores, where the latter are predicted by regressing them on the covariate time of measurement. In this way, one may arrive at an adjusted total sum of squares, where the effects associated with the covariate time of measurement have been removed. On closer inspection, however, the initial enthusiasm for applying ANCOVA to, say, an age × cohort data matrix soon dissipates. Consider, for example, the simple situation in which there are repeated measures on one cohort over time. A one-way ANCOVA would attempt to subtract the variance associated with the covariate time of measurement from the total variance, leaving the residual variance associated with age. This would effectively result in there being *no* variance left associated with age, given the dependencies between age, cohort, and time of measurement. Similarly, it would be absurd to apply ANCOVA to the complete age × cohort data matrix, since statistically controlling the covariate time of measurement would effectively eliminate the variance associated with either age or cohort, depending upon whether one regressed time of measurement on the dependent variable across cohort or age, respectively.

Paradoxically, then, ANCOVA as applied to, say, an age × cohort data matrix would eliminate the effects associated with one of the independent variables considered of prime interest. Because of the dependency among age, cohort, and time of measurement, ANCOVA cannot effectively control the third confounded variable. The problem here is related to the violation of a necessary assumption of ANCOVA— namely, that the covariate be unaffected by the independent variable. To the extent that the independent variable (e.g., age and/or cohort) affects both the values on the covariate (e.g., time of measurement) and the dependent variable, removing variance associated with the covariate involves eliminating variance associated with the independent variable. What is unique is the *total* removal of variance associated with one of the independent variables, given the dependent relationship among age, cohort, and time of measurement.

It was previously argued that ANOVA cannot be used on any of Schaie's bifactorial designs either singly or in concert since it is not reasonable to assume that the third confounded variable has zero effects. There is one kind of ANOVA specifically geared toward statistically controlling for a confounded or concomitant variable (ANCOVA), but this design is completely inappropriate, given the intrinsic relationship of age, cohort, and time of measurement. ANOVA for the description of cross-sectional sequentially gathered data must be abandoned.

REGRESSION ANALYSIS FOR THE DESCRIPTION OF DEVELOPMENTAL PHENOMENA

Let us now consider the descriptive question in regard to employing regression techniques in developmental data analysis. How might one analyze an age × cohort data matrix avoiding the problems associated with ANOVA? ANOVA in a split-plot design necessitates making inferences about differences in means, where the mean differences are associated with the independent variables and their interaction. Since time of measurement is confounded in such an analysis and cannot reasonably be assumed to have zero effects in any developmental study, the description of mean differences as "due" to age, cohort, and/or their interaction becomes untenable. If one did a regression analysis on these same data, the problem could be avoided.

What are the inferences afforded by regression analysis? In such an analysis, one attempts to describe and predict the dependent variable on the basis of some function of the independent variables. One may calculate the various sums of squares in a split-plot design for testing linear or quadratic trends in the data (see Kirk, 1968, pp. 270–275). One might try to fit the developmental curves of various cohorts to some theoretically expected curve, or to test for differences in trends for various cohorts (see Lewis, 1960, Chapter 10, for a discussion of the various techniques of curve fitting and detecting trend differences). In all such regression techniques, the *inferences* are not the same as in a typical ANOVA. In regression analyses of the type under discussion, one is interested in *describing* consistencies in the data on the basis of a prediction rule. No inferences are required concerning mean differences being produced by age- and/or cohort-related variables, where it must be assumed that time of measurement effects are zero. In general, it is quite conceivable to have a situation in which an ANOVA performed on independent continuous variables arbitrarily demarcated into various "treatment" levels yields nonsignificant effects, whereas a regression analysis on the same data would detect significant consistencies (linear, quadradic, etc.). In the type of regression analyses being proposed, it is *not* necessary to assume that time of measurement is in fact unrelated to the dependent variable. For those researchers interested in describing developmental change based upon the data in an age × cohort matrix, I strongly recommend giving up traditional bifactorial ANOVA designs, and opting for regression analyses.

What about choice of data matrix when carrying out descriptive regression analyses on cross-sectional sequentially gathered data? For those interested in developmental questions, the age × cohort data matrix is indeed the one to be preferred. Both age and cohort are organismic variables and, as such, are intrinsically of greater interest than time of measurement. The central developmental descriptive question is as follows: What are the life-span developmental or age-related changes for a particular cohort? Further, are there cohort differences in such developmental functions? The age × cohort data matrix subjected to regression and trend analyses nicely answers such a descriptive developmental question. This is not to say that representing some kinds of data in a cohort × time of measurement or an age × time of measurement data matrix would not be useful for other purposes. Thus, Riley, Johnson, and Foner (1972) present several examples of all three Schaie data matrices, where the focus of attention is on data from demographic and epidemiological studies. For example, one might be interested in charting changes in the age structure of a population through time. That is, what are the proportions of various age groups at various points in time? Only the age × time of measurement matrix would be appropriate for addressing this question.

In demographic and epidemiological studies, the unit of analysis is typically a frequency count of individuals possessing a certain categorical property. In other words, the data are nominal in nature, and the description of such data is of necessity limited to histograms, frequency distributions, frequency polygons, and the like. There is no problem of the confounding third variable, since ANOVA cannot be carried out on such data. Different data matrices, of course, will produce different ways of representing the same intrinsic information, and the choice of how to best represent the data (in terms of which two variables) must be guided by the question one is asking. Considerations such as these sound very similar to the kinds of things Schaie and Baltes mention in regard to selecting a bifactorial ANOVA design, but the two situations, of course, are quite different. Whereas these extra design matters do make sense when applied to the description of nominal or categorical data, they do not make sense in the context of carrying out ANOVA on data consisting of interval data for reasons previously outlined.

EXPLANATION AND THE INDIVIDUAL–SOCIETY DIALECTIC

What about the relationship between the methodological designs proposed by Schaie and Baltes and "methodological dialectics?" Attempts to reconcile the view that the organism is a passive receptacle of environmental influences versus the notion that, in contrast, the organism is active and structures and influences the environment has been formulated by the notion of a dialectical relationship between the individual and society. A changing individual in a changing society is viewed as dialectical insofar as each influences and is influenced by the other. Although several people in the social sciences have alluded to such a dialectical relationship (e.g., Berger and Luckman, 1966; Buss in Press a, b; Looft, 1973; Nesselroade and Baltes, 1973; Riegel, 1972, 1975, in press), such an idea, in its modern form, may actually be traced back to Karl Marx. Can the bifactorial ANOVA designs proposed by Schaie and Baltes provide empirical investigation of such a dialectical relationship? Nesselroade and Baltes believe they can, as is clear from the following quote:

Models of development which have emphasized either an active organism in a passive environment or a passive organism in an active environment are being challenged by those of a dialectic orientation which view development and change of the organism and environment as concurrent, mutually influencing phenomena which, in their interaction, are properly studied together. These largely theoretical papers lack substantial empirical support for their views, however, and the writers believe that the evidence provided here on the interactive relationships between individual and historical change components contributes to conceptual and methodological advancement on this point. (1974, p. 57)

The desire to use quantitative methodological designs for uncovering mutually determining or reciprocally causative change agents—that is, the dialectical relationship between the individual and society—is to be applauded. Shcaie's and Baltes's bifactorial ANOVA designs, however, are not logically equipped to address this issue. As pointed out by Overton and Reese (1973), the independent variables in an ANOVA design may interact to produce effects. What this means is that two causal variables (in this instance, age, cohort, and time of measurement are not manipulated so they are causal only in the sense of accounting for variance) interact to produce a difference in the organism. This notion of interaction is conceptually quite different from the kind of interaction in the individual-society dialectic; in the latter, each serves as both cause and effect, rather than both being causal "agents" interacting to produce an effect. Riegel (1972) has also stated that the kinds of bifactorial ANOVA designs proposed by Schaie and Baltes do provide empirical support for the individual-society dialectic, although he has recently acknowledged (personal communication) that in light of a previous discussion of this point (Buss, 1974b), he is no longer willing to equate the two conceptually different kinds of interaction.

CONCLUSION

In conclusion, I would like to emphasize that I believe ANOVA has led us down a blind alley in the search for interpretable description and/ or meaningful explanation of developmental phenomena. ANOVA, like any statistical model, should be only one of many available aids in the researcher's methodological kit. To become fixated on a particular methodological model in light of obvious shortcomings in a given context is to commit that well-known sin of methodological idolatry, or "methodolatry."

References

Baltes, P. B. "Longitudinal and cross-sectional Sequences in the Study of Age and Generation Effects." *Human Development 11;* 145–171 (1968).

Baltes, P. B., Baltes, M. M. & Reinert, G. "The Relationship between Time of Measurement and Age in Cognitive Development in Children: An Application of Cross-sectional Sequences." *Human Development 13:* 258–268 (1970).

Baltes, P. B. & Nesselroade, J. R. "Cultural Change and Adolescent Personality Development: An Application of Longitudinal Sequences." *Developmental Psychology 7:* 244–256 (1972).

Baltes, P. B. & Nesselroade, J. R. "The Developmental Analysis of Individual Differences on Multiple Measures." In *Life-Span Developmental Psychology: Methodological Issues,* J. R. Nesselroade & H. W. Reese, eds., (New York: Academic Press, 1973).

Baltes, P. B. & Reinert, G. "Cohort Effects in Cognitive Development of Children as Revealed by Cross-sectional Sequences." *Developmental Psychology 1:* 169–177 (1969).

Berger, P. L. & Luckman, T. *The Social Construction of Reality: A Treatise in the Sociology of Knowledge* (New York: Irvington Publishers, 1966).

Buss, A. R. "An Extension of Developmental Models That Separate Ontogenetic Changes and Cohort Differences." *Psychological Bulletin 80:* 466–479 (1973a).

Buss, A. R. "A Conceptual Framework for Learning Effecting the Development of Ability Factors." *Human Development 16:* 273–292 (1973b).

Buss, A. R. "Generational Analysis: Description, Explanation, and Theory." *Journal of Social Issues 30(2):* 55–71 (1974).

Buss, A. R. "A General Developmental Model for Interindividual Differences, and Intraindividual Changes." *Developmental Psychology 10:* 70–78 (1974b).

Buss, A. R. "The Emerging Field of the Sociology of Psychological Knowledge." *American Psychologist 30:* 988-1002 (1975a).

Buss, A. R. "More on the Age × Cohort Developmental Model: A Reply to Labouvie." *Psychological Bulletin 82:* 170–173 (1975b).

Buss, A. R. "Psychology's Future Development as Predicted from Generation Theory." *Human Development 17:* 449–455 (1975c).

Cattell, R. B. "The Multiple Abstract Variance Analysis Equations and Solutions for Nature-nurture Research on Continuous Variables." *Psychological Review 67:* 353–372 (1960).

Cattell, R. B. "Separating Endogenous, Exogenous, Ecogenic, and Epogenic Component Curves in Developmental Data." *Developmental Psychology 3:* 151–162 (1970).

Hoyer, W. J. "Aging as Intraindividual Change. *Developmental Psychology 10:* 821–826 (1974).

Jinks, J. L. & Fulker, D. W. "Comparison of the Biometrical Genetical, MAVA, and Classical Approaches to the Analysis of Human Behavior." *Psychological Bulletin 73:* 311–349 (1970).

Kerlinger, F. N. & Pedhazur, E. J. *Multiple Regression in Behavioral Research* (New York: Holt, Rinehart and Winston, 1973).

Kirk, R. E. *Experimental Design: Procedures for the Behavioral Sciences.* (Belmont, Calif.: Brooks/Cole, 1968).

Kuhn, T. S. *The Structure of Scientific Revolutions* (Chicago: University of Chicago Press, 1970).

Labouvie, E. W. "An Extension of Developmental Models: A Reply to Buss." *Psychological Bulletin 82:* 165–169 (1975).

Linquist, E. F. *Design and Analysis of Experiments* (Boston: Houghton Mifflin, 1953).

Looft, W. R. "Socialization and Personality throughout the Life Span: An Examination of Contemporary Psychological Approaches. In *Life-span Developmental Psychology: Personality and Socialization*, P. B. Baltes & K. W. Schaie, eds. (New York: Academic Press, 1973).

Nesselroade, J. R. & Baltes, P. B. "Adolescent Personality Development and Historical Change: 1970–1972." *Monographs of the Society in Child Development 39* (1, Serial No. 154) (1974).

Nesselroade, J. R., Schaie, K. W. & Baltes, P. B. "Ontogenetic and Generational Components of Structural and Quantitative Change in Adult Behavior." *Journal of Gerontology 27:* 222–228 (1972).

Overton, W. F. & Reese, H. W. "Models of Development: Methodological Implications." In *Life-Span Developmental Psychology: Methodological Issues*, J. R. Nesselroade H. W. Reese, eds. (New York: Academic Press, 1973).

Reese, H. W., & Overton, W. F. "Models of Development and Theories of Development." In *Life-span Developmental Psychology: Research and Theory*, L. R. Goulet & P. B. Baltes, eds. (New York: Academic Press, 1970).

Riegel, K. F. "Influence of Economic and Political Ideologies on the Development of Developmental Psychology." *Psychological Bulletin 78:* 129–141 (1972).

Riegel, K. F. "Adult Life Crises: Toward a Dialectic Theory of Development." In *Life-span Developmental Psychology: Normative Life Crises*, N. Datan & L. H. Ginsberg, eds. (New York: Academic Press, 1975).

Riegel, K. F. "From Traits and Equilibrium toward Developmental Dialectics." In *Nebraska Symposium on Motivation: 1974–75*, W. J. Arnold & J. K. Cole, eds. (Lincoln: University of Nebraska Press, 1900).

Schaie, K. W. "A General Model for the Study of Developmental Problems." *Psychological Bulletin 64:* 92–107 (1965).

Schaie, K. W. "A Reinterpretation of Age-related Changes in Cognitive Structure and Functioning." In *Life-Span Developmental Psychology: Research and Theory*, L. R. Goulet and P. B. Baltes, eds. (New York: Academic Press, 1970).

Schaie, K. W. "Methodological Problems in Descriptive Research on Adulthood and Aging." In *Lifespan Developmental Psychology: Methodological Issues*, J. R. Nesselroade and H. W. Reese eds. (New York: Academic Press, 1973).

Schaie, K. W., & Baltes, P. B. "On Sequential Strategies in Developmental Research and the Schaie-Baltes Controversy: Description or Explanation?" *Human Development*, in press.

Schaie, K. W. & Labouvie-Vief, G. "Generational versus Ontogenetic Components of Change in Adult Cognitive Behavior: A Fourteen-year Cross-sequential Study." *Developmental Psychology 10:* 305–320 (1974).

Schaie, K. W. Labouvie, G. V. & Buech, B. V. "Generational and Cohort-specific Differences in Adult Cognitive Functioning: A Fourteen-year Study of Independent Samples." *Developmental Psychology 9:* 151–166 (1973).

Schaie, K. W. & Strother, C. R. "A Cross-sequential Study of Age Changes in Cognitive Behavior." *Psychological Bulletin 70:* 671–680 (1968a).

Schaie, K. W. & Strother, C. R. "The Effect of Time and Cohort Differences on the Interpretation of Age Changes in Cognitive Behavior." *Multivariate Behaviorial Research 3:* 259–294 (1968b).

Wohlwill, J. F. "The Age Variable in Psychological Research." *Psychological Review 77:* 49–64 (1970).

Wohlwill, J. F. *The Study of Behavioral Development* (New York: Academic Press, 1973).

Chapter 11

Educational Theory and Values: Mastery Learning and Computer-Assisted Instruction

Within the social sciences today there is a growing realization that a value-free science is impossible and that it is necessary to develop a philosophy for the social sciences which accommodates the value-laden nature of all "facts." The early positivists had hoped to make pre-inferential facts the basis for a positive science—a science which banished anything metaphysical from within its boundaries and adhered to a strict dualism of facts separate from values. The climate today in the philosophy of science is one of "theory-laden" observations (e.g., Feyerabend, 1972). Few contemporary social scientists would deny that values enter into the knowledge-seeking process at the very beginning and serve to affect the facts. Thus, for example, experimenter bias, problem selection, theoretical perspective, etc., all serve to dispel the myth of a value-free science.

The above rather obvious comments seem hardly worth making were it not for the observation that social scientists in general and educational theorists in particular have not yet absorbed their full impact. The facts one observes within an educational setting are to a great extent a function of one's theoretical perspective and values. However, there is another twist to this basic idea which merits some explication: Educational theory itself, and the technologies it gives rise

Greg P. Kearsley co-authored this chapter. Reprinted with permission from the *Journal of Instructional Psychology* 3 (1976): 41–48; original title, "Underlying Values in Bloom's Theory of Mastery Learning as Compared to CAI."

to, selectively endorse certain human values of the prevailing sociocultural milieu. Human beings are, in a general sense, political, and
their activities, including educational theory and practice, are not carried
out in a social vacuum.

The last statement above will ring true to some but most likely upset
the majority. Those professionals working on the frontiers of educational
theory and practice would, in all probability, not care to have their
activities characterized as "political" or value-laden in the more radical
sense. But if we probe beyond the natural science approach to the study
of educational problems and the development of educational theory, we
begin to encounter the real human dimension underlying our theoretical
practice.

A natural science model of educational theory and research emphasizes the ideal of a strict separation between the subject and object and
claims to be engaged in a "detached" search for truth—supposedly
bracketing human values and personal beliefs while wearing the cloak of
the scientist. However, the natural science model will just not do in
educational research to the extent that a major human dimension of the
inquiry process is suppressed. The values and presuppositions which
underlie educational theories may not take the form of conscious willful
acts, but this is not to say that they are absent. Rooted in the assumptions
of the natural science model is a predisposition for the scientist to
suspend human values, attitudes, and, in general, a critical spirit vis-à-
vis the human dimension of inquiry. Thus, the natural science model
dictates that scientists should be critical of all aspects of the research
endeavor except the cultural and political values upon which their
theories rest, and in turn, affirm.

That knowledge in the social sciences is value-laden in the more
radical manner hinted at above, and linked in complex ways to certain
aspects of the underlying social structure, is the major thesis of the
sociology of knowledge (e.g., Mannheim, 1936). While sociologists have
turned the field of the sociology of knowledge upon themselves (e.g.,
Gouldner, 1970), and psychologists are beginning to appreciate the social
basis of their theories (e.g., Buss, 1975), thus far there has been little
analysis of the value-laden nature of educational theory and technology
in terms of the relationship of the latter to political ideologies and the
sociocultural structure. Educational theory and practice must revolve
around a specific image of humanity and an implicit, if not explicit,
prescription as to what "ought to be" the case. A particular image of
humanity is culturally conditioned—influenced by a particular set of
sociocultural forces. Educational theory, in turn, is also intimately

concerned with bringing into existence a certain social reality (via achieving certain educational objectives) based upon a culturally conditioned image of humanity. In this way there is a dialectical relationship between the goals and image of humanity inherent in a particular educational theory and the sociocultural context—each serves to influence and be influenced by the other via reciprocal interactions.

The intent of the present chapter is to take some of the rather abstract ideas expressed above and, using two concrete examples on the frontiers of educational research, attempt to illustrate the interaction of educational theory and technology with certain aspects of the social-cultural context and underlying values. More specifically, it will be argued that the educational foundations of computer-assisted instruction (CAI) and Bloom's mastery learning theory are premised on different images of humanity. Thus, CAI as a theory and technology of instruction is based upon a view of humanity and value orientation which historically has been called "individualism," and stresses the importance of individual freedom. Mastery learning, on the other hand, is a theory of instruction which is premised upon an image of humanity and a value system which historically may be identified as "egalitarianism"; that is, the belief in the equality of all individuals.

The underlying values of CAI and mastery learning may be seen as embedded within different value systems of ideologies which have sociopolitical implications. In other words, since educational theory is prescriptive by nature, different theories based on different values lead to differing political conclusions. While it is neither possible nor desirable to try and avoid the value-laden and prescriptive nature of educational theory and the resultant educational practice, those in the field should become more self-conscious and aware of the implicit values of their theories. In this way, values in educational theory may assume an important *conscious* role rather than an important *unconscious* role. Educational theory and practice must be evaluated in terms other than the "facts" they purport to explain. Behind every theory of education lies an image of humanity and a value system which shapes their implementation. One must penetrate beyond the "facts," beyond surface appearances, and get to the essence or the underlying values of a theory. In other words, where theories are prescriptive, as they must be in the area of education, it is values rather than facts which must be first evaluated. Consider, then, the underlying values in CAI and Bloom's mastery learning.

COMPUTER-ASSISTED INSTRUCTION (CAI)

Computer-assisted instruction involves the man-machine interaction in which the computer serves the active role of teaching without the intervention of a human instructor. This situation differs from other essentially administrative uses of the computer in education (computer-managed instruction or computer-assisted testing or counselling) in that the computer provides the major means of instruction rather than simply serving as a teaching aid. CAI has been in existence for more than a decade now and a number of large-scale systems are in daily use with many different student populations and curriculums. A recent survey (Hoye and Wang, 1973) lists approximately 2000 instructional programs available at over 30 major CAI centers.

The *Raison d'être* of CAI lies in its potential to individualize education by tailoring the instructional sequence to individual differences in abilities, interests, motivation, and/or objectives. A CAI system should provide "optimal" instruction by catering to the particular learning rate and style of the individual. At the most elementary level, CAI provides "personalized" instruction insofar as students may schedule the "what" and "when" of instruction (within limits) to suit themselves. Students may also set their own pace in covering the material, thereby avoiding the regimentation of traditional classroom instruction. Each individual proceeds independently of others. Furthermore, all CAI systems provide for some form of different branching decisions based on the particular response (or patterns of responses) of the individual to questions or problems embedded in the instructional sequence. Such branching decisions may result in a review or remedial instruction if the performance is poor, or may lead to more sophisticated material if the performance (or single response) is good. In addition to such "local" control of the instructional sequence, more "global" control is possible by having the program take account of the student's performance history to choose instructional levels or strategies in the instructional sequence.

Even though the degree of individualization achieved by current CAI systems is impressive with respect to traditional classroom practice, much more ambitious ideas have been under development. For example, Stolurow (1969) has proposed an "idiographic" programming model in which contingency statements or teaching rules are used to control the selection and presentation of material and which are related to individual differences in such variables as reading rate, memory abilities, motivation level, and various aptitude/personality dimensions. Self (1974) has suggested the idea of "student models" which are representations of the hypothesized knowledge state of each student via a set of teaching procedures. Presumably the computer would adapt to the spectrum of idiosyncratic learning preferences and abilities by having a separate "model" of each student. Furthermore, there are a number of systems currently under development (e.g., Bunderson, 1974) which have the goal of giving the student control of the way in which the material is to be learned. This involves the provision for learner specification of preferred modes or levels of presentation (e.g., abstract principles versus concrete examples, visual aids) as well as allowing the student to direct the interaction (via question-asking or dialogue, rather than being tutored in an essentially passive manner.

Implicit in the different approaches to CAI is a theory of instruction which places a premium on adapting the educational means to the individual rather than having the individual adapt to a particular style of instruction. In fact, the original impetus for CAI (Skinnerian learning theory), which was based on the importance of immediate reinforcement, has given way to what may be characterized as a humanistic goal: CAI as a means of allowing each individual to realize their full educational potential by developing their idiosyncratic talents. This has been heralded as a "deep" view of individualization corresponding to a "deep" view of educational technology (Dwyer, 1974).

What are the underlying values upon which CAI is premised? The emphasis upon individualization and the more recent developments of allowing students to determine their own educational goals and course of instruction serves to emphasize the value of individual freedom within the educational process. The recognition and emphasis placed upon pre-entry individual differences explicitly accepts the inequality of individuals.[1] While CAI can remain neutral with respect to the interpretation of the major sources (genetic and environmental) of individual differences, it is engaged in a policy of increasing even further initial individual differences and thereby the educational inequality of all. Thus, the instructional philosophy of CAI may be seen as committed to the values of individual freedom and inequality.

The underlying values of CAI as a theory and technology of instruction are quite compatible with the more general concerns of the political ideology of capitalism. Rokeach (1973) has recently proposed a two-value model for discriminating between different political ideologies. This model consists of the two orthogonal dimensions of high-low equality and high-low freedom. Capitalism is considered to fall into that quadrant characterized by high individual freedom and low equality—values which are indigenous to CAI. CAI may be viewed as reifying the capitalist image of humanity in a theory and technology of instruction. Thus the underlying values of the theory and practice of CAI have their basis in the more general ideology of capitalism, and further, CAI may be seen as an educational system which is ultimately geared towards serving the interests of capitalism by making concrete the values of individual freedom and inequality in supposedly nonpolitical spheres. In fostering an image of humanity which stresses the values of individual freedom and inequality, CAI nicely exemplifies the relationship between educational theory and the political ideology of capitalism. Although the relationship is not a conscious and deliberate one, this does not make it any less real.

That capitalism as a political ideology endorses the twin values of individual freedom and the inequality of people may be appreciated in historical perspective. During the rise of capitalism in eighteenth-century England, there arose a *laissez-faire* political and economic policy which stressed individual freedom in the context of a self-regulating market. Individuals were, in principle, free to develop their potential in diverse directions—a view which implicitly accepted the extant socioeconomic class structure as reflecting the inherent inequality of individuals. Here we see the isomorphism between inherent individual differences in aptitudes and individual differences in socioeconomic status. Socioeconomic inequality is a logical outcome of, and justified by, inequality in natural aptitudes, perserverance, and motivation. Capitalism required highly specialized individuals for both carrying out the monotonous and mundane aspects of production and, at the other extreme, for advancing technology in order to maintain competition. Thus the inequality of humanity as reflected in the scientific study of individual differences went hand in hand with the requirements of capitalistic production (Buss, 1976; Riegel, 1972).

BLOOM'S MASTERY LEARNING

Mastery learning, as explicitly espoused by Bloom (1971, 1974), implied earlier by Carroll (1963), and elaborated and reviewed in Block (1974), is another exciting theory and technology of instruction and learning of recent vintage. Egalitarian in spirit and intent, it promises to provide not just equal educational opportunity but equal educational *achievement* as well. Bloom's theory of Mastery learning is premised on the belief or assumption that, given the right circumstances, the majority of individuals will be able to master to criterion a specified learning task in an educational setting. Traditional educational practice assumes that there will be large variability on the learning criterion variable and, according to Bloom, such an assumption permits educators to abdicate what he believes is their major responsibility—namely, to provide the necessary instructional means to ensure that the majority of students learn to mastery.

Bloom believes that the prevalent educational assumption, the assumption that there must be large variability in learning performance, is maintained and reinforced by the actual practice of educators. Thus the traditional approach to instruction involves the following sequence: large variability on input variables (abilities, interests, aptitudes, motivation, work habits, etc.) ▶ uniform "treatment" effect (essentially identical duration and kind of instruction) ▶ large variability maintained on output variable (learning-performance criterion variable). In other words, large initial individual differences in, say, aptitudes, are reflected in the learning and performance variable to the extent that there are no differential "treatments" (instruction).

Whereas traditional approaches to instruction assume that there must be large variability on the criterion variable, according to the philosophy of mastery learning, instruction may be considered unsuccessful to the extent that there are large individual differences in learning-performance outcome. The latter state of affairs implies that, traditionally, only a small proportion of students achieve criterion. Mastery learning is committed to the goal of having the majority of students (80% is the frequent proportion mentioned) perform at a level which, under traditional procedures, only about 20% of the students achieve. Mastery learning for the majority of students is achieved by providing sufficient *time* during which additional and/or differential instruction on the learning task occurs.

Time is a central concept in the theory of mastery learning, where the belief that the majority of individuals can achieve high levels on a learning criterion variable becomes operationalized through a strategy of providing sufficient time as needed for all individuals. Individual differences in aptitudes becomes conceptually transformed into individual differences in time required for learning, the implication being that given sufficient time, most individuals should be able to reach criterion. This shift in the conceptualization of aptitudes within the educational context (which is based on Carroll's 1963 model of learning) permits entertaining the possibility of taking steps to ensure that all of the majority rather than a minority of students achieve mastery learning. Whereas under conditions of both uniform duration and kind of instruction individual differences in aptitudes for learning are directly translated into a normal probability curve on the criterion variable, this is not the case in mastery learning. Rather than keeping duration and kind of instruction constant (and of necessity allowing criterion performance to vary), in mastery learning both duration and kind of instruction are permitted to vary and achievement is held constant.

In other words, one may accommodate individual differences in aptitudes for learning by adjusting the time and nature of instruction. In this way large variability or individual differences on such organismic input variables as aptitudes and abilities need not necessarily be reflected in large individual differences on the learning criterion variable but, rather, may be reflected in the time and nature of instruction necessary to reach a given mastery level on the criterion variable. However, varability in the duration and nature of instruction is thought to approach zero and mastery learning progresses, and so Bloom is claiming more than that he is simply accommodating individual differences in the educational process. He is claiming to *eliminate* individual differences in learning rate, instructional time, or school achievement as mastery learning programs unfold. While a complete critical appraisal of Bloom's theory is beyond the scope of this chapter, it will suffice for present purposes to appreciate the underlying logic of mastery learning and the value-laden nature of the theory.

While there may be some *prima facie* similarity between CAI and mastery learning insofar as they allow individuals to vary the duration of instruction, they are predicated on different images of humanity. The underlying values of mastery learning include the belief in the desirability of human equality as exemplified by Bloom's notion of vanishing individual differences. Whereas CAI accepts and attempts to amplify existing individual differences, mastery learning considers such differences to be largely a function of the failure of instruction. Mastery learning may be seen as an educational theory and technology which reifies an egalitarian or socialist image of humanity, that is, the values of equality and freedom are paramount. By attaining educational equality, the way is open to achieve economic and social equality. In removing supposedly inherent inequality (individual differences), mastery learning is implicitly committed to removing socioeconomic inequality.

While the attainment of educational equality will presumably go some distance towards the achievement of economic equality, it should be noted that bidirectional influences are probably more realistic and effective. Thus, mastery learning as an educational theory of practice could probably be better implemented in a socialist society. Halsey, for example, has argued "that the society of equals has to be created by economic and political reform and that the role of education must largely be to maintain such a society once it has been achieved" (1975, p. 10). In other words, Halsey is arguing for the transformation of the underlying socioeconomic structure in order to make it compatible with such educational theory and practice (e.g., mastery learning), which endorses the value of equality.

Rokeach (1973), in his two-value model of political ideologies, considered socialism to be in that quadrant characterized by equality and freedom. While both socialism and capitalism endorse freedom, it is apparent upon closer inspection that each has a different view as to its meaning. For socialism, freedom involves outside intervention and controls in order to ensure socioeconomic equality for all. For capitalism, freedom entails socioeconomic inequality, that is, the lack of outside intervention and controls which allows for the attainment for some of superior wealth, status, and power at the expense of others. Mastery learning may be seen as based on a socialist image of humanity, where explicit intervention and controls are set up to enhance the possibility of bringing about greater equality. Since major differences in educational level become translated into social and economic inequality, mastery learning is commited to an image of humanity which places a high priority upon eradicating unjust inequalities in society. Important to note in this theory of education is that the goal of educational equality is realized by attempting to bring the majority of students up to the level of the more advanced. There is no attempt to achieve educational equality by holding down the top students. Economic leveling does not entail educational leveling, but, rather, can be achieved by "educational raising."

CONCLUSION: TOWARD CRITICAL EDUCATIONAL THEORY

CAI and mastery learning may be viewed as theories of instruction which are based upon differing images of humanity as revealed by their implicit and underlying values. Theories of instruction are in essence political insofar as they are prescriptive in nature and attempt to bring into being a specific social reality. The radical value-laden nature of theories of instruction implies that one should evaluate such theories, in part, in terms of the image of humanity they assume and propagate. Only when the political and ideological aspects of educational theory are revealed can one provide a truly adequate and complete critical analysis of such theories.

The foregoing is consistent in many respects with the educational philosophy of John Dewey (e.g., Dewey, 1900, 1916). One of Dewey's major themes was that education should be looked upon as a social process—that education is the transmission of culture. In developing this theme, he took cognizance of the fact that educational theory and practice were interwoven with the sociocultural milieu. In particular, he advocated a "progressive" educational system which he felt would be in tune with a truly democratic society and culture. Moreover, Dewey's view of the scientific method (as elaborated in Dewey, 1930) was much broader that the traditional one in that it encompassed the critical study of both meaning and values in relation to the social system. The educational philosophy of Dewey was an important attempt to make clear the underlying values of educational theory and practice and a step in the direction of the type of critical educational theory we are advocating herein.

Attempting to go beyond the mere appearance of a phenomenon or theory in order to penetrate to its true essence is the goal of critical theory (e.g., Horkheimer, 1972). Critical theory, as developed by the Frankfurt School, is, in part, committed to revealing the social, political, and economic forces underlying theory. Human values and interests are intimately connected to the knowledge-seeking process, and a greater awareness of these interrelationships permits a more conscious and directing influence in managing the future course of society with respect to certain prescriptive educational theory and practice. Although the importance of the reciprocal interactions between education and society has been recongized of late (Glaser, 1972), critical theory goes beyond this point and attempts to establish the interrelationships between both theory and facts to the underlying socioeconomic relationships and human values.

Critical theory accepts and endorses the individual's own partiality in social theory and itself makes a conscious commitment to theory which leads to an emancipatory practice based upon nonexploitive relations between individuals (economic or otherwise), as well as to theory which restores the individual as a self-conscious, self-managing subject within social reality. In other words, awareness of the partisanship underlying theory is a prerequisite to *transcending* the enslavement of social theory and practice based on the mere recording of facts. It is in this sense that educational theory should become critical theory in order that it truly become "critical."

Notes

1. The term "equality" is open to several interpretations within the context of education (e.g., see Warnock, 1975). Throughout this chapter, by equality we mean equal educational results.

References

Block, J. H. (ed.) *Schools, Society, and Mastery Learning.* (New York: Holt, Rinehart and Winston, 1974).

Bloom, B. S. "Mastery Learning." *Mastery Learning: Theory and Practice,* J.H. Block, ed. (New York: Holt, Rinehart and Winston, 1971).

Bunderson, C. V. "The Design and Production of Learner Controlled Courseware for the TICCIT System; A Progress Report. *Man-Machine Studies 6:* 479–491 (1974).

Buss, A. R. "The Emerging Field of the Sociology of Psychological Knowledge." *American Psychologist 30:* 988–1002 (1975).

Buss, "Galton and the Birth of Differential Psychology and Eugenics: Social, Political, and Economic Factors, *Journal of the History of the Behavioral Sciences 12:* 47–58 (1976).

Carroll, J. B. "A Model of School Learning." *Teachers College Record 64:* 723–733 (1963).

Dewey, J. *The School and Society (Chicago: University of Chicago Press, 1900).*

Dewey, J. *Democracy and Education* (New York: Macmillan, 1916).

Dewey, J. *Individualism: Old and New* (New York: Macmillan, 1930).

Dwyer, T. A. "Heuristic Strategies for Using Computers to Enrich Education." *Man-Machine Studies 6:* 137–155 (1974).

Feyerabend, P. K. "How To Be a Good Empiricist—A Plea for Tolerance in Matters Epistemological." *Challenges to Empiricism,* H. Morick, ed. (Belmont, Calif: Wadsworth, 1972).

Glaser, R. "Individuals and Learning: The New Aptitudes." *Educational Researcher,* 5–13 (1972).

Gouldner, A. W. *The Coming Crisis of Western Sociology.* (New York: Basic Books, 1970).

Halsey, A. H. "Sociology and the Equality Debate." *Oxford Review of Education 1:* 9–23 (1975).

Hoye, R. E., and Wang, A. C. *Index to Computer-based Learning* (Englewood Cliffs, N.J.: Educational Technology Publishers, 1973).

Mannheim, K. *Ideology and Utopia* (New York: Harcourt, Brace and World, 1936).

Riegel, K. F. "Influence of Economic and Political Ideologies on the Development of Developmental Psychology." *Psychological Bulletin* 78: 129–141 (1972).

Rokeach, M. *The Nature of Human Values* (New York: Free Press, 1973).

Self, J. A. "Student Models in Computer-assisted Instruction." *Man-Machine Studies* 6: 261–276 (1974).

Stolurow, L. M. "Some factors in the Design of Sytems for Computer-assisted Instruction." In *Computer-assisted Instruction*, R. Atkinson & H. A. Wilson, eds. (New York: Academic Press, 1969).

Warnock, M. "The Concept of Equality in Education." *Oxford Review of Education 1:* 3–8 (1975).

Chapter 12

The Trait-Situation Controversy and the Concept of Interaction

Within the last few years a number of major articles have examined the interrelationship of traits and situations in predicting and/or understanding behavior (e.g., Bowers, 1973; Ekehammar, 1974; Endler, 1975; Endler and Magnusson, 1976; Mischel, 1973). While differing in their orientation, emphasis, and conclusions, these particular articles all attempt to resolve the trait "versus" situation controversy by resorting to some form of *interactionism*. A careful reading of the recent articles by Bowers, Ekehammar, Endler, and Mischel on the trait-situation issue reveals that, while each advocates an interactionist position, they do not all mean the same thing by this term. Moreover, in certain instances these authors advocate incompatible formulations in the same article. If the continuing debate surrounding the trait-situation controversy is to proceed in a meaningful way, then it is extremely important that the term "interaction" be clearly understood in order to avoid using inappropriate empirical evidence to support a particular view, and to avoid constructing what, upon closer inspection, turn out to be inherently contradictory arguments. Thus the purpose of the present chapter is to contribute to clearer thinking about the various interactionist solutions to the trait-situation controversy which have been proposed.

Reprinted with permission from *Personality and Social Psychology Bulletin* 3 (1977): 196–201.

THE CONCEPTUAL STRUCTURE OF THE TERM "INTERACTION"

Psychologists tend to use the term "interaction" in at least two major and mutually contradictory ways. In order to develop an analytic basis for distinguishing between the two meanings of the term "interaction" within the context of the trait-situation controversy, it is first necessary to characterize what may be called four major subperspectives.

The "pure" *situationist position* may be characterized by $B = f(E)$, that is, behavior is a function of the environment. This view tends to be of the stimulus-response variety, where causality is considered in terms of the situational stimuli determining or evoking behavior. The "pure" *trait position* may be characterized by $B = f(P)$, that is, behavior is a function of the person, personality, or traits. In this view, it is the relatively permanent properties of people, that is, dispositions, which determine behavior. The "pure" *cognitive position* may be characterized by $E = f(P)$, that is, the environment or situation is constructed by the person via certain cognitive processes and structures. In this view, the focus is upon the means by which an individual cognizes his/her world, rather than upon behavior per se, where the meaning of a situation is determined by what is *in* the organism. The "pure" *social learning position* may be characterized by $P = f(E)$, that is, person or individual difference variables are a function of the environment or social learning history of the individual. Here it is the environmental contingencies which are considered to shape relatively enduring psychological structures.

Of the four subperspectives mentioned above, the first two specify *behavior* as a function of either the environment or the person. Taken together $B = f(E)$ and $B = f(P)$ are the basic components of one interactionist model—a model which may be interpreted as specifying behavior as some joint function of both the environment and the person, or $B = f(E,P)$. In other words, the environment and the person interact in producing or determining behavior. While this concept of interaction leaves open the specific function through which the environment and the person *co* determine behavior, that which is not left open is the nature of the causal relationship—it is unidirectional. That is to say, causality is from the environment *and* person *to* behavior. Both environmental variables and person variables are independent variables, while behavior is a dependent variable.

Within the context of the trait-situation controversy, the $B = f(E,P)$ type of interaction has been almost exclusively formulated in terms of the analysis of variance (ANOVA) model, where the variability in the behavioral dependent variable is partitioned into additive sources associated with environmental variables, person variables, and an interactional component. Thus, many authors have attempted to settle the trait "versus" situation controversy by reviewing those empirical researches which permit the evaluation of the relative proportion of variance associated with environmental variables, person variables, and their interaction (for recent reviews, see Argyle and Little, 1972; Bowers, 1973; Ekehammar, 1974; Endler and Magnusson, 1976). The general conclusion of these reviews has been that the interactional component accounts for the highest proportion of variance, thereby supporting an interactionist position. However, as noted by Overton and Reese (1973), the ANOVA model is a linear model, and by the term "interaction" within the ANOVA model, one *means* specifying the *nonreciprocal relationship* between environmental and person variables which best accounts for, predicts or "explains" the behavioral variability.

The second major type of interaction is bound up in the remaining two major subperspectives previously characterized, that is, $E = f(P)$ and $P = f(E)$. In contrast to the first type of interaction, which makes use of a *common* dependent variable (i.e., behavior is a joint function of environmental and person variables), kthe second major type of interaction focuses upon the psychological environment and the person as these affect and are affected by each other. In other words, the *relationship* between environmental and person variables is one of *reciprocal* or bidirectional causation, where each is at the same time both a dependent and independent variable. This type of interaction, which is an interaction between cause and effect variables, rather than simply between two different kinds or classes of causal variables, can be loosely characterized by jointly considering $E = f(P)$ and $P = f(E)$, or more simply, E◆P. A well-known example of the use of this meaning of interaction from developmental psychology would be Piaget's notion of assimilation-accommodation.

Building upon the previous work of von Bertalanffy (1968) and Bunge (1963), Overton and Reese (1973) have developed the argument that the two types of interaction (as exemplified by ANOVA and by what might be termed a systems view) are *incompatible* insofar as they are embedded in two differing metaphysical systems. Thus Overton and Reese have linked each of the above two concepts of interaction to the mechanistic model and organismic model, respectively, thereby implying that each type of interaction carries along with it certain modal and ontological assumptions which are basically inconsistent with each other. Such inconsistency between basic concepts is thought to be unresolvable, where neither logical argument nor empirical studies of the "crucial experiment" type can be brought to bear in arbitration. In Kuhn's terminology, each concept of interaction is embedded in a distinct paradigm, and each involves a commitment to a certain perspective through which to view reality (1962).

INTERACTION IN THE TRAIT-SITUATION CONTROVERSY

In light of the above discussion, the question now arises as to how the concept of interaction has been employed by those writing on the trait-situation issue. One might well wonder if the discussion has recognized and kept separate the two distinct kinds of interaction—or, has there been a fundamental confusion undermining intelligent debate? Let us examine separately the major contributors who have recently advanced an interactionist position on this issue.

Bowers' Interactionism.

Bowers' (1973) scholarly article criticized what has been called here the "pure" situationalist view, or $B = f(E)$, and argued for an interactionist position. In so doing Bowers made an unjustifiable shift from the linear, unidirectional, codetermination notion of interaction to the bidirectional, organismic conception. Thus, Bowers opened on the issue of interactionism by developing a persuasive argument for the $B = f(E,P)$ interaction model, and more specifically, the ANOVA version. After reviewing 11 articles published since 1959 which allow for the assessment of the relative importance of environmental variables, person variables, or their interaction in terms of accounting for behavioral variance, Bowers concluded that "interaction of persons and settings accounts for a higher percentage of variance than either main effect in 14 of 18 possible comparisons, and in 8 out of 18 comparisons the interaction term accounts for more variance than the sum of the main effects" (Bowers, 1973, p. 321). Thus it is apparent that Bowers was initially committed to the $B = f(E,P)$ type of interaction, stating that "Obviously, and to some considerable extent, the person and the situation are codeterminers of behavior, and they need to be specified simultaneously if predictive accuracy is desired" (Bowers, 1973, p. 322).

Towards the end of Bowers' article, however, it is not clear as to what type of interactionism is being advanced. Bowers notes that "An interactionist or biocognitive view denies the primacy of either traits or situations in the determination of behavior" (p. 327). However, just two sentences later conceptual confusion over the concept of interaction becomes apparent when he emphatically states what in the end will undermine his endeavor, namely, "Interactionism argues that *situations are as much a function of the person as the person's behavior is a function of the situation*" (Bowers, 1973, p. 327, original emphasis). In this statement there has been a definite shift from the previous kind of interactionism Bowers had outlined, namely, from a linear and unidirectional model of codetermination of behavior to an interactionism which emphasizes reciprocal causation between the environment and the person, that is, from $B = f(E,P)$ to the joint consideration of $E = f(P)$ and $P = f(E)$. Thus Bowers argues "that people do indeed foster consistent social environments, which then reciprocate by fostering behavioral consistency" (Bowers, 1973, p. 329).

As is evident in the above quote, Bowers has now fully embraced an organismic view of interactionism. In accepting the Overton and Reese view that the two types of interactionism are embedded in incompatible metaphysical systems, then it is true that Bowers has generated two incompatible answers while giving a semblance of unity to his article with the ambiguous term "interactionism." Bowers' article is confusing insofar as it advanced an initial interactionist position which, by the very nature of its conceptual structure, cannot be used to bolster a second and incompatible interactionist position.

Endler's Interactionism.

In contrast to Bowers, Endler (Endler, 1975; Endler and Magnusson, 1976) has kept separate the two interactionist positions. Thus in one place he has stated that:

A useful paradigm . . . for the trait versus situation issue is an interactionist one that assesses the relative variance contribution by situations and persons to behavior, and examines how situations and persons *interact* in evoking behavior. (Endler, 1975, p. 17, original emphasis)

At no point did Endler use the findings from ANOVA studies to support an organismic view of interaction, and he explicitly acknowledged (Endler, 1975; Endler and Magnusson, 1976) the two concepts of interaction as outlined by Overton and Reese (1973). In the more recent article, Endler and Magnusson seem to favor the bidirectional, organismic interpretation of "interaction." However Endler does, in the author's opinion, incorrectly characterize the organismic view of interaction when he states that it "would refer to the mutual interdependence of persons-situations and behavior so that the persons-situations influence behavior and vice versa" (Endler, 1975, p. 18). Thus, as previously set out, the organismic view of interaction focuses upon the reciprocal influence between persons and situations and *not* persons-situations and behavior. Contrary to Endler's view, in the organismic sense of interaction person and situation variables are different *kinds* of variables which interact with each other, rather than together interacting with behavior.

Mischel's Interactionism.

Like Endler, Mischel (1973) puts forth a logically consistent interactionist position, although it falls within an organismic bidirectional perspective. Mischel's "cognitive social learning" view of interaction combines the two perspectives $E = f(P)$ and $P = f(E)$ into a unified $E \spadesuit P$. Thus Mischel states his position clearly:

The person continuously influences the "situations" of his life as well as being affected by them in a mutual, organic two-way interaction. . . . The person continuously selects, changes, and generates conditions just as much as he is affected by them. The mutual interaction between persons and conditions . . . cannot be overlooked. (1975, p. 278).

While Mischel (1973, pp. 255–258) does consider the value of the $B = f(E,P)$ type of interaction in the form of ANOVA designs and "moderator variables," he largely dismisses the predictive utility of such interactions and ultimately dismisses the concept of interaction underlying that body of empirical research. This strategy is quite consistent with his later proposal for an organismic cognitive social learning theory of interaction. Mischel, then, has implicitly recognized the two kinds of interactionism in his article, and has been successful in keeping them conceptually separate.

Ekehammar's Interactionism.

In a recent historical review of interactionism in personality theory and research, Ekehammar (1974) has argued that interactionist ideas were alive and well 40 to 50 years ago. Ekehammar also argued that such interactionist ideas have not been empirically tested until quite recently since they had to await the development and refinement of certain statistical models, namely, ANOVA. Unfortunately, Ekehammar, like Bowers, confuses the two major types of interaction previously outlined.

While Bowers at one point clearly changes direction in going from one interactionist model to the other and never looks back, Ekehammar creates much more uneasiness in the reader by slipping back and forth from the linear, unidirectional, codetermination interactionist position to the organismic, bidirectional, interactionist model.

In his historical review of interactionism, Ekehammar cites Kantor, Lewin, Angyal, Murray, and others as specifically advancing an interactionist position in the organismic, bidirectional, systems sense of that term. From the discussion of that historical material, it would seem that Ekehammar was paving the way for looking at modern versions of a particular kind of interactionism. However, in reviewing modern interactionist positions, Ekehammar (1974, pp. 1032–1041) is almost exclusively concerned with ANOVA researches and the linear, unidirectional, codetermination model of interaction. This would be acceptable if one ignored the beginning section on the historical roots of the organismic systems view of interaction, and the summary and conclusion section in which Ekehammar attempts to glue the two incompatible interactionist concepts together. A paragraph in the last section of the article is telling, for here statistically significant person-situation interactions in ANOVA models are mentioned, along with a plurality of organismic and phenomenological concepts such as "man-world reciprocal implication" and "circular causality." Ekehammar's attempt to demonstrate that recent statistical studies, which assume a linear, unidirectional, codetermination of behavior, provide the empirical support for the "older" organismic, reciprocal causation type of interactionism. is a misguided adventure based upon a failure to appreciate that a particular term may stand for different, and in this case, contradictory, concepts. Although Ekehammar (1974, p. 1041) demonstrates an awareness of the Overton and Reese (1973) article, and recognizes certain "limitations" of ANOVA, he still fails to appreciate that he is dealing with two different *kinds* of interactionism which cannot speak to each other. Thus I believe Ekehammar is in error when he states that "analysis of variance components seems to be the best of the mentioned approaches for testing *the* interactionist hypothesis" (1974, p. 1041, emphasis added). Contrary to Ekehammar's intention, he is not addressing a *single* hypothesis or concept of interactionism, but, rather, two different and contradictory types.

SUMMARY AND CONCLUSION

Recent debate on the trait-situation issue has been plagued by a failure on the part of some of the contributors to distinguish between two radically different concepts of interaction. Such conceptual confusion has resulted in offering inappropriate empirical evidence generated within one framework as supporting what in fact is a very different position. If one does not accept the Kuhnian position that the two concepts of interaction are incompatible, then an argument must be made for using empirical evidence generated within one interactionist framework as supporting another. Neither Bowers or Ekehammar have done the latter.

Progress in an area is dependent upon the clarity of one's basic concepts. Those interested in advancing our knowledge about interactionism within personality theory would be wise to explicitly make the conceptual distinction between the two major and contradictory types of interactionism discussed here.

References

Argyle, M. & Little, B. R. "Do Personality Traits Apply to Social Behavior?" *Journal for the Theory of Social Behavior 2:* 1–35 (1972).

Bertalanffy, L. von. *General Systems Theory* (New York: George Braziller, 1968).

Bowers, K. S. "Situationism in Psychology: An Analysis and a Critique. *Psychological Review 80:* 307–336 (1973).

Bunge, M. *Causality: The Place of the Causal Principle in Modern Science* (New York: World, 1963).

Ekehammar, B. "Interactionism in Personality from a Historical Perspective." *Psychological Bulletin 81:* 1026–1048 (1974).

Endler, N. S. "The Case for Person-situation Interactions." *Canadian Psychological Review 16:* 12–21 (1975).

Endler, N. S. & Magnusson, D. "Toward an Interactional Psychology of Personality." *Psychological Bulletin 83:* 956–974 (1976).

Kuhn, T. S. *The Structure of Scientific Revolutions* (Chicago: University of Chicago Press, 1962).

Mischel, W. "Toward a Cognitive Social Learning Reconceptualization of Personality." *Psychological Review 80:* 252–283 (1973).

Overton, W. F. & Reese, H. W. "Models of Development: Methodological Implications." In *Life-span Developmental Psychology: Methodological Issues*, J. R. Nesselroade & H. W. Reese, eds. (New York: Academic Press, 1973).

Chapter 13

A Conceptual Critique of Attribution Theory

The confusion and barrenness of psychology is not to be explained by calling it a "young science"; its state is not comparable with that of physics, for instance, in its beginnings. . . . For in psychology there are experimental methods and *conceptual confusion*. . . .

The existence of the experimental method makes us think we have the means of solving the problems which trouble us; though problem and method pass one another by. (From the last page of Wittgenstein's *Philosophical Investigations*).

THE ARGUMENT IN BRIEF

1. Causes and reasons are logically distinct categories for explaining different aspects of behavior.
2. Causes are that which bring about a change.
3. Reasons are that for which a change is brought about (e.g., goals, purposes).
4. Behavior that happens *to* a person, that is nonintentional, that a person "suffers," is an *occurrence*, and is explained by both actors and observers with causes.
5. Behavior that is done *by* a person, that is intended, that has a goal or purpose, is an *action*, and is explained by the actor with reasons. The

I would like to thank Baruch Fischhoff and Lita Furby for reading and commenting on an earlier draft of this chapter. Reprinted with permission from the *Journal of Personality and Social Psychology* 36 (1978): 1311–1321. Copyright 1978 by the American Pyschological Association.

observer may use either causes and/or reasons in explaining action.

6. Thus, the kinds of attributions made depends upon what kind of behavior is to be explained (occurrence or action) and the status of the explainer (observer or actor).

7. Attribution theorists have tended to project an exclusively causal framework onto the lay explanation of *all* behavior and *all* explainers, and are thus confused and confusing regarding causes and reasons.

8. Progress in an area is, in part, dependent upon the adequacy of that area's key concepts. Attribution theorists need to become more self-conscious about the correct use of the terms "cause" and "reason" in the explanation of behavior.

Attribution theory (e.g., Bem, 1972; Harvey, Ickes, and Kidd, 1976; Heider, 1958; Jones and Davis, 1969; Jones et al., 1972; Kelley, 1973; Shaver, 1975) involves the attempt to explain how ordinary people explain behavior by making attributions. "Attribution theory" is actually a rather loose term standing for a general perspective and/or problem orientation rather than for a single theory.

With few exceptions, attribution theorists have interpreted "the making of an attribution" as "the making of a *causal* attribution." The largely implicit assumption that has served to guide research in this area is that the layperson explains behavior exclusively in causal terms. The latter assumption is implicit in the sense that it is rarely, if ever, called into question. In explaining explanations, attribution theorists have uncritically and unconsciously projected their own (causal) explanatory self-image onto everyone. In this way, attribution theorists have fallen victim to the ideology of causality.

This chapter questions the attribution theory notion that when people explain behavior they do so by making exclusively causal attributions. This idea is critically examined by making the crucial distinction between *causal* and *reason* explanations. The cause-reason distinction has been put into sharp focus within philosophical psychology or the philosophy of mind, which is in the tradition of ordinary language analysis. Reviewing the cause-reason distinction within the philosophy of mind sets the stage for reconceptualizing the nature of attributions. The latter, in turn, provides the framework for undertaking a conceptual critique of two representative areas of research: (1) Jones and Nisbett's (1972) theory of actor-observer differences in the making of causal attributions, and (2) Kruglanski's (1975) critique of the internal-external distinction, and his reformulation involving endogenous versus exogenous attributions.

PREPARING THE WAY

Causes and Reasons

The cause-reason issue turns in part on exactly what is meant by the term "cause." Aristotle distinguished between four different uses of "cause" for purposes of explanation (e.g., see Rychlak, 1968; Taylor, 1967). These were (1) *efficient* cause, or that which brings about some change; (2) *final* cause, or the end, purpose, or telos for which a change is produced; (3) *material* cause, or that in which the change comes about; and (4) *formal* cause, or the pattern or shape of that which is changed. These distinctions can be better appreciated by noting Taylor's example of sculpturing:

A statue is produced by a sculptor (its efficient cause) by his imposing changes upon a piece of marble (its material cause) for the purpose of possessing a beautiful object (its final cause), the marble thereby acquiring the form, or distinctive properties, of a statue (its formal cause). (1967, p. 56)

With the rise of modern science, causality has tended to be exclusively identified with that which makes things happen, or brings about change, that is, *efficient* causality. Both *material* and *formal* causality have been largely abandoned in more recent discussions of this topic. However, in considering the social or human sciences, Aristotle's *final* cause (i.e., purpose, motive, intention) has continued to exert a strong presence in some quarters. Thus, the notion of *final* cause within the social sciences poses somewhat of a challenge to those who would attempt to explain social behavior, and more specifically action (which is intended behavior), exclusively in terms of *efficient* causes. Rychiak's insightful comment in this regard is worth quoting, especially since he is talking about attribution theory: "Although modern attribution theory purports to deal with causal analysis, the only formal theoretical cause used to explain these researches—so fraught with telic overtones—is an efficient cause" (1976, p. 7). In adopting more recent terminology, Aristotle's "efficient cause versus final cause" becomes the "cause versus reason" controversy in regard to the explanation of human action.

Heider and Causal Explanation

In 1958, Fritz Heider's *The Psychology of Interpersonal Relations* was published, and that event has generally been considered as establishing the field of attribution theory. Heider's program for psychology was to be one based upon the "point of view . . . that scientific psychology has a good deal to learn from common sense psychology" (Heider, 1958, p. 5). In order to appreciate the theoretical significance of Heider's goal of building a scientific psychology upon the foundations of commonsense psychology, it is necessary to situate his work within a broader intellectual climate.

Heider was probably one of the first psychologists who shared some of the same concerns of a recent splinter group then emerging from within analytical philosophy. Logical atomism, logical positivism, and logical constructionism were all being attacked by Ludwig Wittgenstein and Gilbert Ryle. Those analytical philosophers who were skeptical of a reductionistic program for explaining behavior in terms of an ideal physicalistic language emphasized two ideas of particular significance in the present context: (1) the necessity for teleological concepts such as purpose, motive, and intentionality (i.e., *reasons*) for explaining intended behavior (i.e., *action);* and (2) that the major task of the philosopher should be one of clarifying how our ordinary language actually works, and to engage in conceptual analysis in order to eliminate conceptual confusion. With respect to this chapter, (1) relates to its content and (2) to its methodology.

It is true that, like the philosophers of mind, Heider was committed to "a careful analysis of language expressions" in order to "arrive at concepts that will enable us to clarify the implicit relations among words referring to psychological phenomena" (1958, p. 10).[1] Unlike the former, however, Heider unfortunately did not distinguish between causes and reasons—the two different kinds of explanations that have their basis in ordinary language. Lay explanation for Heider was assumed to be entirely causal in nature, in spite of the fact that he gave considerable attention to the commonsense use of such reason concepts as purpose, motive, and intention in the explanation of action. It has been the perpetuation of Heider's exclusively causal interpretation of action that has contributed to some of the serious conceptual confusion in the field. Paradoxically, the cause-reason distinction was boldly made in the same year as Heider's book was published in two separate and widely discussed monographs: R. S. Peters's *The Concept of Motivation*, and Peter Winch's *The Idea of Social Science*.

More on Causes and Reasons

Both Peters (1958) and Winch (1958) argued that reason explanations are not of the same logical type as causal explanations—they belong to different categories, to different discourses of speech, or to use Wittgenstein's term, to different "language games." In direct opposition to Heider's view, Peters's main thesis was that an analysis of ordinary language explanations of human action revealed that these were not causal in nature, but rather consisted of reasons. Giving a reason explanation of action involves stating one's intention or goal and/or justifying the means used in attaining that goal. For Peters, a causal explanation of human action would be in terms of bodily movements. As such, it would fail as a sufficient explanation since one could never set down all the various ways an end state could be arrived at. In other words, lay explanation of purposeful behavior (i.e., action) must be in terms of means and ends (i.e., stating the reasons), in order for that behavior to be intelligible to another human being. Peters (like Ryle before him) also allowed for a second class of causal explanations that was required only when it was necessary to explain behavior that is unintelligible or irrational—that is, deviant from purposive rule-following action. Thus, a reason explanation of mad behavior would be a contradiction of terms (unless, like R. D. Laing, one is attempting to demonstrate that madness is a rational reaction to an irrational situation). In the case of irrational behavior, something happens *to* the individual (a "happening"), rather than something being done *by* the individual (action).

Winch, like Peters, stressed the qualitative difference between ordinary language explanations of human action and the causal explanation of the natural sciences. Winch, however, offered a thesis that was much higher in shock value. Whereas Peters did allow for causal explanations of human behavior under certain circumstances, Winch banished outright the entire notion of causality from the explanation of human social behavior. Like Heider, Winch had arrived at his conclusions concerning commonsense psychology only after going through an analysis of ordinary language mentalistic concepts.

Let me now round out the discussion of the cause-reason issue within the philosophy of mind, and then summarize where we stand. The more recent technical literature on causal versus reason explanations of human action contains the debate concerning the possibility of monism—that is, reducing reasons to causes (e.g., Ayer, 1946; Daveney, 1974; Madden, 1975). Although that debate is certainly not settled (e.g., see Donnellan, 1967, for an excellent discussion of the issues), there is a consensus emerging that reasons are logically distinct from causes. Within the dualistic position, there have been two views: (1) those individuals who have explicitly argued that the gulf between causal and reason explanations is unbridgeable (e.g., Louche, 1966; Taylor, 1964; Winch, 1958); and (2) those who have argued that, although distinct, causes and reasons are not incompatible (e.g., Harre and Secord, 1972; MacIntyre, 1971a, 1971b; Q. Skinner, 1972; Toulmin, 1970). In fact, some of the latter (see especially MacIntyre, 1971b; Q. Skinner, 1972) have also argued that causes and reasons are both required for an adequate explanation of human action. According to this view, it is necessary to bring in causal matters that involve explaining what has also happened *to* the person. In other words, reason explanations of actions must be given in light of, or in the context of, causal explanations of what the individual has "suffered."

In summary, then, we can conclude that causal and reason explanations of behavior are conceptually distinct; that is, they are different ways of talking about different kinds of behavior. The major cases involving reason explanations of human action include: (a) justifying, evaluating, or appraising the action; (b) stating the goal, end, or intention of the action; and (c) stating the means or instrumentality of the goal, end, or intention of the action. All these reason-type explanations help to make an action intelligible by attaching meaning to the action in terms of the rules for social behavior; as such, they are not causal explanations. By causal explanation we mean lawfulness and predictability, where an event is explained by reference to a general principle. Although there are many controversial issues surrounding the causality notion (e.g., see Feigl, 1953; Taylor, 1967), for present purposes it will suffice to associate this kind of explanation with such connotative "attributes" as lawfulness, determinism, antecedent-consequent relationship, predictability, and replicability. With respect to explaining behavior, causes are necessary when dealing with either (a) unintelligible or irrational intended behavior, or (b) unintended behavior. They *may* be used when an observer is explaining the action of another (see below).

THE ARGUMENT IN DETAIL

Actors, Observers, and Attributions

Jones and Nisbett have advanced what would appear to be a startling thesis—namely, *"There is a pervasive tendency for actors to attribute their actions to situational requirements, whereas observers tend to attribute the same actions to stable dispositions"* (1972, p. 80, original emphasis). Documented by much research, Jones and Nisbett argue in a convincing manner that the type of attribution made depends upon whether an actor or an observer is doing the explaining. Although actors' and observers' explanations are clearly thought to differ, Jones and Nisbett do believe that both explanations are of the same logical type; that is, both involve making *causal* attributions. Although I certainly agree that the attributions made by actors and observers are very different, I also believe that such differences have their locus in the fact that actors and observers may each be offering logically different *kinds* of explanations. Thus, I disagree with Jones and Nisbett that the meaningful issue in explaining the actors's action involves "the proposition that actors attribute cause to situations while observers attribute cause to dispositions" (p. 82). My criticism of alleged actor-observer differences in the making of causal attributions is conceptual rather than empirical. And it is for this reason that recent studies (e.g., Arkin and Duval, 1975; Miller and Norman, 1975; Regan and Totten, 1975; Storms, 1973; Taylor and Fiske, 1975) that have found and/or manipulated actor-observer attributions do not escape the conceptual critique I will now lay out.

In the first three paragraphs of their chapter, Jones and Nisbett (1972) illustrate the kind of situation they have in mind for comparing actor-observer causal attributions. Each paragraph describes a different situation, and it will be instructive to give a brief sketch of each. The first involves a failing student discussing his academic problems with, and trying to explain his behavior to, a faculty advisor. The second paragraph portrays thirty-nine witnesses of a New York murder attempting to explain their failure to intervene on behalf of the victim. The third refers to the autobiographical accounts of politicians and their explanations of past actions. In each of these cases, Jones and Nisbett believe that the actor (the student, the eyewitnesses, and the politician, respectively) will offer an explanation of his/her action which involves making causal attributions to the environment. The observer, on the other hand (the faculty advisor, news commentator, and the public, respectively), is thought to be more likely to explain the same action by making causal attributions to the actor in the form of behavioral dispositions. Now, in light of the cause-reason distinction made earlier, it should be immediately apparent that the actors (the student, eyewitness, and politician) are all engaged in attempting to *justify* their actions, provide a *rationale* for their actions, make their actions *intelligible* to others, and offer a *moral* explanation of their actions—all in the context of their society's rules for "proper" conduct. In short, they are in a situation where a reason, and not a causal explanation of their action, is required. To construe an actor's self-explanation to be fundamentally causal in nature, where the actor supposedly divides his/her causal attributions disproportionately to self and the environment, is to make a serious category mistake.

Like Ryle's (1949) analysis of the "ghost in the machine,"[2] the basis for misconstruing the actor's explanation as being causal in nature relates to the grammar of language. Identical surface structure of language does not necessarily entrail identical deep structure or a single category. When an actor is asked "why" with respect to his/her action and retorts with statements all beginning with "because," neither the question nor the answer is necessarily of the same logical type as those in a situation in which an observer is asked "why" with respect to another's action, and also gives statements beginning with "because." Even if an actor should explain his/her own action by using causal terminology (and the reader may have already been prompted to construct such prima facie counterexamples in opposition to the present thesis), such explanations should not be accepted at face value as constituting a causal explanation. Rather, in such instances, the term "cause" is being used in the sense of a reason, as when an actor says, "What caused me to walk out of class was the boring lecture." The latter idea can more accurately be expressed in this way: "The reason I walked out of class was that I found the lecture boring."

In asking an actor to explain his/her action, the "why" is a request to justify, or to make rational or intelligible, his/her action vis-à-vis society's norms for "proper" conduct. The actor's "because" statements consist of giving his/her reasons for an action—that is, matters that were weighed in his/her deliberation. By definition, in giving one's reasons for an action only matters that are *consciously* available to the actor can occur. In contrast, the observer who is asked to explain "why" in regard to an actor's action can include causal attributions that operate *out* of the consciousness of the actor. Thus, while an observer can make causal attributions in explaining the action of an actor (see below), the actor's explanation could not include such kinds of attributions—even if, as already noted, the actor should happen to use the term "cause."

The upshot of this discussion is that language identity does not reflect logical identity. Thus, I believe that Jones and Nisbett are in error when, in referring to some relevant research, they state that "The experiments by Jones et al. present data for actors and observers in *identical* situations" (1972, p. 81, emphasis added). Far from being in identical situations, actor and observer are engaged in fundamentally (i.e., logically) different situations when each attempts to explain the same action. It is the actor's unique situation which requires the conclusion that his/her self-explanations of action are exclusively reason and not causal in nature. In the words of Donnellan (who uses the term "agent" rather than "actor" in outlining two unique characteristics of the actor's situation):

First, the agent seems to have a privileged position concerning the reasons for his actions. . . . He does not, at any rate, utilize evidence and empirical investigation in the normal case to establish what his reasons are. Second, we seem to accept reason explanations, without supposing the necessity for some generalization to a larger class of cases. If a man acts from certain reasons in this instance, we may, but do not have to, suppose that either he or others will act in this way when they have these reasons. In other cases. These two facts . . . seem foreign to causal explanation. (1967, p. 88)

Thus, the actor gives a reason explanation rather than a causal explanation of his/her own action.

Even though Jones and Nisbett recognize that the difference in actor-observer explanations of the actor's behavior "often stems in part from the actor's need to justify blameworthy action" (p. 80), they still frame this need to justify within the context of making causal rather than reason attributions. Thus, they do not consider the justificatory dimension of the actor's explanation as being a *crucial* attribute on which hinges actor-observer differences in explanation.[3] Rather, they believe that such differences "may also reflect a wide variety of other factors having nothing to do with the maintenance of self-esteem" (p. 80). Of particular importance in this regard is the authors' account of differences in information processing between actors and observers in regard to alleged differences in their causal explanations of the actor's action. Although I am very sympathetic to the idea that actors and observers are processing different information, I do not think that such an interpretation is a contribution toward explaining actor-observer differences in the making of *causal* attributions. Rather, I think its importance lies in its being a valuable description of two fundamentally different kinds of explanations of the "same" action.[4]

Although actors must give reason explanations, the observer has the option of giving either a reason and/or a causal explanation of the actor's action. The causal option would consist of the observer attributing either internal or external causes to the actor or environment, respectively, where such causes may operate out of the actor's consciousness. The typical observer's explanation of the actor's action would probably contain both causal and reason components. Of course there is no "reason" why an observer could not be instructed to give an exclusively reason explanation of an actor's action. Such an explanation could be given in two different forms: (1) The observer could be requested to reconstruct on the basis of available evidence the *actor's* reasons for acting; or (2) the observer could be asked for his/her *own* reasons—that is, to justify or make intelligible the action in a way that he/she believes would not necessarily be in accord with the actor's reason account. Either of these observer reason explanations would be of the same logical type as the actor's own explanation of his/her action. *These* kinds of actor-observer differences would be meaningful and directly comparable, and it would seem that a useful line for future research on actor-observer differences in the explanation of the actor's action would be to set the experimental task demands so that the explanations would be directly comparable.

But although *direct* comparability of actor-observer differences is conceptually possible for true reason explanations of action, it is not for causal explanations of action. When we ask an actor to explain his/her actions, we are asking for a reason rather than for a causal explanation. However, if we are talking about the nonaction that a person suffers— that is, occurrences that happen *to* a person (e.g., headache, blushing, perspiring, emotional arousal, etc.)—rather than things done *by* a person (i.e., action), then, of course, an "actor" could, in principle, give a causal explanation of his/her own nonaction behavior.

In regard to actor-observer differences in the explanation of occurrences, consider the well-known study by Storms (1973) on experimentally reversing actor-observer causal attributions. Under certain conditions in that study, actors gave explanations involving a greater proportion of trait dispositional attributions than would be normally expected, whereas observers gave explanations consisting of more than the usual proportion of situational attributions. Also in that study, as well as in extensions of it (e.g., Regan and Totten, 1975; Taylor and Fiske, 1975), actors and observers were explicitly asked for a *causal* explanation of the actor's behavior. What was to be explained was the actor's style characteristics while becoming acquainted with another person— namely, ratings along the dimensions of friendliness, talkativeness, nervousness, and dominance. It is important to note that in the Storms study, and extensions of it, the aspect of the actor's behavior that was being causally explained by both actor and observer was *not* exclusively intentional—that is, *action*. It is easily seen that nervousness is something that happens *to* an individual rather than being something done *by* the individual. To the extent that friendliness, talkativeness, and dominance are not consciously and deliberately sought after in oneself, then they too are also occurrences rather than action—that is, events that happen *to* the person. Thus, the term "actor" as used by Storms (1973), Regan and Totten (1975), Taylor and Fiske (1975), and probably others is really a misnomer with respect to the behavior upon which they are focused.[5] It would seem that they are really concerned with *sufferer*-observer differences in causal explanations of *occurrences*. Such being the case, their results would appear to lie outside the issue relating to actor-observer differences in the explanation of *action*. On the other hand, we can also note that friendliness, talkativeness, and dominance *can* be construed as intended behavior, and there may be some individuals who do consciously and deliberately strive to be friendly, talkative, and dominant in a "getting acquainted" situation. When such individuals are explicitly asked for a causal explanation within the experimental situation, although experimenter and subject may both use the term "cause," in actual fact such indivuls will produce reason explanations! The extent of the latter category mistake will depend upon the extent to which friendliness, talkativeness, and dominance are actions rather than occurrences. This, in turn, will be partly a function of individual differences. Given such individual differences, plus the fact that nervousness is definitely not action, the use of the term "actor" by Storms and others is conceptually inaccurate vis'à-vis the causal inferences they wish to draw from their results.

Unfortunately, these criticisms regarding actor-observer differences in the making of attributions are also applicable to other studies that have attempted to test the Jones and Nisbett thesis. In the original chapter by Jones and Nisbett, they discussed their ideas in the context of the following kinds of behavior: responses on intelligence tests, the expression of attitudes and opinions, the translation of sentences, and decision behavior. It is clear that these behaviors are intentional, conscious, willed *actions*, not occurrences, and Jones and Nisbett are certainly justified in using the term "actor." Such is not the case in the study reported by Taylor and Koivumaki (1976), who clearly confound action and occurrence when they amalgamate such target behaviors as helping someone carry parcels (an action), and looking happy (an occurrence). A much more serious category mistake is made in those studies that consist exclusively of occurrence target behaviors, yet are framed within the Jones and Nisbett theory of *actor*-observer differences in the making of attributions. I have come across two such researches. In a study by Hansen and Lowe (1976), the behavior that was explained by "actors" and observers was physiological *reactions* (galvanic skin responses and electromyograms) to music—clearly not intentional behavior or action![6] In a study by Snyder and Frankel (1976), the target behavior that observers were to explain consisted of the emotional state (anxiety) of an interviewee—again, behavior that is clearly an occurrence rather than action. In the latter two studies one should be talking about *sufferer*-observer differences in causal attributions. Thus, contrary to their stated intention, these investigations do not shed light on the Jones and Nisbett notion of *actor*-observer differences in explanations.

Let me now briefly summarize the conclusions that we have arrived at thus far and, along the way, develop an additional point or two. In asking an actor to explain his/her action, he/she can do nothing but offer a noncausal explanation or a "good-reason-assay"—that is, state the reasons for his/her actions in order to justify and/or make rational and intelligible those actions in light of society's norms and rules for "proper" behavior. *If* the observer's task is designed so that he/she is asked for a reconstruction of the actor's reasons for engaging in that action, or is asked for an interpretation based upon his/her own reasons, then both actor's and observer's explanations are noncausal and directly comparable. Similarly, the explanation of things happening *to* the "actor" (who now becomes a sufferer) would be exclusively causal in nature, and such sufferer-observer differences in explanation would be directly comparable. To the extend that current research on actor-observer differences in the making of attributions has involved the confounding of action and occurrence components, such results yield no unambiguous implications for either actor-observer or sufferer-observer differences in explanation. And, of course, to the extent that attribution theorists have considered the *true* actor's explanation of his/her action as being causal in nature (and that extent would appear to be total), such actor-observer comparisons have been seriously misconceived, and thus are illegitimate.

I believe that the cause-reason distinctions discussed above illustrate rather dramatically that actor-observer differences in attributions may involve diverse *kinds* of attributions. The message here is that attribution theorists must take cognizance of the cause-reason distinction in order to be able to talk meaningfully about true actor-observer differences in attributions. Also implied in this conclusion is that research in this area cannot get by by simply making an internal-external (i.e., actor-situation) attributional distinction. Kruglaski (1975) has also arrived at the latter conclusion, although he has based it upon his endogenous-exogenous distinction. Let us now briefly consider the internal-external and endogenous-exogenous distinctions in the context of the cause-reason issue. Such an exercise will, among other things, permit an even more analytical statement concerning the kinds of attributions actors and observers can make.

FROM INTERNAL–EXTERNAL TO ENDOGENOUS–EXOGENOUS AND BEYOND

In what is undoubtedly an important theoretical article within attribution theory, Kruglanski (1975) has recently argued that an endogenous-exogenous distinction should replace the well-entrenched internal-external dichotomy for classifying lay attributions made to explain human actions. According to Kruglanski, the endogenous-exogenous distinction roughly corresponds to the end-means or goal-instrumentality distinction. The internal-external dichotomy refers to attributions made to either the actor or the situation (environment), respectively. Briefly, it is Kruglanski's contention that the internal-external designation is only appropriate for the lay explanation of occurrences rather than actions. The former are involuntary; the latter are voluntary. Since all human action comes about by conscious deliberation—that is, it is willed by the actor—the lay explanation of action involves only internal attributions. Both endogenous and ex-ogenous attributions are internal attributions—that is, are attributed to the actor.

I believe that in presenting his endogenous-exogenous distinction Kruglanski has, unfortunately, muddied further already muddy waters vis-à-vis the cause-reason confusion within the attribution literature. The latter confusion has been deepened by Kruglanski's article in spite of the fact that the reader had, with "reason" come to expect the very opposite. Consider his postulate 1:

Postulate 1. For the naive attributor, *actions are explicable in terms of reasons or purposes*. That is, the lay explanation of actions is teleological *rather than causal*. (p. 389, second emphasis added)

In order for postulate 1 to make any sense at all, and thus serve a useful "purpose" in the theory, the reader must assume that there is in fact a sharp contrast to be made between causes and reasons. Furthermore, one would expect such a contrast to be subsequently explicated to some extent by the author. However, the postulate is not subsequently amplified, even though its content demands amplification. Indeed, what directs the reader back to considering the postulate at all is not its later discussion, but rather the fact that it is contradicted in several places throughout the text. For example:

In the present section a theory is developed about the inferences that may follow from *causally* attributing actions in contrasting ways, designated here as *endogenous* and *exogenous* (p. 389, first emphasis added).

These two quotes, which are separated by only one sentence, are obviously contradictory. How is it possible that lay explanations of action be reason "rather than causal" explanations, yet at the same time consist of "causally attributing actions in contrasting ways?" Contrary to postulate 1, Kruglanski in several places dissolves outright the cause-reason distinction. Consider the following:

The present theory of endogenous attribution suggests that in explaining actions the layman draws the endogenous-exogenous distinction between the actions' *causes (reasons)* rather than the internal-external distinction. (p. 392, emphasis added)
      . . . an endogenous attribution is made when the action is considered to be its own reason and an exogenous attribution is made when the reason is foreign (exogenous) to the action. The above definitions contain three distinct components: the action, its *cause (or reason)*, and the relation (of endogeneity or exogeneity) assumed to connect the two. (p. 402, emphasis added)

The last two passages communicate the message that causes and reasons are synonymous and are to be used interchangeably. Since in both occurrences of the stated equivalency the concept of cause is given primacy, it would seem that Kruglanski, like others working in the area, has not been able to break out of the prison of a totalizing notion of causality. In collapsing reasons into causes, one is robbed of the critical cutting edge of that distinction.

CONCLUSION

We are now in a position to supplement the conceptual distinctions arrived at in the previous section, and thereby steer a course that will lead us out of the conceptual fog with regard to causes and reasons in the attribution process. Needless to say, causes and reasons do not belong in the same category. In maintaining their separate identities, we can proceed to make some further distinctions. Thus, Kruglanski's very useful endogenous-exogenous distinction is best thought of as yielding endogenous and exogenous reasons for explaining action. This external-internal distinction applies only to *causal* attributions. However, contrary to his restricting internal-external causal attributions to occurrences, these kinds of attributions can be used to explain action *if* it is an observer who is doing the explaining. In summary, then, in explaining action the actor must employ either endogenous and/or exogenous reasons. The observer, on the other hand, could employ any of the following: the inferred actor's endogenous and/or exogenous reasons; the observer's own endogenous and/or exogenous reasons; and finally, internal and/or external causes.

The conceptual confusion surrounding the cause-reason issue within attribution theory demands critical notice, as well as an attempt to develop a more adequate framework for employing these terms. In light of the present discussion surrounding the cause-reason, internal-external, endogenous-exogenous, action-occurrence, actor-observer, and sufferer-observer distinctions and their interrelationships, I believe that those working within the area may now use these concepts in a much more precise and meaningful way. The latter is a prerequisite if attribution theorists themselves are to make valid attributions.

Part of my goal in this chapter is to demonstrate that attribution theorists have been both too naive and not naive enough in explaining naive psychology. They have been too naive in the sense that they have uncritically made an absolute out of a useful idea (causal explanation), remaining unaware of the consequences of that "action." They have not been naive enough in the sense that they need to approach the phenomenon they wish to explain (naive psychology) with less of their own restricting assumptions, and more of an openness to be guided by the way lay explanation actually works.

Finally, let me conclude this essay with a brief consideration of what should now be the obvious question on the reader's mind: Why? Why have the terms "cause" and "reason" been used so incorrectly by those working within attribution theory? The deep answer to that question is rooted in a consideration of the causality notion as ideological, and the encapsulating, partialist, limiting metascience within which attribution theorists move. Causality is a useful and necessary notion in regard to explaining social behavior. When it is totalized and thus transformed into unquestioned dogma, however, it becomes an ideology that obscures and hides, rather than enlightens and informs.

Notes

1.   Some of the ordinary concepts and their grammar that Heider analyzed were these: causing, can, trying, wanting, suffering, belonging, ought, may, and others.

2.   For Ryle, *the* major category mistake in talking about the mind had been the conceptual confusion surrounding "the ghost in the machine." The basic argument here involved the notion that superficial grammatical similarities and differences are not *ipso facto* indicative of logical similarities and differences. More specifically, although the grammar of ordinary language treats mind as an entity on equal footing with body, and further, mental activities as being on a par with bodily activities, in reality these are not two independent and simultaneous activities falling within the same category. They belong to different categories—

to different discourses of speech, to different ways of talking about an organism.

3.   For the extreme but interesting view that *all* explanation of human action is moral explanation, and that "the idea of a science of man is untenable," see Loche (1966, p. viii).

4.   However, some recent refinements of the Jones and Nisbett information-processing hypothesis in regard to actor-observer differences in the making of attributions (e.g., Regan and Totten, 1975; Taylor and Fiske, 1975; Taylor and Koivumaki, 1976) necessitate critical notice and conditional enthusiasm. To the extent that those later researches are actually *not* unambiguously focused upon *action*, then they are not, strictly speaking, dealing exclusively with *actors*.

5.   I do not deny that the Storm subjects were actors; that is, it is true that they were engaged in action (e.g., saying *certain* things in getting acquainted). However, when the nonaction or occurrence dimensions of the actor's behavior are studied (e.g., nondeliberate talkativeness as a general trait), such results do not have a direct bearing on the actor qua actor in actor-observer differences in explanations.

6.   At least not in this situaton. Conceivably such behavior could be regarded as intentional, conscious, willed action in a biofeedback experiment.

References

Arkin, R. M. & Duval, S. "Focus of Attention and Causal Attributions of Actors and Observers." *Journal of Experimental Social Psychology 11:* 427–438 (1975).

Ayer, A. J. *Man as a Subject for Science* (London: Athlone Press, 1964).

Bem, D. J. "Self-perception Theory." In *Advances in Experimental Social Psychology,* L. Berkowitz, ed., Vol. 6 (New York: Academic Press, 1972).

Daveney, T. K. "Intentional Behavior." *Journal for the Theory of Social Behavior 4;* 111–129 (1974).

Donnellan, K. S. "Reasons and Causes." *Encyclopedia of Philosophy 7:* 85–88 (1967).

Feigl, H. "Notes on Causality." In *Readings in the Philosophy of Science,* H. Feigl & M. Brodbeck, eds. (New York: Appleton-Century-Crofts, 1953).

Harre, H. & Secord, P. F. *The Explanation of Social Behavior* (Totowa, N.J.: Littlefield, Adams, 1973).

Harvey, J. H., Ickes, W. J. & Kidd, R. E. eds. *New Directions in Attribution Research* (Vol. 1) (Hillsdale, N.J.: Lawrence Erlbaum, 1976).

Heider, F. *The Psychology of Interpersonal Relations* (New York: Wiley, 1958).

Jones, E. E. & Davis, K. E. "From Acts to Dispositions: The Attribution Process in Person Perception." In *Advances in Experimental Social Psychology*, L. Berkowitz, ed. (Vol. 2) (New York: Academic Press, 1969).

Jones, E. E., Kanouse, D. E., Kelley, H. H., Nisbett, R. E., Valins, S. & Weiner, B. eds. *Attribution: Perceiving the Causes of Behavior* (Morristown, N.J.: General Learning Press, 1972).

Jones, E. E. & Nisbett, R. E. "The Actor and the Observer: Divergent Perceptions of the Causes of Behavior." In *Attribution: Perceiving the Causes of Behavior*, E. E. Jones, D. E. Kanouse, H. H. Kelley, R. E. Nisbett, S. Valins & B. Weiner, eds., (Morristown, N.J.: General Learning Press, 1972).

Kelley, H. H. "The Processes of Causal Attribution." *American Psychologist 28:* 107–128 (1973).

Kruglanski, A. W. "The Endogenous-Exogenous Partition in Attribution Theory." *Psychological Review 82:* 387–406 (1975).

Louche, A. R. *Explanation and Human Action* (Berkeley, Calif.: University of California Press, 1966).

MacIntyre, A. "The Antecedents of Action." In A. MacIntyre, *Against the Self-Images of the Age* (New York: Schocken, 1971a).

MacIntyre, A. "The Idea of a Social Science." In A. MacIntyre, *Against the Self-images of the Age* (New York: Schocken, 1971b).

Madden, E. H. "To Justify or Explain in History or Social Science." *Journal for the Theory of Social Behaviour 5:* 3–16 (1975).

Miller, D. T. & Norman, S. A. "Actor-observer Differences in Perceptions of Effective Control." *Journal of Personality and Social Psychology 31:* 503–515 (1975).

Peters, R. S. *The Concept of Motivation* (London: Routledge & Kegan Paul, 1958).

Regan, D. T. & Totten, J. "Empathy and Attribution: Turning Observers into Actors." *Journal of Personality and Social Psychology 32:* 850–856 (1975).

Rychlak, J. F. *A Philosophy of Science for Personality Theory* (Boston: Houghton Mifflin, 1968).

Rychlak, J. F. "Can Psychology Be Objective about Free Will?" *Philosophical Psychologist 10 (2):* 2–9 (1976).

Ryle, G. *The Concept of the Mind* (London: Hutchinson, 1949).

Shaver, K. G. *An Introduction to Attribution Processes* (Cambridge, Mass.: Winthrop, 1975).

Skinner, Q. "'Social Meaning' and the Explanation of Social Action." In *Philosophy, Politics and Society*, P. Laslett, W. G. Runciman & Q. Skinner, eds. (Fourth Series) (New York: Barnes & Noble, 1972).

Storms, M. D. "Videotape and the Attribution Process: Reversing Actors' and

Observers' Points of View." *Journal of Personality and Social Psychology* 27: 165–175 (1973).

Taylor, C. *The Explanation of Behavior* (London: Routledge & Kegan Paul, 1964).

Taylor, R. "Causation." *Encyclopedia of Philosophy* 2: 56–66 (1967).

Taylor, S. E. & Fiske, S. T. "Point of View and Perception Causality." *Journal of Personality and Social Psychology* 32: 439–445 (1975).

Taylor, S. E. & Koivumaki, J. H. "The Perception of Self and Others: Acquaintanceship, Affect, and Actor-observer Differences." *Journal of Personality and Social Psychology* 33: 403–408 (1976).

Toulmin, S. "Reasons and Causes." In *Explanation in the Behavioral Sciences*, R. Borger and F. Cioffi, eds. (Cambridge, Eng.: Cambridge, University Press, 1970).

Winch, P. *The Idea of a Social Science* (London: Routledge & Kegan Paul, 1958).

Chapter 14

A Metascience Critique of Attribution Theory

In a previous chapter I explored the extent to which attribution theorists (e.g., Heider, 1958; Jones and Nisbett, 1972; Kelley, 1973; Kruglanski, 1975) have tended to misuse the terms "cause" and "reason." I noted there that, in explaining how laypersons explain behavior, including intended behavior or action, attribution theorists have unfortunately adopted an exclusively *causal* framework. Thus, *reason* attributions or explanations are either misconstrued by attribution theorists as being causal in nature, or denied altogether.

My earlier critique of the cause-reason distinction within attribution theory was based on a conceptual analysis. Thus, I drew heavily from the tradition of ordinary language philosophy and certain philosophers of mind (e.g., Peters, Ryle, Winch, Wittgenstein). I would now like to offer a critique of attribution theory launched from a higher altitude. A conceptual critique of the cause-reason distinction within attribution theory is a very important one, but I believe it is only a way station along a route leading to a more ultimate destination. The abstract conceptual critique needs to be transformed into a critique based upon content (i.e., human values and interests). This move will involve a consideration of metascience. *This tack is necessary since the roots of the cause-reason confusion within attribution theory are firmly planted in the soil of empiricist metascience.* In calling for a drastic overhaul of the metascience of attribution theory, we ultimately arrive at a similar conclusion

I would like to thank Baruch Fischhoff and Lita Furby for reading and commenting on an earlier draft of this chapter.

187

as in the previous conceptual critique—namely, that causes and reasons are both necessary for explaining social behavior. However, in contrast to the empiricist metascience of attribution theorists, the metascience to be proposed is able explicitly to *legitimize* that conclusion.

CRITIQUE OF THE TOTALIZING ATTITUDE

The underlying philosophy of science of attribution theory is patterned after the natural science model—that is, empiricism.[1] Implicit in this model is the lief that the social, behavioral, or human sciences are not different in kind from the natural sciences. Explanation, according to the unity of science view, is exclusively causal in nature. Philosophers of science subscribing to the unity of science program are rather explicit in their rejection of reason explanations for the social or behavioral sciences. For example, Dray's (1957) proposal that historical explanation involves giving reasons has been reduced to a "special case" of the covering law model of scientific explanation (Hemple, 1966). The important point to note here, then, is the link between the underlying philosophy of science that guides attribution theory (empiricism), and the exclusive "attribution" of causal explanations to the lay attributor by attribution theorists.

What attribution theorists have done is to project their own ideal explanatory self-image onto the lay attributor. Just as Piaget conceives of the child to be operating on reality as an imperfect scientist and the telos of cognition to be the scientific method, lay explanation is considered by attribution theorists to approximate that ideal of scientific explanation—causal explanation. Kelley, for example, has explicitly stated the latter assumption as underlying his theory of causal attribution:

The assumption is that the man in the street, the naive psychologist, uses a naive version of the *empiricist method* used in science. Undoubtedly, his naive version is a poor replica of the scientific one—incomplete, subject to bias, ready to proceed on incomplete evidence, and so on. (1973, p. 109, emphasis added)

Although Kelley has probably been the most explicit in stating the layperson-as-an-imperfect-scientist theme, the assumption is widely shared by others in the field. As previously argued (Chapter 13), the one serious attempt within attribution theory to consider reasons (Kruglanski, 1975) ended by collapsing them into the category of causes. Undoubtedly part of the problem there was the difficulty of climbing out from under the debilitating weight of the causality ideology.[2] We thus arrive at the following important conclusion: *It is the underlying metascience of attribution theory (empiricism) that totalizes what is a useful and important idea (causal explanation), with the consequence that reason explanation is either misconstrued or denied altogether, thereby obscuring and misrepresenting lay explanation.*

We can with profit dig still deeper in the attempt to unearth and reveal the ideological role the causality assumption has played within attribution theory. In order to do the latter task adequately, it is necessary to consider a major alternative to empiricism for the social sciences. The alternative metascience that places reasons at the base of explanation has gone under various names, including the method of *verstehen,* "hermeneutics," and *"geistewissenschaften."*

Historically, the rise of a distinctive method and philosophy for the human and cultural sciences emerged in late nineteenth-century Germany. The growing disillusionment at this time with the natural science model and the mechanical billiard ball conception of the individual and society led to the development of the method of *verstehen* or (reason) understanding of cultural activities. Although Dilthy is most closely associated with the term *geistewissenschaften,* or human studies or sciences (in contrast to the physical sciences), his method of *verstehen* was developed by the sociologist Max Weber. *Hermeneutics* incorporates the method of *verstehen,* and is closely associated with the *geistewissenschaften.* Hermeneutics roughly involves the interpretation of a text, where the goal is to arrive at intersubjective or shared meanings.

Thus, the major alternative metascience for the study of the human or social sciences is one that aims at reason understanding and interpretation, rather than causal explanation in the attempt to make intelligible a text, text analogue, or action. In this view, the program of the human sciences should be one that attempts to make explicit either (a) the significance of a text or an individual's action in terms of the intended meaning on the part of the writer or the actor, or (b), the contemporary meaning or significance that the text or action may now have. Such a task requires arriving at valid intersubjective meanings. The latter procedure involves, in the words of Charles Taylor,

An ultimate appeal to a common understanding of the expressions, of the "language" involved. This is one way of trying to express what has been called the "hermeneutic circle." What we are trying to establish is a certain reading of text or expressions, and what we appeal to as our grounds for this reading can only be other readings. (1971, p. 6)

In a hermeneutic study, the problem is not to escape *from,* but to get properly *into* the circle. For useful discussions in English on hermeneutics and understanding in the social sciences, see Ihde (1971), Radnitzky

(1970), Rickman (1967), Ricoeur (1974), Taylor (1971), and the recently established journal *Cultural Hermeneutics*. And for specific treatments of psychology as a hermeneutic science, see Beshai (1975), Gadlin (1975), and Taylor (1973).

The logic of the hermeneutic enterprise holds the key to revealing the ideolgical function of an attribution theory founded upon the totalization of causal explanation. That is to say, hermeneutics is explicitly committed to arriving at valid intersubjective meanings, *and thereby facilitating communication and enhancing greater understanding*. Thus, a text in the form of an actor's self-explanation is an occasion for greater self-understanding, *given* a dialogue situation consisting of the search for *inter*subjectively valid meanings or *reasons* vis-à-vis the actor's action. The logic of causal explanations of lay explanations of human action, on the other hand, does not require—and, in fact, ultimately denies—the more liberating and democratic function of knowledge. The unity of science metascience makes no provision for the researcher to communicate or dialogue with the object of study. This aspect of the natural science model is certainly not a deficiency when the objects of study are not capable of reflecting upon the results of the research involving them. However, when natural science metascience is carried over in toto to the study of objects that are also subjects in the *true* sense of that term,[3] then the logic of the experiment itself does not provide for facilitating communication between experimenter and experimentee (see Gadlin and Ingle, 1975, for a dicussion of this point).

Thus, the study of the attribution process based upon the metascience of empiricism reinforces the following suppressive tendencies: (a) there is no commitment to reveal the intersubjective (i.e., between experimenters) meaning of the experimental subject's action to the subject; (b) there is no attempt to arrive at the intersubjective meaning of the subject's action based upon the intersubjectivity between experimenter and experimentee. Such knowledge-suppressive practices on the part of attribution theorists could not be otherwise, given the *totalization* of the natural science model of empiricism in this field of inquiry. Since the latter statements are critical for the main argument of this chapter, it is necessary to expand further on the theme they express.

Like any study carried out within the natural science model, attribution theory is founded upon and presupposes a hermeneutic dimension—attribution theorists *themselves* must share intersubjective meanings before it is possible for them to even attempt causal explanations of phenomena. The latter, in turn, geed back to *their* pool of intersubjective meanings, which form the foundation for further causal explication. In this way, attribution theorists are locked into a hermeneutic spiral. However, and this is the critical point, the hermeneutic spiral in which attribution theorists practicing the metascience are locked into locks *out* the objects of study from participating in a "meaningful" way. In the words of Radnitzky:

The interpretation-community of behavioral or social scientists must be limited to those who explain and are allowed to know the results of predictions; and forecasts of social events must not be publicized outside this group in order to prevent "self-influencing" prophecies and feeding "secret" information to the rest of society. (1970, p. 66, vol. II)

It would thus seem that there is a built-in undemocratic and suppressive bias in the metascience of empiricism (when applied to the study of human behavior) to the extent that it does not explicitly condone (and may prevent) the widespread dissemination of research results. Although this epistemic bias is mainly (but not exclusively) pursued by practicing social scientists in an unconscious, nondeliberate, and passive manner, it is apparent that, as a secondary goal and/or implicit assumption, it is neither tenable nor justifiable. The reflexivity of the social sciences—the fact that the object of study is also a true subject, and can therefore change its objectivity by acting in the future partly on the basis of self-knowledge gleaned from publicized research findings—has been the basis for major criticism of natural science metascience as applied to the social sciences (e.g., Friedrichs, 1970; Gadlin and Ingle, 1975; Gergen, 1974; Gouldner, 1970).

Carrying out a *successful* totalization of the natural science program for the social sciences would only work in a totalitarian society—that is, where behavioral research findings were made the sole property of the researchers and those in power. However, this is not to say that there are not ideological forces at work in nontotalitarian societies where there is a prevalence of empiricism in the human sciences. Thus, while the actual reflexivity of the human sciences in nontotalitarian sciences may undermine the totalization of the empiricist program, the undesirable forces may still operate to a considerable extent. In other words, the reflexivity of the social sciences in nontotalitarian societies is presently not being realized as fully as would be desirable due to the ideological forces that accompany the totalizing attitude of natural science metascience. The closed society demands, and in part is founded upon, the totalization of natural science metascience for the human sciences, whereas the open society demands, and in part is founded upon, the maximization of the reflexivity of the human sciences. Unfortunately, current theory and practice of attribution theory is based upon a metascience that is fundamentally not compatible with the open society. In the open society, knowledge gained with respect to lay attributions would be consciously and deliberately fed back to the objects of study. Although attribution theorists have not hesitated to point out the liberating and emancipatory value of their findings for *themselves* and their theories, they have thus far failed to affirm those same rights for the objects of their studies.[4]

What needs to be done, then, is to recognize *explicitly* the reflexivity of the objects of study within the human sciences, and to realize that in such reflexivity lies the basis for democratizing knowledge, and thus achieving greater liberation and emancipation from previously unconscious causal forces. The reflexivity issue should not just be used in a negative way as an argument that invalidates the totalization of the natural science program within the social sciences. Rather, it should be recognized for the positive role it can play—namely, the securing of a metascience for the social sciences in general, and attribution theory in particular, which is founded upon the democratization of knowledge, and thus the values of human liberation and emancipation. A few years back, George Miller called for psychologists to "give psychology away" to the people who need it (1969). In light of the present discussion, it should be apparent that, if such a program is to succeed, it must be founded upon a metascience quite different from the natural science model of empiricism.

Thus far I have been building up to the idea that there is a more appropriate metascience for attribution theory. Before becoming a little more concrete about that metascience and its implications for attribution theory, one issue must be dealt with briefly and laid to rest: the totalization of the hermeneutic program. Just as the totalization of the natural science program for the social sciences (that is, exclusively causal explanation) is untenable, so is the hermeneutic approach. Radnitzky (1970) has made available to English readers the ideas of K.-O. Apel on this issue. Apel, according to Radnitzky, was the first to criticize the totalization of the hermeneutic program. His contention was that an exclusively hermeneutic approach to the understanding of human action and cultural activities would only be justified if, in fact, individuals were *completely* transparent to themselves. To the extent that a person's action is, say, judged to be inconsistent with his/her professed reasons for that action, a hermeneutic approach alone will not be sufficient to understand that action. To the extent that unconscious motives and conflicts affect action, they will function as *causes* and will not, so long as they remain *unconscious* causes, be available for inclusion in arriving at intersubjective meanings between actor and observer. Thus, a totalization of the hermeneutic program for understanding human action shares a deficiency similar to the totalization of the natural science model: *Each transforms a valid and important aspect of the growth of knowledge into an absolute, and thereby obscures, hides, and denies another equally important dimension for understanding and explaining social reality.*

RESOLUTION: TOWARD A MODIFIED CONVERSION MODEL

Each of the two major alternative metasciences for the human sciences has been considered by Habermas (1971, 1973) as being based upon different research-motivating and research-guiding interests. According to Habermas, the natural sciences are based upon a *technical interest,* and the hermeneutic sciences upon a *hermeneutic* (i.e., reason understanding) interest. The problem, as Habermas sees it, is to bring these two metasciences together by grounding them both on a third interest—human emancipation. It isthe job of this third metascience, referred to as a *hermeneutic-dialectic* one by Radnitzky (1970), to oversee the technical and hermeneutic interests by making them subordinate to the emancipatory interest. Whereas the type of knowledge generated by the experiment social sciences and hermeneutic studies are information and interpretation, respectively, the hermeneutic-dialectic metascience engages in critique. What distinguishes the latter type of critique from the kind of criticism to be found in the metascience of empiricism, or even in my abstract conceptual critique of the cause-reason distinction within attribution theory, is that it is legitimized by the interest of human emancipation.

Given the emancipatory interest that should guide the development of knowledge within the social or human sciences, it is clear that such knowledge should aim to yield greater self-understanding and greater awareness of the hypostatized forces acting upon the individual. A model that illustrates the relationship between causes and reasons in the context of arriving at increased knowledge of self has been developed and described by Apel (in Radnitzky, 1970), Habermas (1971), Ricoeur (1970), as well as Taylor (1973). Essentially the model involves the dialogue between patient (actor) and therapist (observer) within the psychoanalytic encounter. As long as the actions of the patient can be understood by his/her offering reasons (thereby arriving at valid intersubjective meanings—that is, the *point* of the action is intelligible to both patient and therapist), there is no need for the therapist (observer) to introduce hypostatized causal forces. But when there is a breakdown in a reason account of action, it is necessary to resort to causal analysis;

the therapist (observer) attempts to formulate a causal explanation involving unconscious or hidden motives. To the extent that these causal factors are brought into the patient's (actors's) consciousness (through the technique of appropriately timed interpretations), they *cease functioning as causes* and become matters for deliberation—that is, reasons. Thus, the road toward greater self-(reason) understanding and emancipation from hypostatized causal forces lies in converting causes into reasons. In this way, causal analysis mediates, or is in the service of, greater (reason) understanding.

The psychoanalytic encounter and the growth of self-knowledge operates at the individual level, and Habermas in particular has generalized this basic paradigm to the collective enterprise of the growth of knowledge in the social or human sciences. Revealing the underlying social forces or causes of nonliberation requires criticism grounded in the emancipatory interest. At the social level, bringing previously unknown hypostatized forces, causal forces that hinder greater self-(reason) understanding at a social level, into consciousness will, of necessity, take the form of a critique of ideologies. Bringing previously hidden social forces into consciousness transforms them into matters of deliberation; that is, they are converted into reasons, and are thereby made not to function causally.

We can be somewhat critical of the boldness of the claims of Apel, Habermas, Ricoeur, and Taylor regarding the conversion of causes into reasons, thereby supposedly neutralizing their causal efficacy. If only things were that simple and straightforward! Unfortunately, as critics of the role of insight in psychotherapy have pointed out (e.g., Hobbs, 1962), there is often no change in maladaptive behavior even after sufficient insight has been demonstrated by the patient—that is, after previously unconscious causes are brought into consciousness. According to what we might aptly dub the "conversion model," the causes should cease to function once they enter consciousness and become matters for deliberation (reasons). Since the latter is often not the case in the psychoanalytic encounter situation, and most certainly is not the case vis-à-vis becoming conscious of previously hidden social forces, it is necessary to add a very important qualification to the "conversion model": The bringing of previously hidden causes into consciousness, and thereby instituting or creating new reasons, does not ipso facto neutralize or destroy the original cause. Rather, in converting a cause into a reason, the cause may still operate, but now the awareness of that cause may *potentially* lead to eventual elimination of that cause qua cause. Important in the latter process, and another consideration entirely missed by proponents of the "conversion model," is that new reasons (based upon an awareness of previously hidden causes) will figure in altered forms of behavior or new action. That is to say, such new reasons will be instrumental in bringing about effective neutralization of the previously unconscious causes. Thus, the conversion of causes into reasons may (but not necessarily will) deflate previously unconscious causes of their causal power.

IMPLICATIONS FOR ATTRIBUTION THEORY AND PRACTICE

The implications of a hermeneutic-dialectical metascience for attribution theory should now be becoming apparent. A program for attribution theory founded upon the emancipatory interest would make the technical interest of causal explanation subordinate to the hermeneutic interest of arriving at intersubjective meanings *beyond the scientific community*. The totalization of causal explanation, as applied to lay understanding and explanation of human action, must be supplanted by a program that has the following goal: *To understand and explain lay understanding and explanation of human action by tacking back and forth from causes to reasons*. The largely *unconscious* causalty ideology within attribution theory itself must be converted from its present causal status to becoming a conscious reason, thereby establishing the potential for making it causally impotent. Within the social sciences, causal explanation should mediate reason understanding; and in this capacity, the function of causal explanation should be to help reveal, and thus make possible, the neutralization of previously unconscious causes. Consider, for example, the research on perceiving the causes of one's own behavior (e.g., Nisbett and Valins, 1972). When an actor's self-understanding of his/her action (as revealed by his/her reasons for the action) does not match the known causal factors at play (as determined by the experimental manipulation), an attribution theory based upon a hermeneutic-dialectical metascience would *facilitate* the process of such causes being made into objects of contemplation for the actors, and eventual conversion into reasons. Such a democratization of knowledge would provide the potential for greater self-knowledge and emancipation from hypostatized causal forces that operate as either unconscious motives (internal causes), or unknown social determinants (external causes).

The modified "conversion model" proposed here permits the taking of a critical step forward in terms of going beyond the implications of attribution theory for psychotherapy that have thus far been considered. Storms (1973), Storms and Nisbett (1970), and Valins and Nisbett (1972) have all discussed both the desirability and the means for having the patient (actor) adopt more of an observer perspective with respect to his/her action. In this way, the patient (actor) would tend to give more dispositional or self-attributions in explaining his/her inappropriate or maladaptive actions (see note 4), and thereby assume greater responsibility for it (and thus, presumably, greater responsibility for changing it). The modified "conversion model" permits us to be a little more sophisticated in understanding how, in fact, a greater frequency of internal attributions made by the patient (actor) can work toward the goal of greater self-understanding and emancipation. That is to say, in becoming more self-conscious of previously unconscious internal causes vis-à-vis maladaptive behavior, such causes *may* be made causally impotent by converting them into reasons.

It should be noted, however, that a higher frequency of internal causal attributions on the part of the patient (actor) is not in and of itself desirable if they are not valid attributions. Storms (1973; see also Galper, 1976) did recognize that increasing the number of self-attributions may actually lead to an exacerbation of the pathological behavior if the causes of such behavior are external. The modified "conversion model" also goes beyond abstract individual liberation by incorporating unconscious social causes of nonliberation within its framework. Thus, one must guard against the reification of abstract internal causes (dispositions), as well as abstract external causes (situations), and adopt more of a dialectical view of subjective (internal) and objective (external) forces. In this way, the successful conversion of causes into reasons, and thus the achievement of greater human emancipation, is two-dimensional, rather than one-dimensional.

Finally, I would like to note some recent views within attribution theory which indicate that perhaps the present critique may find a receptive audience at this time. In a recent chapter, Orvis, Kelley, and Butler (1976) have questioned the exclusivity of the layperson as an imperfect scientist model within attribution theory, and have distinguished between "causal understanding" and "social context" explanations. Thus, they state:

What if this view (layperson-as-an-imperfect-scientist model) is essentially wrong? What if the person learns and is motivated to make attributions not for some abstract understanding of the world, but, rather, to explain his own actions . . . in the social context of justification of self and criticism of others? (p. 379)

Although Orvis, Kelley, and Butler do not base their distinction between the two types of attributional processes on the cause-reason framework, I believe that this is the underlying issue with which they are struggling. But, having alluded to two different attribution models, their proposed resolution falls short of being satisfactory. Thus, Orvis, Kelley, and Butler make the ontological claim that a "reasonable judgment would be that the truth lies somewhere between the two models," yet advocate, on pragmatic grounds, that "it may be more constructive to pose clearly alternative models, rather than to move immediately to some ambiguous mixture of them" (p. 382). I do not believe that the truth on this issue lies in the direction of holding a middle of the road position, and thereby robbing each model of its uniqueness and potency. Equally inadequate is the setting up of a false dualism that inevitably splits and isolates concepts, and thereby splits and isolates reality. Rather, I believe that we can get closer to the truth by thinking dialectically, and by attempting to relate, integrate, and synthesize what may at first appear to be contradictory and irreconcilable concepts. The latter tack does not imply collapsing or reducing one category into another, but rather placing them within a *dialectical* unity.

More compatible with the present approach than the views of Orvis, Kelley, and Butler are those of Fischhoff (1976). Fischhoff has argued for a broader perspective in trying to explain lay explanation by suggesting, as do Orvis, Kelley, and Butler, that we consider the nature of historical (as opposed to scientific) explanation as a potentially useful analogy. However, although Fischhoff himself does not attempt it, he does at least indicate that we should transcend the false dualism of a scientist "versus" nonscientist model for lay explanation. Consistent with the hermeneutic-dialectical metascience program for attribution theory developed here, Fischhoff recommends an interdisciplinary approach. The last sentence of his article is indeed a fitting programmatic statement to end a book on attribution theory:

We might get a good deal of mileage out of thinking of ourselves as intuitive historians and attempting to produce an integrated psychology of predictive and explanatory behaviour that accommodates the historians' observations, the philosophers' formalizations, and the psychologists' and sociologists' theories and empirical findings. (1976, p. 445)

SUMMARY

Let me now summarize the main conclusions and argument of this chapter. The critique of natural science metascience as adopted by attribution theorists in the explanation of human action turns out to be a

critique of the totalization of causal explanations. However, the totalization of reason explanations of action is equally unjustified. In denying the
absolutization of either causes or reasons for explaining human action, we
arrive at a position that attempts to bring each of these categories
together within the metascience of the hermeneutic-dialectic approach.
The latter does not simply assimilate both causes and reasons, but
accommodates them in setting out their interrelationship in the context
of prescribing a specific plan of "action" (the modified "conversion
model") based upon the belief that knowledge should be liberating. *Both
the previously developed abstract conceptual critique and the present
value-laden metascience critique of attribution theory converge onto the
same conclusion: Attribution theorists must effectively distinguish between, as well as accommodate, both causes and reasons.* To the extent
that attribution theorists are to distinguish effectively between, and
accommodate, both causes and reasons; it is necessary that they
legitimate their theory and practice by a hermeneutic-dialectical metascience based upon the values of the democratization of knowledge and
human emancipation.

Notes

1. It is important to appreciate that I am *not* claiming here that empiricism
reflects current natural science metascience. Rather, attribution theory and
research can be viewed as being guided by that philosophy of science. There are,
of course, more enlightened philosophical positions than empiricism in regard to
explaining social behavior (e.g., Harre and Secord, 1973). However, it is
unfortunately true that attribution theorists as a group have not assimilated these
more advanced positions.

2. I am using the term "ideology" in the sense of an unquestioned assumption
that not only affects one's world view, but poisons it.

3. The term "subjects," as used to designate the objects of study within an
investigation in the behavioral sciences, is one of the more curious anomalies of
language convention. Unfortunately, empiricism cannot take seriously the true
meaning of what they call those individuals who participate as objects of a study.
By true "subject" it is meant one who can act, as well as react; plan, as well as
recall; or, in short, contemplate, as a subject, its own objectivity, and thereby
change that objectivity (see below).

4. For example, Jones and Nisbett's (1972) findings that observers make more
trait dispositional attributions and actors make more situational ones in explaining the actor's behavior (I bracket the validity of this claim for present purposes)
have been discussed in terms of their implications for the trait-situation

controversy (e.g., Bem, 1975; Jones and Nisbett, 1972; Kelley, 1973). The point these authors make here, of course, is that psychologists are observers of behavior, and may therefore be biased toward making trait rather than situational attributions.

References

Bem, D. J. "Social Psychology." In E. R. Hilgard, R. C. Atkinson & R. L. Atkinson, *Introduction to Psychology* (New York: Harcourt Brace Jovanovich, 1975).

Beshae, J. A. "Is Psychology a Hermeneutic Science?" *Journal of Phenomenological Psychology 5*: 425–439 (1975).

Buss, A. R. "Causes and Reasons in Attribution Theory: A Conceptual Critique." *Journal of Personality and Social Psychology 17* (1978).

Dray, W. *Laws and Explanation in History* (New York: Oxford University Press, 1957).

Fischhoff, B. "Attribution Theory and Judgment under Uncertainty." In *New Directions in Attribution Research*, J. H. Harvey, W. J. Ickes & R. F. Kidd, eds. (Vol. 1) (Hillsdale, N.J.: Lawrence Erlbaum, 1976).

Friedrichs, R. W. *A Sociology of Sociology* (New York: Free Press, 1970).

Gadlin, H. "Toward a Dialectical Psychology: Theoretical Self-consciousness and Hermeneutic Understanding." Paper presented at the conference "Dialectics: A Paradigm for the Social Sciences," Glendon College, York University, Toronto, 1975.

Gadlin, H. & Ingle, G. "Through the One-way Mirror: The Limits of Experimental Self-reflection." *American Psychologist 30*: 1003–1009 (1975).

Galper, R. E. "Turning Observers into Actors: Differential Causal Attribution as a Function of 'empathy'" *Journal of Research in Personality 10*: 328–335 (1976).

Gergen, K. J. "Social Psychology as History." *Journal of Personality and Social Psychology 26*: 309–320 (1973).

Gouldner, A. W. *The Coming Crisis of Western Sociology* (New York: Basic Books, 1970).

Habermas, J. *Knowledge and Human Interests* (Boston: Beacon Press, 1971).

Habermas, J. "Introductio: Some Difficulties in the Attempt to Link Theory and Praxis." In J. Habermas, *Theory and Practice* (Boston: Beacon Press, 1973).

Harre, H. & Secord, P. F. *The Explanation of Social Behavior* (Totowa, N.J.: Littlefield, Adams, 1973).

Harvey, J. H., Ickes, W. J. & Kidd, R. E. (eds.). *New Directions in Attribution Research* (Vol. 1) (Hillsdale, N.J.: Lawrence Erlbaum, 1976).

Heider, F. *The Psychology of Interpersonal Relations* (New York: Wiley, 1958).

Hemple, C. G. "Explanation in Science and History." In *Philosophical Analysis and History,* W. H. Dray, ed. (New York: Harper & Row, 1966).

Hobbs, N. "A New Cosmology." *American Psychologist 17:* 18–34 (1962).

Ihde, D. *Hermeneutic Phenomenology* (Evanston, Ill.: Northwestern University Press, 1971).

Jones, E. E. & Nisbett, R. E. "The Actor and the Observer: Divergent Perceptions of the Causes of Behavior." In *Attribution: Perceiving the Causes of Behavior,* E. E. Jones, D. E. Kanouse, H. H. Kelley, R. E. Nisbett, S. Valins & B. Weiner, eds. (Morristown, N.J.: General Learning Press, 1972).

Kelley, H. H. "The Processes of Causal Attribution." *American Psychologist 28:* 107–128 (1973).

Kruglanski, A. W. "The Endogenous-exogenous Partition in Attribution Theory." *Psychological Review 82:* 387–406 (1975).

Miller, G. A. "Psychology as a Means of Promoting Human Welfare." *American Psychologist 24:* 1063–1075 (1969).

Nisbett, R. E. & Valins, S. "Perceiving the Causes of One's Own Behavior." In *Attribution: Perceiving the Causes of Behavior,* E. E. Jones, D. E. Kanouse, H. H. Kelley, R. E. Nisbett, S. Valins & B. Weiner, eds. (Morristown, N.J.: General Learning Press, 1972).

Orvis, B. R., Kelley, H. H. & Butler, D. "Attributional Conflict in Young Couples." In *New Directions in Attribution Research,* J. H. Harvey, W. J. Ickes & R. F. Kidd, eds. (Vol. 1) (Hillsdale, N.J.: Lawrence Erlbaum, 1976).

Radnitzky, G. *Contemporary Schools of Metascience* (Vols. I and II) (Stockholm: Scandinavian University Books, 1970).

Rickman, H. P. *Understanding and the Human Sciences* (London: Heinemann, 1967).

Ricoeur, P. *Freud and Philosophy: An Essay on Interpretation* (New Haven, Conn.: Yale University Press, 1970).

Ricoeur, P. *The Conflict of Interpretations: Essays in Hermeneutics* (Evanston, Ill.: Northwestern University Press, 1974).

Storms, M. D. "Videotape and the Attribution Process: Reversing Actors' and Observers' Points of View." *Journal of Personality and Social Psychology 27:* 165–175 (1973).

Storms, M. D. & Nisbett, R. E. "Insomnia and the Attribution Process." *Journal of Personality and Social Psychology 16:* 319–328 (1970).

Taylor, C. "Interpretation and the Sciences of Man." *Review of Metaphysics 25:* 3–51 (1971).

Taylor, C. "Peaceful Coexistence in Psychology." *Social Research 40:* 55–82 (1973).

Valins, S. & Nisbett, R. E. "Some Implications of Attribution Process for the Development and Treatment of Emotional Disorders." In *Attribution: Perceiving the Causes of Behavior*, E. E. Jones, D. E. Kanouse, H. H. Kelley, R. E. Nisbett, S. Valins & B. Weiner, eds. (Morristown, N.J.: General Learning Press, 1972).

Index

actors, attributions of, 174-180
Adams, H., 104
Adorno, T., 20, 61, 110, 121, 122, 123
age-groups, *see entries under* generation
alienation: humanistic psychology,103; religion, 3; sociological theory, 101
Allport, G., 79, 93
Altbach, P. G., 89
American Psychological Association (APA), 104
American Psychologist, 44
ANCOVA design, descriptions by, 141-142
Anderson, W., 102
Angyal, 167
ANOVA design: applications of, 135-137; critique of, 129-130; developmental change description, 130-135; inefficiency of, 140-141; interactionism, 163, 164, 165, 166, 167; logic of, 127; variables in, 128
Apel, K.-O., 192, 194
Argyle, M., 163
Aristotle, 117, 171
Arkin, R. M., 175
Aron, A., 107, 108, 110
attribution(s), actor/observer dichotomy, 174-180

attribution theory: critique of, 187-193; definition of, 170; Heider and, 172
authoritarian personality, Fromm, 62
authority: family, 68; individual-society dialectic, 63
Ayer, A.J., 173

Bachrach, P., 109, 110
Baltes, M. M., 136
Baltes, P. B., 45, 127, 128-129, 130, 132, 133, 134, 135, 136, 137, 138, 139, 141, 144, 145
Barclay, 132
Becker, Carl, 21
behavior: attribution theory, 169-170; interaction concept and, 161-164; trait-situation controversy, 161
"behavioral sciences," term of, 15
behaviorism: humanistic psychology, 102-103; paradigm of, 2, 5-6, 8; political science and, 15; reality, 104; subject-object relationship,6
Beit-Hallahmi, B., 81, 92, 104
Bem, D. J., 170
Bengston, V. L., 45
Bentham, J., 30, 34

Berger, P. L., 145
Bernstein, E., 55
Bernstein, R. J., 78, 82, 117
Bertalanffy, L. von, 163
Beshai, J. A., 190
bifactorial analysis of variance, *see*
    ANOVA
Birnbaum, N., 102
birth control, 46-47, 96
Black, K. D., 45
Blacker, C. P., 32, 34, 37, 39
Block, J. H., 154
Bloom, B. S., 151, 154-157
Blumenthal, A., 5, 7
Boring, E. G., 28, 32, 37, 90
Bowers, K. S., 161, 163, 164-165, 167
Brandt, L. W., 90
Braungart, R. G., 89, 94
Brown, N. O., 103
Buck-Morss, 75n; commodity struc-
    tures, 121; contradiction in,
    120-121; cross-cultural studies,
    115-119; neo-Marxists and, 123-124
Buech, B. V., 136
Bunderson, C. V., 153
Bunge, M., 163
bureaucracy: capitalism, 35; so-
    ciological theory, 101
Burt, C., 32
Buss, A. R., 28, 44, 45, 55, 94, 96,
    98, 101, 115, 129, 130, 132, 137,
    138, 145, 150, 154
Butler, D., 196, 197
Butterfield, H., 14, 21

capitalism: class structure, 36; com-
    puter assisted instruction, 153-154;
    Darwinism, 33; individualism,
    29-30; mastery learning, 157; psy-
    chology, 91; quantification, 35
Carroll, J. B., 154, 155
Cattell, R. B., 45, 129, 138
cause-reason dichotomy, 187; at-
    tribution theory, 170, 171
character structure, 61-63
childhood, historicity of, 60
Childhood and Society (Erikson), 65
child-rearing, individual-society di-
    alectic,59

civilization, Freud, 57
civil liberties, individualism, 30
class antagonism: neo-Marxists, 122;
    see also conflict
class structure: capitalism, 36; cogni-
    tive structure, 18; Darwinism, 33
cognition: historicity of, 18; interac-
    tion, 162; Wundt, 5; *see also*
    consciousness; thought
cognitive development, Marx,
    116-117
cognitive psychology, as paradigm, 6
cohort(s): generational theory, 95;
    life-span studies, 127-128, 129
cohort differences, 45, 46
collectivism, Plato, 40
commodity structures: con-
    sciousness, 120-121; neo-Marxists,
    123-124
communism, consciousness, 120
communist parties, 108
community, sociological theory, 101,
    102
computer assisted instruction (CAI),
    151, 152-154, 156
Comte, A., 90-91, 94, 102
Concept of Motivation, The (Peters),
    172
conflict: dialectic and, 75, 76; Erik-
    son on, 66, 69; Freudianism, 57;
    Fromm on, 61; generational the-
    ory and, 94; neo-Marxists and,
    122; Reich on, 60
conformism, Erikson, 68-69
consciousness: actor, 176; Durk-
    heimian, 120; neo-Marxists, 55-56;
    see also cognition; self-con-
    sciousness; thought
conservatism: Freud, 103; humanis-
    tic psychology, 102
contradiction: Buck-Morss, 120-121;
    dialectics, 77, 78, 84; Kruglanski,
    181-182; Maslow, 108, 109, 110
conversion model, modification of,
    196
Cornford, F. M., 40
Cowan, R. S., 32, 37
Critical Theory (Horkheimer), 63
critical theory: emphasis of, 122;
    fact-theory relationship, 19-21

cross-cultural differences, neo-Marxists, 123-124
cross-cultural studies, Durkheim,
120
Cultural Hermeneutics (journal), 190
culture, ego psychology, 65

Darwin, C.: Freud and, 58; Galton
and, 32-33, 37
Datan, N., 45
Daveney, T. K., 173
Davis, K. E., 170
decision-making, Maslow, 111
de Mause, F., 60
democracy: liberalism, 31; Marxism,
54-55; Maslow, 107-109
demography, regression analysis,
144
developmental phenomena: AN-
COVA design, 141-142; description
of, 130-135; explanation of,
137-139; regression analysis for,
143-144
Dewey, John, 158
dialectic(s): critical theory, 20; definition, 75; Erikson, 68; family/
society, 63; Galton, 39, 40; generation theory, 49; Hegelian, 76-82;
history of, 53-54; Marxism, 54-57;
82-85; Maslow, 110; methodology,
76, 144-145; psychological paradigm, 8-9
Dilthy, 189
Dollard, J., 8
dominance, Frankfurt School on, 61
Donnellan, K. S., 173, 176-177
Dray, W., 188
Durkheim, Emile, 101, 120
Duval, S., 175
Dwyer, T. A., 153

Eckhardt, W., 93
*Economic and Philosophic Man-
uscripts* (Marx), 17
economics, ego psychology, 65
educational theory, values, 149-150

egalitarianism, educational theory,
151
ego psychology: Erikson, 65, 70;
post-Freudians, 64; stage model
of, 67
Eisenstadt, S. N., 94
Eisenstadt-Parsons functionalist
model, 94
Ekehammer, B., 8, 161, 163, 166-167
elitism: democracy, 109; Maslow,
108
empiricism, 19; attribution theory,
188, 190; critique of, 16, 20;
natural sciences, 15
Endler, N. S., 161, 163, 165-166
endogenous-exogenous distinction,
attribution theory, 181-182
Engels, F., 83, 84
English. A. C., 37
English, H. B., 37
English Men of Science (Galton), 32
Enlightenment, 103, 123
entelechy, generation theory, 46,
49, 96
environment, Maslow, 106
epidemiology, regression analysis,
144
equality, Galton, 34-35
Erikson, Erik, 58, 64-70, 71
Escape from Freedom (Fromm), 61,
63
Essence of Christianity (Feuerbach),
3
ethics: ego psychology, 65; Maslow,
106
eugenics: definition, 37; Galton, 32;
perfectibility, 34; as religion, 38;
social context of, 28; as social
policy, 38-39
existentialism: dialects, 81; humanistic psychology, 93
existential statement, Galton, 38
experience, generational theory, 95
exploitation, neo-Marxists, 56

fact(s): Hegel, 77, 78; values, 149
fact-theory relationship: critical theory, 19-21; Marxian tradition,
16-19; social/natural sciences, 13

family: Erikson, 66, 68; Frankfurt
    School, 61; Freudianism, 57-58;
    individual-society dialectic, 59;
    society dialectic, 63
Fascism, 108; family and, 59;
    Fromm, 62
Feigl, H., 174
fetishism, religion, 3-4
Feuerbach, L., 2-4, 82, 84
Feyerabend, P. K., 16, 149
Fichte, J. G., 78
Fischoff, B., 1n, 169n, 187n, 197
Fiske, S. T., 175, 178
Flacks, R., 89, 96
Foa, U. G., 44
Foner, 144
Frankel, 179
Frankfurt School, 14, 20, 123, 158;
    emphasis of, 121-122; individual-
    society dialectic, 60-63
freedom: Fromm, 62; Galton, 34;
    Hegel, 79; Marxism, 54-55; Mas-
    low, 105, 107
French Revolution, positivism, 91
Freud, S., 6, 7, 57, 58, 70; dialec-
    tics, 53; Erikson and, 64-65;
    Fromm and, 61, 62; human na-
    ture, 103; individual-society di-
    alectic, 65-66, 70-71; Maslow and,
    106; post-Freudians and, 64;
    Reich and, 60
Freudianism, Marxism and, 57, 61
Friedrichs, R. W., 191
Fromm, E., 58, 61-62, 63, 64, 66,
    79
Fulker, D. W., 138
Furby, L., 96, 97, 169n, 187n
futurists, 43

Gadlin, H., 190, 191
Galper, R. E., 196
Galton, F., 28; biography, 32; eu-
    genics, 37-41; hedonism, 34;
    liberalism, 33; paradox in, 35
geistewissenschaften, 189
generation, Freudianism, 57
generational differences, 96-97
generational theory, 45-49, 94
genetics, 37; see also eugenics

Gergen, K. J., 18, 28, 191
Giddens, A., 84
Gillis, J. R., 60
Giorgi, 79
Girvetz, H. K., 29-30, 31
Glaser, R., 158
Glass, J. F., 81, 104
Goertzel, T., 94
Goodman, P., 97
Gouldner, A. W., 150, 191
Goulet, 132
government, see state
Gramsci, A., 55
groups, sociology, 19
group differences, neo-Marxists, 124

Habermas, J., 118, 122, 123, 193, 194
Halsey, A. H., 156-157
Hampden-Turner, C., 102, 110
Hanson, N. R., 16, 18, 179
Harman, W. W., 104
Harre, H., 174
Harvey, J. H., 170
Hay, 132
hedonism, Galton, 34
hedonistic calculus, 30
Hegel, G. W. F., 3, 9, 81; dialec-
    tics, 76-82; Feuerbach on, 4;
    Freud and, 58; Horkheimer and,
    63; Marx and, 82
Hegelianism, Marxism, 55
Heider, F., 170, 171-172, 187
Hemple, C. G., 188
Hereditary Genius (Galton), 32, 33,
    34
heredity, developmental phe-
    nomena, 138
hermeneutics, 189-193
Himmelfarb, G. 31
historicism, critical theory, 20
history (intellectual), 27-28
History and Class Consciousness
    (Lukacs), 16, 121
Hobbs, N., 194
Hobhouse, L. T., 107
Hook, S., 3, 75, 80, 82, 83
Horkheimer, 20, 58, 60, 61, 63, 66,
    118, 121, 122, 123, 158
Horney, K., 64

Houghton, W. H., 29
Hoye, R. E., 152
Hoyer, W. J., 133
Hull, C., 6
humanism, Marx, 83
humanistic psychology: critique of,
   85; dialectics, 76, 79-82; human
   nature, 104; as paradigm, 7; social
   context, 101; sources of, 93-94,
   101-105; youth movement, 93,
   97-98
human nature: educational theory,
   150-151; Freud and, 103; Fromm
   and, 61; humanistic psychology,
   104; Marx and, 116; Maslow and,
   106; positivism, 93; psychoanalysis, 64
Hutchison, K., 31

Ickes, W. J., 170
idea, social sources, 27-28
Idea of Social Science, The (Winch),
   172
Identity and the Life Cycle
   (Erikson), 65
ideology: attribution theory, 188;
   cohort differences, 46; computer
   assisted instruction, 153-154; cgo
   psychology, 65; family, 59;
   Fromm, 61; mastery learning, 157;
   neo-Marxists, 55-56; notion of, 18
Ihde, D., 189
individual: clinical psychology, 92;
   conception of, 28; dialectics, 80;
   educational theory, 152, 155, 156;
   Fromm; 62; generational theory,
   48; humanistic psychology, 81;
   Maslow, 105, 106, 107-108; neo-
   Freudians, 64
individual differences: capitalism,
   36; eugenics, 40-41
individualism: community, 102; Darwinism, 33; eugenics, 39; as
   normative doctrine, 29-31
individual-society dialectic, 53-54;
   Erikson, 64-70; explanation and,
   144-146; Fromm, 61-62; ontogeny/
   phylogeny theory, 70-72
industrialization, Erikson, 66

Ingle, G., 190, 191
Inquiries into Human Faculty
   (Galton) 32, 37
instinctoid concept, 106
interaction: conceptual structure of,
   162-164; trait-situation controversy, 161, 164-167
intergenerational conflict, psychology, 48
intergenerational interaction, 46
internal-external dichotomy, 181-182

Jacoby, R., 66, 103, 122
Janousek, 84
Jay, M., 122
Jinks, J. L., 138
Johnson, 144
Jones, E. E., 170, 174-175, 176-177,
   179, 187
Jourard, 79
Jung, C. G., 53

Kant, I., 83
Kantor, 167
Kantsaywhere (Galton), 35, 39
Kaufmann, W., 78
Kearsley, G. P., 149n
Kelley, H. H., 170, 187, 188, 196, 197
Kerlinger, F. N., 141
Kidd, R. E., 170
Kirk, R. E., 133, 140, 143
knowledge, Marxian dialectics, 83
Koivumaki, J. H., 179
Kojeve, A., 81
Kolakowski, L., 17, 83-84, 116
Korsch, K., 55, 56
Kruglanski, A. W., 170, 180, 181,
   182, 187, 188
Kuhn, T. S., 1, 2, 16, 18, 48, 90,
   139, 164

labor (division of): Darwinism, 33;
   sociological theory, 101
Labouvie, E. W., 45, 130
Labouvie, G. V., 136
Labouvie-Vief, G., 135
Laing, R. D., 173

laissez-faire: civil rights, 31; individualism, 30
Lambert, T. A., 94
Langman, L., 89, 97
language: attribution theory, 173, 176; cognitive psychology, 6; fact/theory relationship, 18; paradigms, 15,16
Lasswell, H. D., 91
Laufer, R. S., 89
law and order, ego psychology, 65
learning theory, paradigm of, 8
Left (Young) Hegelians, 3, 8
Leiss, W., 122
Lenin, V. I., 55
Lewin, 167
Lewis, 143
Liberalism (Hobhouse), 107
liberalism: affirmative state, 31; Darwinism, 33; Galton, 40; humanistic psychology, 101, 103; individualism, 29, 31; Maslow, 108; self-actualization and, 105-107; sociological theory, 102
Lichtman, R., 104, 106
life-span studies, data for, 127
Lindquist, E. F., 133, 140
Little, B. R., 163
Lobkowicz, N., 77, 117
Logic (Hegel), 78
logic, dialectics, 78
Looft, W. R., 91, 145
Louche, A. R., 173
Lowe, 179
Luckman, T., 145
Lukacs, G., 16-17, 19, 55, 119, 120
Lyons, 79

MacIntyre, A., 174
Madden, E. H., 173
Magnusson, D., 161, 163, 165
Mannheim, Karl, 18, 19, 90, 150; generational theory, 45-47, 94, 95-96; intelligentsia, 97
Marcuse, H., 20, 61, 77, 78, 79, 103, 121, 122, 123
markets, individual, 30, 31
Marx, K., 3, 9, 19, 101, 145; cognitive theory, 116; consciousness,

120; dialectics, 54, 76, 82-85; epistemology of, 16-17, 18; Hegel and, 82; ideology, 104; Horkheimer and, 63; Piaget and, 118; presentism, 21
Marxism: Freudianism and, 57, 61; individual-society dialectic, 54-57
Maslow, A. H., 7, 79, 85, 93, 101, 102, 105-111
Mass Psychology of Fascism, The (Reich), 59
mastery, Erikson, 69
mastery learning, 151, 154-157
materialism, Watson, 6
Matson, 79
McCarthyism, 108
McLellan, D., 54
measurement, capitalism, 35
methodology: developmental data analysis, 128; dialectics, 76, 144-145; sociological theory, 102
Meyers, 133
Mill, J. S., 30, 31, 107
Miller, D. T., 175
Miller, G., 192
Miller, N., 8
Mills, C. W., 111
Mischel, W., 161, 166
modernity, sociological theory, 101
morality: birth control, 96; changes in, 47
motivation, psychoanalytic paradigm, 6-7
Motivation and Personality (Maslow), 108
Murray, 167

Naess, A., 16, 18
Natural Inheritance (Galton), 32
naturalism, Marxian dialectics, 84
natural science model: attribution theory, 190, 193; educational theory, 150; fact-theory relationship in, 13; social sciences and, 15
nature, neo-Marxists, 122-123
Nazism, 62, 108
neo-Freudians, emphasis of, 64
neo-Marxists, 121; emphasis of, 120; family, 59; Marxism, 55

Nesselroade, J. R., 132, 133, 134, 139, 145
Neugarten, B. L., 45
Nisbett, R. E., 101, 102, 170, 174-175, 176-177, 179, 187, 195
Nord, W., 104
Norman, S. A., 175
normative statements, Galton, 38

observers, attributions of, 174-180
Oedipus conflict, 58
On Liberty (Mill), 30, 107
ontogenic change, 45
ontogeny/history theory, 65, 71
ontogeny/phylogeny theory: Freudianism, 58; Fromm, 62; individual-society dialectic, 70-72
operationalism, natural sciences, 15
original sin, Galton, 37
Origin of Species, The (Darwin), 32, 37
Orvis, B. R. 196, 197
Overton, W. F., 139, 145, 163, 165, 167

Packard, V., 97
paradigm(s): generation theory, 48-49; in psychology, 2
Parsons, T., 94
Party, Lenin, 55
Pearson, K., 32, 35, 37, 38, 39
Pedhazur, E. J., 141
perception, organismic determinants of, 17
personality, neo-Freudians, 64
Peters, R. S., 172, 173, 187
phenomenology, humanistic psychology, 93
Phenomenology of Mind (Hegel), 78
Philosophical and Economic Manuscripts (Marx), 116
Philosophical Investigations (Wittgenstein), 169
Philosophy for Personality Theory, A (Rychlak), 53
Piaget, J., 49, 71, 188; learning, 117; categories, 120, cognitive develop-
ment theory, 116; interaction, 163; praxis, 117-118
Piagetian tests, cross-cultural differences, 115
planning, establishment of, 43
Plato, eugenics, 39-40
pluralism: individualism, 31; Maslow, 108
political science, paradigms in, 15
Popper, K. R., 9, 16, 40
positivism, 19; clinical psychology, 92; critique of, 16, 20; dialectics and, 77, 83; human nature, 93; Mannheim rejects, 94; Maslow rejects, 105; natural sciences and, 15; Piaget, 119; social sciences, 102
post-Freudians: emphasis of, 64; individual-society dialectic, 57; ontogeny/phylogeny theory, 58
power, Mill on, 30
praxis: Marx, 117; Marxian dialectics, 83-85; Maslow, 110
prediction, 43
presentism: critical theory, 20-21; social sciences, 14
Primal Horde theory, 58
progress, Freudianism, 58
Protestantism, individualism, 29
psychoanalysis: attribution theory, 193-194; Erikson on, 64; humanistic psychology and, 102-103; individual-society dialectic, 57-59; neo-Marxists, 56, paradigm of, 6-7, 8; reality, 104
psychology (as discipline): assumptions of, 90; generation theory and, 45-49, 96; job market in, 44-45; youth movement and, 97
Psychology of Interpersonal Relations, The (Heider), 171

quantification, capitalism, 35

Radnitzky, G., 189-190, 191, 192, 193
reality: absolute/current, 104; dialectics, 77, 82-83; Hegel, 78-79; humanistic psychology, 80

reason: Hegel, 79; *see also* cause-reason dichotomy
received view, theory, 15-16
reductionism, Freudianism/Marxism, 57
Reese, H. W., 139, 145, 163, 165, 167
Reformation, 29
Regan, D. T., 175, 178
Reich, C. A., 89, 96
Reich, W., 58, 59-60, 61, 63, 64, 66, 103
Reinert, G., 136
religion: ego psychology, 65; eugenics as, 38; Feuerbach, 3; Galton, 37; individualism, 29; science, 91
repression: Erikson, 64; Frankfurt School, 61; Freudianism, 57; neo-Marxists, 56
Republic, The (Plato), 39, 40
revisionism: Marxism, 55; of psychoanalysis, 64
revolution: individual-society dialectic, 54; Marxism, 56
Rickman, H. P., 190
Rocoeur, P., 190, 193, 194
Riegel, K. F., 35, 47, 48-49, 53, 76, 77, 145, 154
Riley, 144
Roazen, P., 66, 103
Robinson, P. A., 103
Rogers, C., 79, 93
Rokeach, M., 153, 157
Rousseau, J. J., 106
Russian Revolution, 54-55
Rychlak, J., 53, 75, 171
Ryder, N. B., 45
Ryle, G., 172, 173, 176, 187

Saint-Simon, C. H., 90-91, 94
Samelson, F., 14
Schaie, K. W., 45, 127-130, 132, 133, 134, 135, 136, 137, 138, 139, 140, 141, 144
science: religion, 91; values, 149; youth movement, 89-90
scientism, epistemology, 118
Secord, P. F., 174

Self, J. A., 153
self, Maslow, 107-108
self-actualization: clinical psychology, 92; co-optation of, 104; dialectics and, 81-82; liberalism and, 101, 105-107; Maslow, 109
self-consciousness: Hegel, 82; Marxian dialectics, 84; *see also* consciousness
sexuality: Erikson, 64; Freudianism, 58
Shaver, K. G., 170
situation, behavior, 161
Skinner, B. F., 6
Skinner, Q., 174
Skinnerian learning theory, 153
Smith, Adam, 30
Smith, D. G., 29
Smith, M. B., 105, 106
Snyder, 179
Social Darwinism, 31
Social Democratic Party (Germany), 55
socialism, mastery learning, 157
social learning position, interaction, 162
social psychology, historicity of, 18
social sciences: fact-theory relationship, 13; natural sciences and, 15; paradigms in, 2; universalist assumptions, 18
social status, eugenics policy, 39
social structure, character structure, 61-62
specialization: capitalism, 35-36; Darwinism, 33
Spencer, H., 31, 106
Starr, J. M., 89, 97
state: eugenics policy, 39; liberalism, 31
statistics, Galton, 32
Stocking, G. W., Jr., 14, 20-21
Storms, M. D., 175, 178, 195, 196
Stolurow, L. M., 152
Stromberg, R. N., 27-28, 31
Strother, C. R., 135, 136
structuralism, as paradigm, 5-6
Structure of Scientific Revolutions, The (Kuhn), 1
Studies on Authority and Family

(Frankfurt Institute), 61, 63
subject-object relationship: behaviorism, 6; dialectics, 82;
  Feuerbach, 3-4; Marxism, 55-56,
  85; natural/social sciences, 15; paradigms and, 5-9; psychology, 4-5
Sullivan, H. S., 64

Taylor, C., 173, 189, 190, 194
Taylor, R., 171, 174
Taylor, S. E., 175, 178, 179
technology: ego psychology, 65;
  Erikson, 66; neo-Marxists,
  122-123; youth movement, 90
Terman, 32
theory, received view, 15-16
theory/practice relationship: democracy, 109; Marxian dialectics, 83
thought: Habermas, 123;
  Horkheimer, 122; see also
  consciousness
Tolman, E., 6
Tönnies, 101
Totten, J., 175, 178
Toulmin, S., 174
trait(s), behavior, 161
trait-situation controversy, interaction in, 164-167
transformative method, 2-4
Trotskyism, 9
truth, dialectics, 76
Turner, J. L., 44
Tyler, F. B., 92

utilitarianism, capitalism, 30

Valins, S., 195
value(s): computer assisted instruction, 154; critical theory, 21;
  educational theory and, 149-150,
  151; Galton, 39; generation theory, 46; liberals, 109; Maslow,
  105-106, 108; positivism, 91; psychology, 92; science, 149; youth
  movement, 96-97
verstehen, 189
Victorianism, individualism, 29
Vienna Circle, 20
Vietnam War, 97

Wang, A. C., 152
Watson, J. B., 6
Weber, M., 18, 19, 101, 189
Weimer, W. B., 14
Wellmer, A., 122
Westkott, M., 102
Whig interpretation, 21
Whyte, W. H., 97
Winch, P., 172, 173, 187
Wittgenstein, L., 169, 172, 173, 187
Wohlwill, J. F., 130, 132, 133
Wolff, R. P., 107
Wolman, 90
World War I, Marxism, 54-55, 63
World War II, 109
Wundt, W., 5-6, 7, 49

Young (Left) Hegelians, 3, 8
youth movement: generational theory, 96; humanistic psychology,
  93; impact of, 89; paradigms, 90

Zeitlin, I. M., 91
Zinn, H., 21